OUT OF
THE STORM

Holocaust to Hope

OUT OF THE STORM

Holocaust to Hope

Michael Halperin

CHERRY ORCHARD BOOKS

2025

Library of Congress Cataloging-in-Publication Data

Names: Halperin, Michael, 1934- author
Title: Out of the storm : Holocaust to hope / Michael Halperin.
Description: Boston : Cherry Orchard Books, 2025.
Identifiers: LCCN 2025020145 (print) | LCCN 2025020146 (ebook) |
  ISBN 9798887198514 hardback | ISBN 9798887198538 adobe pdf |
  ISBN 9798887198545 epub
Subjects: LCSH: Roslan, Alex | Roslan, Mela | Gilat, Jacob | Righteous
  Gentiles in the Holocaust—Poland—Biography | Holocaust, Jewish
  (1939-1945)—Poland | Gilat, David ǂc (Mathematics professor) |
  Holocaust survivors ǂz Poland ǂv Biography | LCGFT: Biographies
Classification: LCC D804.65 .H34 2025 (print) | LCC D804.65
  (ebook) | DDC 940.53/18092 $a B—dc23/eng/20250714
LC record available at https://lccn.loc.gov/2025020145
LC ebook record available at https://lccn.loc.gov/2025020146

ISBN 9798887198514 hardback
ISBN 9798887198538 adobe pdf
ISBN 9798887198545 epub

Cover design by Ivan Grave
Book design by Tatiana Vernikov

Published by Cherry Orchard Books, an imprint of Academic Studies Press
1007 Chestnut Street
Newton, MA 02464
press@academicstudiespress.com
www.academicstudiespress.com

Contents

Names of individuals used with permission.
Selected names changed to protect privacy.

"They not only rescued David and Jacob, they rescued God."

—Rabbi Harold Schulweis
Jewish Institute for the Righteous

Acknowledgments

Altruistic Personality and Prosocial Behavior Institute

American Jewish Joint Distribution Committee

BBC Written Archives Centre Benton Arnovitz

Center for Jewish History

Embassy of the Republic of Poland, Washington, DC

Yoram Gutgeld, PhD

Habricha HIAS

Jewish Agency for Israel

Judah L. Magnes Memorial Museum

Donia Schaumann

United States Holocaust Memorial Museum

Yad Vashem The World Holocaust Remembrance Center

YIVO Institute for Jewish Research

Original funding for *Out of the Storm* provided
   by a grant from the National Endowment
   for the Humanities

Appreciation

David Gilat (**Gutgeld**) shared recollections of his traumatic post-Holocaust years. The incidents and dialogue are drawn from memory, recreating David and Jacob Gilat's reality.

Jacob Gilat (**Gutgeld**) provided critical points of view, correspondence, translations, photos, and recollections of the years traversing Europe following the Holocaust.

Foreword

An offhand remark from innovative philosopher the late Rabbi Harold Schulweis, upending Jewish thought in the twentieth- and twenty-first century, opened the doors to an unexpected adventure. An Israeli PhD candidate in mathematics from the University of California, Berkeley, David Gilat, related a remarkable story of sacrifice, life-threatening danger, and love.

Two exceptional individuals, Alex and Mela Roslan, Polish Catholics struggling under Nazi occupation, rescued him and his brothers Jacob and Shalom from the Warsaw Ghetto, hiding them from certain death. In a tragic turn of events, Shalom succumbed to scarlet fever raging through the city. With rare altruistic compassion, the precocious children bonded with the Roslans, their daughter Marisia and older son Jurek.

In the post-Holocaust years, Alex and Mela Roslan refused to abandon the boys, remaining with them as antisemitism erupted across Europe, eventually reuniting them with their surviving family. It became one of the origin stories for the establishment of the Foundation for the Righteous by Rabbi Schulweis, dedicated to supporting the unsung heroes who risked their lives saving Jews during the Holocaust.

The Writers Guild of America invited an acquaintance from the National Endowment for Humanities to address its members; the representative encouraged writers to apply for grants exploring the human spirit. After mentioning the Roslan story, he suggested it fit NEH guidelines.

Fascinated by the unique, almost mythical, self-sacrificing story, I contacted David and Jacob living in Tel Aviv, Israel. They maintained contact with their rescuers, whom they considered surrogate parents, just as the Roslans, who immigrated to the United States and lived in Florida, looked upon them as their sons.

The Roslans did not accept the appellation 'hero.' The elderly, unassuming couple living a quiet life in Clearwater, Florida, did what they felt necessary to protect the lives of two vulnerable children. In twelve hours of recorded recollections, they calmly described events taking place from 1943, when they rescued the children, hiding them from death squads at the risk of their own lives, until 1947, when they made their farewells, watching tearfully as the two children they loved as their own boarded a train taking them on the first leg of a journey to a father who loomed only as a shadow, living in a land the boys did not know.

Via email and phone conversations between Los Angeles, Tel Aviv, and Florida, the story took shape. The Gutgeld brothers and Roslans became part of our family, whether visiting in Tel Aviv, Florida, or California. Alex's sly humor and Mela's genuine warmth were gifts we treasured. Jacob and David shared their academic achievements in the fields of mathematics and physics, shaping science and medicine.

As their story unfolded, every incident and adventure unsealed doors to forgotten and suppressed memories of a remarkable love story between children in peril and their rescuers, ordinary people who fought evil with their wits, winning against enormous odds.

—*Michael Halperin*

Chapter One

Judenrein

The fourth-century CE Roman Empire, centered in Byzantium, stretched from Britannia in the north, southwards to North Africa, and eastwards across the Adriatic Sea to Dalmatia. Romans worshipped the Capitoline Triad—Jupiter, Juno, Minerva—in their temples. They tolerated worship of other gods, including the invisible god of the Jews. Polytheism proved a great leveler. The elevation of Roman commander Constantine to emperor of the Roman Empire brought the nascent Christian sect, born out of Judaism, into prominence. It created tension between believers in their living god, who was sacrificed and resurrected, and worshippers of an incorporeal god who inspired human beings to write their basic text the Torah. As early as the second century CE, rabbis insisted the writings not be taken literally, but as poetry, where truth hides in blank spaces between the lines. The schism grew wider when Constantine recognized Christianity as the state church. In 325 CE he called bishops to a gathering at Nicaea in what is now Turkey to formulate a statement of belief. The first version of the creed made no mention of crucifixion or reference in gospels supporting Jesus's resurrection.

The emperor's mother, Helena, an ardent convert to Christianity, traveled to Jerusalem searching for the "True Cross" upon which Jesus had been crucified. Stories of miracles attributed to her discovery of the relic spread, inaugurating a period of fervid conversion among Roman citizens. The majority of Jews rejected the notion of death and resurrection.

Seen as a repudiation of Christianity, Constantine needed the Church's blessing to make Judaism a pariah religion. The conclave of 381 CE demanded bishops rewrite the Nicaean Creed. The council added portions of three Gospels and Paul's letters to the Thessalonians, placing primary responsibility for the death of Jesus on Jews: "for you suffered the same things from your own countrymen as they did from the Jews, who killed both the Lord Jesus and the prophets, and drove us out, and displease God and oppose all mankind" (Thess. 1:14-15).

Vicious hordes torched synagogues, shouting for death. As time went on, the empire, instigated by the Church, stripped away rights from Jews. Those who played prominent roles in government were dismissed. Death was meted out to any Roman who married a Jew. The Church cleverly permitted impoverished Jews to survive in miserable gated communities as proof their god was impotent and the ascendant Church bore the truth.

Eastern Roman emperor Theodosius II built on the Nicaean Creed. In his bitter, vicious Codex Theodosianus (439 CE), he presaged the attempted destruction of a people fifteen centuries later:

> "[W]e ordain by this law to be valid for all time: No Jew . . . shall obtain offices and dignities; to none shall the administration of city service be permitted; nor shall any one exercise the office of a defender of the city. Indeed, we believe it sinful that the enemies of the heavenly majesty and of the Roman laws should become the executors of our laws—the administration of which they have slyly obtained and that they, fortified by the authority of the acquired

> rank, should have the power to judge or decide as they wish against Christians, yes, frequently even over bishops of our holy religion themselves, and thus, as it were, insult our faith."

It fermented the perennial seesawing relations between Jews and Christians. At times the Church maintained a benign tolerance often exploding into disaster, expulsion, and death. Through it all, Judaism survived, hanging onto the core belief God created, not warring supernatural beings, but the divinity of the human soul.

Reports of plague, the Black Death, in 1349 were rapidly disseminated throughout Europe. In Germany, Brandenburg burghers issued an edict: "the Jews have elsewhere dispatched many persons through poisoning." Emperor Charles IV ordered the requisition of silver and gold held by Jewish moneylenders. The royal treasury became the prime beneficiary. Citizens of Brandenburg, Nuremburg, and Trier took the emperor's statement as permission to slaughter "their" Jews.

Martin Luther began his ministry early in the sixteenth century, appalled at the animus toward Jews, who had given the ancient texts prophesying Jesus's bringing peace to the world. In his treatise *Jesus Was Born a Jew*, he denigrated those who "treated Jews in such a fashion that if a man wanted to be a true Christian he might be better to become a Jew. . . . [W]ere I a Jew and saw what blockheads and windbags rule and guide Christendom, I would rather be a sow than a Christian." Luther's use of the word "sow" refers to a sculpture on Wittenberg's parish church that he knew only too well; it depicts Jews on their knees suckling the teats of a female pig.

Luther ends the pamphlet with the following: "we must give them a friendly hand, letting them work and thrive in our midst, in order that they have reason and occasion to become us and with us."

Jews rejected the offer "to become us and with us." Thwarted, angry, this stiff-necked people did not see the light, Luther embarked on savage anti-Judaic campaigns, culminating in his odious and malignant polemic *Concerning the Jews and Their Lies*, based on the Codex Theodosianus. With the help of the new technology of Gutenberg's printing press, it was read throughout Europe. "How dare the Jews complain of the bitter captivity among us," he wrote:

> "For three hundred years now they persecuted and martyred us Christians, and even today we do not altogether know what deviltry they have brought into our land. Since they live among us and we know about their lying and blasphemy and cursing, we cannot tolerate them. . . . Let me give you my honest advice. First, their Synagogues or Churches should be set on fire . . . secondly, their homes should likewise be broken down and destroyed . . . thirdly, they should be deprived of their prayer books and Talmuds . . . fourthly, their rabbis must be forbidden under threat of death to teach any more . . . fifthly, you ought not, you cannot, protect them, unless in the eyes of G-d you want to share all their abomination . . . sixthly, they ought to be stopped from usury . . . seventhly, we ought to drive the rascally lazybones out of our system. To sum up, dear princes and nobles who have Jews in your domain, if this advice of mine does not suit you, then find a better one so that you and we may all be free of this devilish burden—the Jews."

Fleeing east to Lithuania and Poland and west to France, Jews searched for safe havens from contempt and hatred.

They found, if not a warm welcome, brief sanctuaries from persecution. Thirteenth-century feudal statutes placed Jews in the precarious position of working as moneylenders. Hostilities broke out when the nobility employed Jewish entrepreneurs to manage their estates. Unlettered peasantry believed this act disgraced society. Those who rejected Jesus controlled treasures built on peasants' backs.

Dependence of kings, dukes, and feudal lords on Jewish financiers led to a need to protect those who helped build empires. Polish nobility adapted Germany's Magdeburg Law, giving Jews the same rights as Christians. It permitted their engagement in all economic activities. The law protected synagogues and cemeteries and forbade forced conversion. Antisemitic crimes were punished. Within a short time, Jews became integral to Poland's resurgence.

With the tacit assent of the Catholic Church, German states attempted to undermine Magdeburg. Bolislaw, a Polish prince, countered by writing A General Charter of Jewish Liberties. It stated: "Accusing Jews of drinking Christian blood is expressly prohibited."

For a hundred years Poland protected its minority with specific statutes. Under penalty of death, no one could force the baptism of children or desecrate Jewish cemeteries. Kings, princes, and administrators of Poland had enlightened views; but statutes and charters protecting equality for Jews ran into animosity promoted by the Church among illiterate priests and peasants who accepted the fiction that Jews joined with the devil to turn light into darkness. This belief remained an undercurrent in Polish religious mythology.

At the end of a ninety-year quiescent period, a series of violent conflicts created an economic depression striking every stratum of Polish society. Looking for the cause, opportunists ignored wars with Russia and Sweden, pointing fingers at Jews who had risen to prominence through their creation of academies of learning and literature, and achievement of unprecedented freedom.

Cossacks, loyal to the Eastern Orthodox Church, rode out of the steppes of Russia in the mid-seventeenth century, dominating and controlling eastern and southern Poland. Rampaging across the land, they massacred thousands of Jews and Roman Catholics in Chelminski. The weakened nation fell prey to the Swedish Empire, sweeping down on the kingdom destroying, plundering in a ferocious assault. After five years of oppressive occupation, Polish king John II Casimir returned from exile with a restructured, stronger Polish army and drove the invaders across the Baltic Sea.

While the Church objected, Polish intellectuals introduced plans for integrating Jews into society. Aided by a newly organized Jewish cavalry, Poland revolted against the Russian Empire. The revolt failed against massive and well-armed Russian forces. One positive outcome, however, was that it solidified the notion Jews not only lived in Poland but were loyal to the nation.

Although under Russian hegemony, Jews rebuilt their lives. The majority returned to the land—farms, orchards, and dairies. Rabbis established schools, wrote religious treatises, developed Hasidic Judaism. Jewish intellectuals contributed to science, medicine, and literature. The nation flourished until Prussia invaded, absorbing part of the country.

Russia, under Catherine the Great, aided Stanislaus II Augustus take the throne as last king of Poland. Expected to be subordinate to Russia, the new king took independent action, introducing major reforms, including the Stanislaw Augustus Code, enhancing the status of Jews in Poland.

The impact of the Enlightenment on German-speaking Europe saw that region's slow move toward tolerance. Culture flourished with the emergence of Bach, Mozart, Haydn, and the poet and historian Friedrich Schiller. Philosophy predicated on rational thought found a home with the support of a cultivated aristocracy and prosperous middle class.

In rare moments, Jews fought for their rights rather than begging for the privilege of being a Jew. The philosopher Moses Mendelssohn, Gotthold Lessing, author of *Nathan the Wise*, and physician Aaron Gumpertz, among others, moved in aristocratic circles. Emperor Joseph II issued the Edict of Toleration for Austrian Jews, in the face of strong resistance from the Church. However, the edict also included a clause for German Jews to "improve." Mendelssohn understood "improve" meant conversion. His response was the essay "Jerusalem," in which he made the forceful and radical argument that freedom of religion meant separation of Church and state. Although a devout Jew, he recognized that ancient traditions could be antithetical to society: "neither church nor state has any right to coerce men's principles and convictions in any way whatsoever." He believed the state would support his view. He was rewarded in the form of a tax he paid for permission to pass through Dresden's gates.

Less affluent working classes did not enjoy or participate in the state's magnanimity. They endured poverty and oppression. Ordinary Jews paid taxes, not to pass through gates, but for the dubious privilege of living in hovels behind locked iron bars. Bankers and merchants in Königsberg lamented that "the word Jew carries a debasing flavor, and its use does us damage."

Bubbling discontent from the Lutheran Church eventually led Prussia to issue the Edict of Religion in the waning years of the eighteenth century. The law banned anyone from opposing the truth of the Holy Trinity and Bible.

The Prussian archivist and Judeophile, Christian Wilhelm Dohm, penned a booklet in which he wrote: "Every craft and trade guild would feel itself dishonored if it admitted a circumcised worker to its ranks. . . . For the most part they remain tied to . . . prohibitions which allow the barest livelihood." The future deputy to the French States General Honoré Gabriel Riquet, count of Mirabeau, despaired over the debasement of Jews in Germany and condemned their subjugation. Asked for his answer to the ancient hatred of Jews, Mirabeau replied, "I will make them human." When the Prussian law was introduced, he called it "a law worthy of cannibals."

The revolution in France panicked monarchies across the continent. Cries of "Freedom, Equality, Fraternity" in the streets and alleys of Paris brought down the king in a bloody rebellion. Austria and Italy's military misjudged Napoleon Bonaparte, who overwhelmed and drove them back, eventually taking control of the Rhineland. Jews had not been allowed to live in Cologne since the fifteenth century. The French commissioner proclaimed: "All traces of slavery are now abolished . . . you shall account to God alone for your religious beliefs, and as to your status, all men stand equal before the law."

Rabbi Abraham Scheur of Mainz welcomed Napoleon in 1811 at Dusseldorf. Although Napoleon said, "Before God all men are brothers. They should love and help one another without regard to differences of religion," he betrayed his true attitude in a letter to his brother Jerome: "I have undertaken to reform the Jews, but I have not endeavored to draw more of them into my realm. Far from that, I have avoided doing anything which could show any esteem for the most despicable of mankind."

Napoleon's politically motivated public statements had little impact on Polish Jews. They continued battling to maintain their rights. The advent of World War I, the collapse in 1917 of czarist Russia, and defeat of Germany in 1918 changed the face of Europe, opening the door to Poland's independence.

Literature, music, art, and business prospered in the country. Jews were half of all physicians, one-third of Polish attorneys, and a major portion of journalists and teachers. They served in parliament and municipalities. Prominent, respected Jewish businessman and philanthropist Wolf Gutgeld sat on Warsaw City Council. Germany enacted the Nuremberg Laws in 1935—race laws classifying Jews as inferior to so-called "pure Aryans" and therefore not eligible for full German citizenship. This sent shock waves through Jewish communities in Europe and America.

The Great Depression and Nazi Germany's increasing militarism convinced Wolf to sell his investment portfolio, although he retained a few real estate holdings providing inexpensive housing for the less fortunate. As political conditions became increasingly dangerous, he purchased gold coins with the money he made from selling equities, even though they'd dropped almost forty percent in the economic crisis. If he fled Poland gold would be a valuable, stable transactional commodity.

On Purim, March 17, 1938, Wolf's daughter-in-law Sara, married to his eldest son Nahum, gave birth to her third child,

David. Eight days later, David's family attended his Brit Milah, circumcision, his entry into the ancient covenant. His mother remained in hospital suffering from a severe infection. Sara Gutgeld passed away on March 27. The child only knew his mother from photos.

David's birth on Purim was prescient. The holiday celebrates the story of a reluctant hero in the fourth century BCE. Hadassah, a young Jewish girl, adopts the name Esther to mask her ethnicity in order to save her people. Years later, David stepped out of the storm, emerging from the unspeakable maelstrom of the Holocaust into an incredible existential adventure with a new identity.

Europe rocked again the same month with the ironically named *Anschluss*—"connection." Accompanied by applause and fervid cheers, the unopposed German army annexed Austria. The dictator of Germany, Adolf Hitler, immediately took steps to conquer and rule a continent swept clean of Jews— *Judenrein* Europe—humiliating and subjugating them with hard labor and destroying their institutions. The Nuremberg Laws made clear Nazi Germany's goals: the "purity of German blood is the essential condition for the continued existence of the German people."

The Third Reich demanded that Czechoslovakia cede the German-speaking region of the Sudetenland. Slovak, British, and French diplomats caved to Hitler's demands. He blithely assured the world he had no further expansionist plans. They signed the Munich Agreement on September 1938. The outfoxed prime minister of Great Britain, Neville Chamberlain, announced "Peace for our time."

Winston Churchill, speaking in the British House of Commons, called the pact an utter catastrophe:

"We have suffered a total and unmitigated defeat. . . . We are in the presence of a disaster of the first magnitude. . . . [W]e have sustained a defeat without a war, the consequences of which will travel far with us along our road. . . . [W]e have passed an awful milestone in our history, when the whole equilibrium of Europe has been deranged. . . . [D]o not suppose that this is the end. This is only the beginning of the reckoning."

Under orders from Hitler and executed by Obergrupenführer Reinhard Heydrich and Minister of Propaganda Josef Goebbels, the paramilitary Schutzstaffel (SS) wreaked havoc on major metropolises, towns, and villages, destroying Jewish businesses, smashing store windows, and inciting citizens to join the assault. The night of November 9, 1938, *Kristallnacht*, the "Night of Broken Glass," ended with thirty-six Jews dead. Three days later Hermann Goering called a meeting at the request of Hitler to plan the forced removal of all Jews from Germany and confiscation of all Jewish property. The *New York Times* reported to the world:

"MUNICH, Germany, Nov. 10—All Jewish families were ordered this morning to leave Munich within forty-eight hours and were instructed to inform the political police by 6 P.M. when they would hand over the keys to their dwellings and garages. Instructions were issued to confiscate all Jewish-owned cars and the sale of gasoline to Jews was forbidden. In some cases Jews were told that they must leave Germany and they were forced to sign a statement to this effect. No notice was taken of the objection that most Jews were without passports. The only Jews with passports are those who have already made preparations to emigrate. . . . So far as can be gathered every Jewish-owned shop in town was completely or partly

> wrecked as well as several "Aryan" businesses, which shared the general fate for having previously belonged to Jews. An orthodox synagogue was set on fire early this morning; the alarm was raised about 8 A.M. but the flames caused much havoc before they could be controlled. The synagogue was reduced to a shell and the Jewish school adjoining it was also completely burned. It was reported that synagogues in Bemberg, Bayreuth and Treutlingen were also burned. Arrests of male Jews began at their homes at an early hour. It was estimated that so far about 400 had been taken into custody and also a half dozen women."

A circular dated January 25, 1939, from the German Foreign Office to German representatives abroad ordered: "All Jews to emigrate from Germany, leaving their property behind; no Jewish state to be formed; wide distribution of Jews desired; Anti-Semitism to be fostered in all countries to greatest possible degree." Jews abandoned everything, leaving them destitute. Nazis incarcerated and murdered those not transported to Dachau, Buchenwald, and Mauthausen concentration camps.

In August the same year, Germany and the Soviet Union signed a secret protocol, the Hitler-Stalin Pact, forming an alliance guaranteeing neither state would open hostilities with the other. The pact carved out Nazi and Soviet spheres of influence in Eastern Europe.

Chapter Two

The Kid Who Didn't Exist

In August 1939, Nazi troops in Polish army uniforms staged an attack on the Gleiwitz radio station in Germany; taking over the transmitter and broadcasting anti-German messages in Polish. They forced concentration camp prisoners to wear German military garb, murdered them, took photos, and claimed the pictures proved the Polish government invaded German territory. In September 1939, the Reich established the first concentration camp, Stutthof, east of Danzig, the same month Hitler launched his assault on Poland.

Guided by Soviet radio transmissions, German bombers hit Warsaw, Łódź, Kraków, and Poznań. Germany, joined in the east by the Soviet Union, decimated the ill-prepared and unde-requipped Polish armed forces, sending shockwaves across the Western world. Wolf Gutgeld and his sons Nahum, Levi, and Natan escaped Warsaw, leaving behind his mother, sisters, and grandchildren in the misguided belief Germany—the land of Bach, Brahms, Beethoven, Heine, and Hesse—would never harm children and women. Hitler's regime had no compunction about persecuting them, along with men. The occupiers cordoned off 759 acres of Warsaw, in a predominantly Jewish area, creating one of the largest ghettoes in Europe. Bank accounts were frozen, businesses shut down.

Rugged blonde, blue-eyed, thirty-five-year-old Alex Roslan, a merchant eking out a living dealing in out-of-date textiles, and his wife Mela watched helplessly four hundred thousand Jews locked behind sealed gates on a squalid island in the midst of the city. Among inmates of the Warsaw Ghetto were the three Gutgeld brothers, their grandmother, and aunts Hanka and Devorah.

The Nazi regime took control of the entire nation, instituted programs to rid Jews from Europe, and crushed Polish independence. It broke the Hitler-Stalin Pact when Germany invaded the Soviet Union in 1941. The Nazis deported three hundred thousand people from the ghetto to death camps. Those left behind formed the Jewish Fighting Organization, determined to battle rather than bend to the will of their captors. Out of conviction or altruism a few people outside the ghetto risked their lives in order to save the oppressed, supplying clandestine shipments of weapons and ammunition to the JFO through tunnels dug beneath the ghetto walls.

An acquaintance of the Roslans, Leopold Zygmunt, brought damaged German uniforms for Alex to refurbish into civilian clothes. He also had a sideline gathering bits of silver and gold from those inside the ghetto to buy German arms and ammunition captured by partisans, delivering them to Jewish fighters.

Zygmunt's fate was sealed when he was caught after curfew with pockets full of precious stones. Troops dragged him by his feet to a telephone pole where they hung him by wire around his neck. The barbaric execution spurred Alex to take Zygmunt's place.

Mela reacted to Alex's news as if slapped in the face. "What about our children? Our welfare? Let the partisans do their job. Stay out of it."

"All my life I fought tyranny with my vote, my voice. Hitler's Third Reich made them meaningless. Jews first. Who comes next? Fighters inside the ghetto need help to show the world they will not go down without defending themselves."

Filled with anxiety, Mela could not dissuade Alex. Under cover of darkness, he met a JFO commander in a shaft, explaining he knew Zygmunt and would take his place buying weapons.

"You're dead if you don't deliver," the commander warned.

"We're all dead if I don't deliver," responded Alex.

On a moonless night, Alex stealthily pushed a handcart to a shattered warehouse tucked away in a dark alley. He rapped on the door. A slit opened.

"What do you want?" asked a gruff voice.

"Zygmunt's dead. I'm replacing him."

Hands dragged Alex inside and he was slammed into a chair. A candle sputtered, illuminating a tough, bearded partisan wearing a khaki jacket, bandolier over his shoulder, holding a gun to Alex's forehead.

"Who the fuck are you?"

"Roslan. Alex Roslan. Zygmunt bartered guns and ammunition. I promised a JFO commander I'd continue his work."

"Trying to run your own goddamned war?"

"You have the goods. I have payment."

A partisan stepped out of the shadows. "You won't remember me. I did business at your shop before the war."

"Kolbek. A long time ago," smiled Alex. "Back in '36, we traveled together to Łódź."

"Roslan's a good guy, Marek. If Jews kill Nazis, what difference does it make?"

Marek slapped his hand on a table. "Put it here."

Alex emptied gold, silver, emeralds, sapphires, diamond rings, and earrings onto the scarred wood.

"The Germans are right. Jews have it all. Kolbek, help with the boxes."

Wehrmacht troopers, indoctrinated to obey orders without question, helped make Alex's plan operational. Night after night he observed sentries rotating at the ghetto walls. For a minimum of five to a maximum eight minutes, they left areas unguarded. Enough time for him to push a small cart to a tunnel entrance and deliver munitions and arms before detection.

On one covert nighttime trek, he demanded a JFO commander permit him to enter the ghetto. Warned he would be executed if discovered, Alex responded with typical bravado. "I survived invasion, bombs, and antisemitic partisans. I helped you, now I'm calling in the debt."

With a yellow six-pointed star pinned on Alex's jacket, they crawled into a dank, narrow space until sunrise. At dawn, Alex and his guide emerged onto an oppressive, overcrowded, narrow street. Emaciated men and women wandered aimlessly. Vacant-eyed beggars slumped against walls, pleading for help.

Starving children grabbed his hand: "piece of bread," "Groschen," they pleaded. In the shadows of scarred buildings, piles of wood. Alex moved closer, staggered at the truth. Children's bodies were heaped against walls. Men, praying as they went about their terrible job, tossed them in wagons.

"We can't feed them all. Typhoid and scarlet fever take most of the young ones," mourned the JFO commander. Overcome with shock and dismay, Alex made a solemn oath to rescue at least one child from certain death. Question: How to find a child in the ghetto? Would a family be willing to give them up, despite hardships behind walls?

A fortuitous visit to Alex's shop by an old friend, Stasek Sokolski, chauffeur for Wolf Gutgeld before the war, gave him the opportunity. Stasek sent packages of food to three boys, their grandmother, and aunts incarcerated behind the walls.

His plan hit a brick barrier. "You're insane!" Mela shouted.

"Papa, only Jews are allowed in the ghetto. They find you, they'll kill you," said Jurek.

"Doing nothing admits we're powerless. Friends suffer behind those walls. We need to do something, anything. I will not stand by. People who helped us, customers, friends, sent to their death."

Troubled, Marisia whispered, "My teacher said Jews made all the trouble we have in Poland."

"You believe friends caused the war? Bombed the city?"

"It doesn't make sense," she replied.

Alex took Mela's hands. "A child's life. If it were Jurek or Marisia, nothing would stop you. My old friend Stasek Sokolski, chauffeur for the boy's grandfather before the invasion, gave me a picture so I could put a face to a name: Jacob Gutgeld."

"I'm supposed to trust Stasek the drunk, the womanizer?" scowled Mela.

"Forget what he was. He helps the Gutgelds survive. What does your Good Book say about sinners? 'Happy is he whose transgression is forgiven, whose sins are covered over.'"

"The atheist quotes the Bible all of a sudden."

"Even a blind squirrel finds an acorn once in a while." He handed the photo to Mela. "We can change Jacob's destiny."

She ran her finger over the image. The boy had soulful, dark eyes, and a mop of unruly hair.

"If this is what you want."

"Only if we all agree."

"Nice to have another boy living with us," said Jurek.

"How old is he?" asked Marisia.

"The same age as you—nine."

"We can study together."

"Two down, one to go. Mela?"

"The picture makes him real. A boy who needs help. Yes."

From the comfort of her home in North Carolina, decades later, Marisia recalled: "If the Germans knew my parents harbored Jewish children, I knew I would be hanged on the balcony and then my parents would be hanged. We did what we had to do."

Stasek slipped a note into his next delivery to the Gutgelds. The children's rescue, one at a time, was imminent. Alex's observation of German soldiers obeying the clock, leaving the gates to go to the munitions factories where they forced Jews to work, gave him a brief window to help Jacob escape.

Hanka Gutgeld stood behind the gate with the nine-year-old boy. The memory imprinted itself in Jacob's mind for the rest of his life. Speaking almost passively sixty years later, he recalled: "My aunt kissed me and handed me over to Alex. He took my hand, like father and son. We walked together to his apartment."

"You can't be Jacob any longer. I have a nephew, Geniek, out in the country. From now on your name is Geniek, not Jacob. Remember: Geniek."

"Will you bring my brothers out of the ghetto?" Jacob asked.

"That's our plan. We have to wait for the right time," said Alex.

They skirted the back of the building. "Keep very quiet," said Alex quietly opening the entrance into a basement filled with odds and ends left behind by people who fled or Jews captured and driven into the ghetto.

Jacob tripped over a metal container, clattering across the floor. Alex halted, pressing his hand over Jacob's mouth. They waited in semidarkness for a few minutes and moved on.

The noise disturbed the janitor, Oleg Korcek, sleeping off a drinking bout. He staggered out in time to see Alex and Jacob disappear through a door to stairs leading up to the Roslan apartment.

They gathered around Jacob. Marisia and Jurek bombarded him with questions.

"What's it like inside?" Marisia asked.

"Did you have enough food?" asked Jurek.

"You must have felt terrible leaving your brothers behind," Marisia said.

Mela interrupted them. "Now is not the time to bother Jacob."

"Use his new name—Geniek," ordered Alex. "Anyone hearing 'Jacob' will know he's Jewish."

"Where are your mother and father?" whispered Marisia.

Jacob sat down, and in a plaintive voice cried, "My mother died after my brother David was born. My father, grandfather, uncles, left us behind."

Mela held his hand. "From now on, I am your mama and Alex is your papa. You are part of our family."

He looked up. "The Germans want to kill us all. I don't know why."

The Roslans had no words. They could not tell Jacob that what they wished and what they could do were miles apart. Their hope lay in Stasek's ability to get messages in and out of the ghetto.

Alex returned to his shop, leaving Mela in charge of the children. A few weeks later, police sergeant Mirosław Komski slipped into the shop. "We've known each other for a hell of a long time. My uniform doesn't represent allegiance to Nazis; I've been working with the partisans. You have to get out of here. The Gestapo's searching for contraband. I'm not doing the Germans' dirty work. You've always been good to me and my family. Now it's my turn. Don't waste time. Get the hell out."

Alex shuttered the windows and locked the doors; he threw stripped German uniforms beneath floorboards, covering them with bolts of fabric, and burned papers in a small stove. Klaxons screeched. Trucks pulled onto the street, disgorging platoons crashing into one store after another. Alex ran into a back alley, watching from a distance as the Gestapo dragged merchants from shops throwing bloody, beaten men into trucks. Polish Blue and Criminal Police abetting the Nazi regime smashed open the door of Alex's shop, ransacking the interior.

"All businesses not supporting the war effort are hereby ordered to cease and desist business within two weeks. We have it on good authority that such businesses may be hiding Jews and other undesirables. Such actions will be met with severe punishment," an officer stated.

Before the deadline, Alex and Jurek dragged out several bolts of fabric, carted them into the apartment building's cellar, and locked the merchandise behind wooden doors hidden by a dilapidated armoire.

"Gives me enough to sell at a market near Otomańska tomorrow."

The Gutgeld chauffeur visited at least once a week, checking up on Jacob, remembering halcyon days before the war when Sokolski drove his grandfather's big American car to the country for picnics in a Warsaw forest. He and Shalom played among the trees. His mother Sara, a delicate woman with porcelain skin, wearing a broadbrimmed straw hat, sitting on a blanket, ate fresh strawberries, giving one to him and one to Shalom, counting "One, two, three. Next year we'll be counting 'One, two, three, four' when the baby's born," she smiled.

Stasek took Alex into a corner of the room. "I have a way of making some real money. There's a barn in the country with a stash of prewar cigarettes. Worth more than gold. You can have a share. Friends and I are making a raid on the place. We'll bring them back and sell them on the black market . . . something you know how to do. I'll come over tomorrow for your answer."

Mela erupted when she heard about Stasek's plan. "Absolutely not. He'll be drunk before you get halfway. You'll be stranded God knows where after curfew."

"Your word is my command," said Alex, kissing her.

She pulled back. "It better be."

A knock on the door, followed by Korcek's voice, called, "Anyone home?"

"What does that nosy son of a bitch want?" asked Alex, hustling Jacob into the bedroom. "Not a sound." He closed the door and ordered Marisia and Jurek to sit on the floor. He tossed a deck of cards to them. "Play something."

"Marisia doesn't know card games," said Jurek.

"Ever heard of pretend? Pretend!"

Alex opened the door. "Can I help you, Korcek?"

The janitor peered over Alex's shoulder and shrugged. "Thought I'd drop in to see if you need anything fixed."

"Come in. Maybe you can end the war."

Korcek saw his son and daughter playing cards. "Gamblers like your father?"

"I don't gamble. Odds are always with the dealer," said Alex.

"Good advice. Wish I listened years ago." He kept looking around, a jackal sniffing for prey. "Seen the posters? Big rewards for handing over Jews. Even their kids."

"If you have any hidden away, trade them for a pair of shoes."

Alex retrieved a bottle of cherry Visniak and poured two glasses. They clinked. "Sto lat. Let me know when you make a killing handing over Jewish babies," said Alex.

Jolted by the statement, the janitor suddenly stood up. "I have to go."

Alex went to work hammering together a narrow space with a trap door under a cabinet beneath the kitchen sink. "Get in," Alex ordered Jacob. He squirmed into the hiding hole and pulled the trapdoor down. "How is it?"

"Dark," came Jacob's muffled voice. The trap door opened, and the boy popped out.

"Problem solved," announced Alex.

A week passed and Stasek did not make his usual visit. Alex had a gnawing feeling this friend's plan hit a snag. If the chauffeur had been successful, he would have pranced in with pockets filled with zlotys.

A stranger tapped on the door. Alex saw an odd sight through the peephole. A bearded man wearing a hat with a feather in its headband, a *Tirolerhut*. "Looking for Alex Roslan," he whispered.

"His Polish told me it wasn't his first language. From the way he dressed, I thought he was Austrian, German, not

Jewish. I almost closed the door when he told me his name," recalled Alex.

"Mr. Roslan, I'm Jacob's uncle, Dr. Avraham Galler. Since the Nazis invaded I've been working with forged papers as Dr. Vladimir Kowalksi. When I didn't hear from Stasek, I decided to take matters into my own hands. I'm sorry to bring bad news. The SS set a trap for him and his friends. They were all killed."

Mela's face turned white. "It could have been you."

"All for a carton of cigarettes," said Alex.

"Can we still bring Jacob's brothers out of the ghetto?" asked Mela.

"With Stasek dead, the plan to rescue Shalom and David needs to be reconsidered. I'll see what I can do. Shalom's in hiding at a farm just outside Warsaw. In a few days, I have a break from the hospital and plan to pick him up."

"Galler, maybe he's better off where he is."

"Can you imagine the psychological damage for them to be separated, not only for Shalom, but for Jacob and David? I've seen how you handled Jacob's escape. You and Mela take this responsibility with remarkable resolution. I'll be in touch."

Time was not on Avraham Galler's side. SS Commander Jürgen Stroop, wary of news young Jews in the ghetto planned to resist, drew up plans to eliminate the Jewish enclave with a massive military attack. Before the war, Galler helped a German Olympic boxer overcome a severe leg injury. He earned a Silver Medal in the 1936 Olympics. After the treacherous invasion by Germany, he changed his name to Hans Müller. The gestapo began sweeping up Jewish lawyers, financiers and doctors. Galler's colleague, 24 C hapter Two Dr. Janusch Masurik, hid him in a cellar beneath his private office. Galler emerged weeks later with a dark beard, a new name and forged papers in the name of Dr. Vladimir Kowalski who practiced alongside Masurik at Warsaw's Ujazdowski Hospital, a military hospital given unusual freedom, treating not only the military, but civilians as well. It was Galler's perfect cover. He hired the former athlete as an ambulance driver who remained loyal for the duration of the war.

They commandeered an ambulance and with hospital papers explaining a need to transport an injured Polish child to the hospital, made it through German inspections.

Arriving at the farm unannounced, Galler was shocked to find skeletal Shalom covered in muck, cowering in a corner of a pig stye. He demanded to know why the farmer maltreated the chld. Before another word the athlete slammed him into a brick wall with a warning, "Next time I won't be this nice."

Galler would not place Shalom in that condition with the Roslans. The child needed medical attention. He brought the boy back to his grandmother and aunts Hanka and Devorah, treating him under cover. With the noose tightening around the ghetto, it became imperative to get Shalom out.

A few days later, Galler reappeared, carrying a large backpack. A thin hand reached out, then the pinched face of an almost skeletal boy.

"Take good care of Shalom. He's frail. Needs food and rest. It's going to be more difficult rescuing David. The SS and Gestapo tightened security around the ghetto. As a Polish physician, I'm allowed inside to prevent the spread of communicable diseases to the outside world. It may prove advantageous, but no promises."

Galler contrived a perilous plan for David's liberation. Müller agreed to assist in the rescue. On a moonless night, he waited in the dark outside the ghetto walls. David stood on the other side in the gloom between two burly men. A church bell tolled two in the morning. Grasping David's arms and legs, they tossed him over the wall into the arms of the attendant, who handed the shaken boy to Alex.

Forty years later, David gave a seminar on probability mathematics at a California university. A local elementary school requested he talk to students about his incarceration in the ghetto. He gave them a vivid description of the incident that saved his life. Students asked if he was afraid. His answer: "Better a broken leg than dying in a gas chamber."

Alex insisted David also change his name. "I gave Jacob the name of a nephew. I have another nephew, Tadek, who lives far away. You look like you could be his brother. From now on you are Tadek. Never use your real name."

Fearing a new name would impact the frail, anxious, sickly Shalom, the Roslans waited until he gained strength.

David had difficulty sleeping. He incessantly asked his brother about the mother and father he never knew. "What were they like? Did they treat you and Shalom nice?"

"Our mother was beautiful. She and our grandmother loved to cook and bake. Especially sweet, delicious coffee babka."

"Tell me about our father?" asked David.

"Always busy. I think he was grandfather's accountant. He started teaching me arithmetic when I was about five or six, a year before you were born."

"I wish I knew them."

"One of these days we might get to see our father."

The boys crawled out on the fire escape. Battle-scarred Warsaw spread to the horizon. German soldiers in work clothes clambered out of trucks below, pasting notices on buildings, sending a terrifying chill through Jacob and David:

"REWARD FOR INFORMATION REGARDING
HIDDEN JEWS. REPORT INFORMATION TO OFFICE
OF JEWISH AFFAIRS DEUTSCHE GESTATZPOLIZEI.
COMMANDER, SICHERHEITZ POLIZEI SD,
WARSAW DISTRICT."

A neighbor spotted the boys. The opportunity to receive additional rations if she reported unusual activity, especially involving Jews, overcame any sense of moral obligation. She eagerly informed the police.

A cadre of troopers, accompanied by a police officer, hammered on the Roslan door. Alex planted Jacob and Shalom beneath the trapdoor in the kitchen cabinet. The front door burst open, splintering the frame. The police officer yelled, "Leave them alone! I know Roslan."

Alex took a close look and broke into a broad smile. "I didn't recognize you in uniform, Rogowski," he said. "How about a drink for old times?" He pointed at the troopers. "Invite your . . . friends."

With a nod from their sergeant, the security force put aside their weapons and joined Alex.

"Sorry about the door. We'll send a repair crew to take care of it," said Rogowski.

Mela, their children, and David watched Alex's cool behavior with amazement at how he manipulated the invaders.

The sergeant bowed to Mela. "Our apologies. The person who made the report will not bother you again." He patted David on his head. "A true Aryan."

Quiet fell in the apartment after they marched out. Shalom and Jacob crawled out of the cabinet. David fell into a chair, exhausted by fear.

April 20, 1943, the first day of Passover, brought increasing dread. On Reichsführer Heinrich Himmler's directive, General Jürgen Stroop ordered the demolition of the Warsaw Ghetto and deportation of the entire population to death camps. In an incredible show of heroism, the Jewish Fighting Organization rose up, mounting a tactical guerilla battle.

The unexpected rebellion inspired partisans to attack German positions. The Roslans watched from a distance as fighters bravely took the offensive, striking down the lie Jews would succumb passively. With daring and an indomitable will never to surrender, they fought back, forcing their jailers out of the enclave. Their short-lived victory ended when the Waffen-SS attacked with flamethrowers and firebombs, burning down the entire ghetto. After a month of brutal hand-to-hand clashes, the ghetto fell to overpowering force.

Jürgen Stroop reported to Heinrich Himmler: "The former Jewish quarter of Warsaw is no longer in existence."

Reduced to ashes, the Warsaw Ghetto inspired uprisings in Lithuania, Ukraine, and Belorussia. Jews in the Treblinka killing center set fire to the camp, a few escaping to join the partisans. Prisoners in Sobibor killed guards, wiped out police auxiliaries, and set the camp ablaze. Short on weapons, lacking numbers, they managed to resist their captors. Warsaw's streets became open sewers. Rats ran in packs. Virulent disease swept through the city, eventually infecting Jurek. Alex raced to the hospital, asking for Dr. Vladimir Kowalski. Informed he was in surgery, Alex paced nervously until Kowalski/Galler came out of the operating room.

"A German soldier. Couldn't save his leg."

"You helped the enemy?" asked Alex.

Galler pulled him aside. "Roslan, you took a great chance because you needed to. That boy in there needed my skills to survive. He'll be sent home. Away from here. He'll never know a Jew saved his life."

"We need you. Jurek is sick, feverish, has difficulty swallowing."

"I'll come as soon as possible. Get soup down his throat. You need to keep his temperature down. Don't wrap him in a blanket."

Avraham Galler arrived carrying a bag filled with medication. "Make sure Jacob, David, and Shalom do not go near him."

Galler palpated Jurek's neck and took his temperature. "Scarlet fever," he announced. "Early stage. He needs hospitalization immediately to keep from getting worse." He scribbled a note on his prescription pad, signing it 'Vladimir Kowalski.' "Get him there first thing in the morning. I'll alert the staff he's a special case."

"Am I going to be all right?" Jurek croaked.

"We'll take good care of you." He gave Mela a packet of pills. "Two every six hours. Every hour a cold compress on his forehead. The hospital, tomorrow, early."

Alex placed his son on a hand cart. He and Mela trundled along streets pitted with bomb craters, past German patrols, into the hospital. Nurses transferred Jurek to a gurney. Alex and Mela followed him to a room occupied with patients coughing, wheezing, suffering from the myriad of diseases rampant in Warsaw.

"Dr. Kowalski ordered a bed near a window. Fresh air is good for him," said a nurse bringing a tray with medications.

Galler examined Jurek once more. "He's strong, in good shape. I have confidence we'll get him back on his feet. Mela, in a few days you can bring him some home cooking."

"How long will he be here?" she asked, worry written on her face.

"Depends on his recovery. A few weeks. I'll keep my eye on him."

Mela hugged him. "May God bless you."

Shaking his hand, Alex whispered to Galler, "I believe in you."

Several days later Shalom developed the same symptoms. Galler rushed to the Roslan apartment confirming the weak, fragile boy developed scarlet fever as well. The Roslans could not risk taking him to a medical facility out of fear hospital personnel would report him.

"Bring us the medicine," said Mela.

Galler, tears in his eyes, put his arms around Alex and Mela. "The Germans ordered all medications locked away. Anyone attempting to take them out of the hospital will be executed. The best you can do is keep his temperature down and place him near a window with sunlight."

Mela stiffened her spine and prepared a meal for Jurek. She told him about Shalom. How Galler no longer had access to medications. "All we can do is pray for a miracle."

Little Shalom's condition preyed on Jurek as he slowly grew stronger. The next time a nurse brought medications in packets, he squirreled half in the empty envelopes.

Mela brought him a potato and a small piece of dry bread. He ate it with relish and asked about Shalom.

"If we had medicine, he might be all right. Right now, he's very weak."

He slipped the packets to Mela. "Come every day and I'll give you more."

Her son's care and concern overwhelmed Mela. "You need medicine to get better."

"Don't worry about me. I'm feeling stronger. Listen to my voice. Normal. Fever's down. Shalom needs the medicine more than me." He held his mother's hand. "Besides, I talked with him. He's smart. One time he told me a story called 'Treasure Island,' all about pirates and a boy who discovers a treasure map. I want him to live so he can finish it."

Under Galler's supervision, Mela administered Jurek's prescriptions to Shalom. Weakened by malnutrition, depression, and anxiety, he succumbed. His death took a major toll on his brothers, the Roslans, Marisia, and Jurek.

Years later, Jacob, with tears in his eyes, recalled, "We put him in a basket and buried him in a cellar. He was a kid who didn't exist."

Chapter Three

Valley of Shadows

Jurek returned home, healthy and energetic. Unknown to his parents, he joined the Polish youth resistance formed as part of the underground Polish Scouting Association, branded criminal by the Nazi regime. The scouts reorganized as paramilitary fighters. Jurek engaged in sabotage, blowing up railway bridges, interrupting transports, and on several occasions, freeing inmates from enemy prisons.

Prodded by Marisia's curiosity to know what he did at night, Jurek confided his scout unit was part of the resistance. "Papa worked hard getting arms and ammunition into the ghetto. The least I can do is join my mates fighting our own way." His dedication made him a hero in her eyes.

Jurek's nighttime excursions took a heavy toll. He looked haggard and tired in the morning.

Alex took Marisia aside. "What's going on with your brother?"

"I don't know," she said, her voice trembling.

"You're not telling the truth."

"What's going on?" Mela asked.

"I promised not to tell," murmured Marisia.

Jurek stumbled into the kitchen, his eyes red.

"Where were you last night?" Alex demanded.

"Working with the partisans," he blurted out.

"Are you insane? You're too young. You could be killed," complained Mela.

"There are boys and girls younger than me."

"I don't care about others. Under my roof you'll do as I say," ordered Alex.

Jurek sat back and swigged a cup of coffee. "*You* do it."

Time stood still. Alex smiled. "Eat your breakfast. Afterwards, I need my hero's help getting fabric to another market near Górczewska Park. You want danger? Work in the black market."

They came home in the evening. Alex placed a container of earnings from sales on the table. "Time for my little accountant to take charge. Geniek, I need your help." Jacob staggered into the room holding his head. His face was flushed, perspiration soaked his clothes.

"My ear. It's agony." They rushed him to bed. Marisia filled a basin with cold water. David bathed his face and chest. Jacob grasped Mela's hand. "My throat's sore."

"Scarlet fever," Marisia stammered.

Fear struck Jacob. "It killed Shalom."

Marisia held him fast. "You're strong. Very strong."

"Listen to Mama Roslan. She knows," said David, trying not to cry.

"Go in the other room, Tadek. We don't want you to get sick," ordered Alex.

"He needs a doctor," Mela pleaded.

Alex found Dr. Galler in the hospital personnel locker room preparing to leave.

"Geniek has a terrible pain in his ear. We don't know how to help him."

"I'll have an ambulance take us to your place."

The ambulance hurried through streets still lit by the setting sun. They sprinted upstairs, where Galler found a groaning, flushed, and perspiring Jacob pressing a hand behind his ear.

"Everyone outside. I need to focus on the boy," Galler instructed. A few minutes later, he came out and washed his hands. "He has an infection of the bone in back of his left ear. It's not scarlet fever. It's mastoiditis. The bone is like a honeycomb, normally clear. Geniek's is filled with bacterial pus. It needs to be drained or the infection will spread. We can only do it at the hospital." He wrote a note on a pad and handed it to Alex. "Give this to Dr. Masurik. We went to medical school together in Vienna. He can be trusted and will explain our options."

A steady drizzle drenched Alex on his search for the doctor's office. He found it near the hospital. A brass plate with the name J. Masurik, MD on a door. He entered a small waiting room.

"Dr. Kowalski gave me Dr. Masurik's name. It's an emergency," Alex informed the receptionist

Masurik, tall, with a short, cropped beard, read Galler's diagnosis and ushered Alex into his office. "Surgery's the only way to help the boy. Bring him to the hospital as soon as possible."

"The boy is Jewish. A nurse, an attendant could report him."

"Mr. Roslan, protecting the boy from the Nazis means nothing if he dies. I can get him into the hospital. I can operate. I have a loyal staff, but they must have something to make it worth endangering their lives."

Alex remained quiet for a few minutes. He nodded in agreement. "How much?"

"At a minimum, three hundred zlotys. I won't take one groschen."

Alex told Galler and Mela the news. "We used everything—money, the goods you rescued from the shop." She emptied the money box on the table. "This isn't enough."

Alex paced the apartment. "There is a way."

Nazi banners flanked the door of the Warsaw Housing Authority. Soldiers patrolling the area cast suspicious eyes over a long line of ill-clad men, women, and children waiting beneath the gray sky.

"Cold enough?" Alex said to a young man in an undersized overcoat, muffler, and fur cap.

"I'm used to it. Been coming every day for two weeks. Never an opening."

"Difficult times. What's your name?"

"Hetman. Karol Hetman. Married a few weeks ago. Trying to find a place, any place, no matter how small."

Alex shook his hand. "Just married. Now there's a person with hope for the future."

"Hope can't provide a roof over our heads. They make it difficult. Permits. Investigations. You need contacts to find a place."

"Maybe we can help each other."

Alex returned home with Karol Hetman. He heard Mela in the modest kitchen preparing lunch.

"Here it is," said Alex.

"Very nice."

Mela peeked through the door. "You brought home a guest?" She pulled him aside. "What about money for the doctor?"

"He wants to buy the apartment."

"What are you talking about?"

"Karol—four rooms. You won't find many like this for six hundred zlotys."

"You have a deal."

Agitated, Mela grabbed Alex. "What deal? What's going on?"

The young man counted out the money and handed it to Alex. "When can we move in. My parents are staying with us until they find their own place."

"A week. Will that do?"

Mela could not believe Alex sold the apartment without talking it over with her. She wanted to stop him, but he forged ahead.

"A week. Thank you," said Hetman, almost dancing out the door.

"You sold the roof over our heads. How could you?"

Alex spread bills on the table. "Enough for Geniek's operation, and some left over. One of my neighbors at the market loaned me a horse and cart."

Mela threw herself into a chair and sobbed. He was right, but at the same time she deserved to be warned.

When Jurek came home from a clandestine scouting meeting, Alex told him his plan. "We're taking Geniek to the hospital. Important we do it with no one noticing."

His son looked around. "The couch. We put him under cushions punched with holes for air and take it on a horse cart."

"You're a genius."

"I'm writing 'genius' down and reminding you every time you get angry."

Mela placed pillows in the frame. Deep within, she knew they were doing the right thing. At the same time, she seethed with anger. Alex had brushed her aside and made a unilateral decision to sell their apartment.

With David's help, they placed Jacob on blankets spread over wooden slats and put the cushions over him. Alex and

Jurek carried the sofa to a horse and cart tied to a lamppost. A German patrol marched by.

"Come on. We have a customer who wants to buy it," Alex said in a loud, bold voice.

They lashed down the sofa when one of the German soldiers paused to pat the horse's muzzle. "Reminds me of our plow horse back home."

"He's a good old boy. I'd like to talk about your farm, but we promised this to a doctor at the hospital," said Alex. He untethered the animal. Jurek climbed into the cart. A Polish police car, sirens screaming, squealed around a corner. The horse bucked. Jurek leaped to steady the sofa.

They reached the rear hospital entrance and carried the sofa down a corridor past patients, nurses, and doctors. "Watch out. Coming through," warned Alex.

The head nurse stopped them. "Where do you think you're going with that?"

"Dr. Masurik's office. He bought it. A real steal," said Alex.

"He bought it?" asked the incredulous nurse.

"An antique. I can get you one. Interested?"

They pushed the sofa into a corner of Masurik's hospital office. An aide and the doctor assisted Jacob onto a gurney. "Wait in the corridor. The operation doesn't take long. It's the preparation and post-operation period that are time-consuming. As soon as we finish, I'll give you a prognosis."

Attendants pushed gurneys back and forth. Men, women, and children suffering shrapnel wounds hobbled past. Two orderlies assisted a blood-covered German soldier no older than Jurek into an operating room. His pale, beardless face registered a complete lack of understand of the war and his part in it. "Partisan attack," one of the orderlies commented to Alex.

Masurik came out of surgery and stripped off his mask. "He can go home in a few days."

They made their way back, skirting rubble hanging from skeletal frames, passing a cracked, dry, red sandstone fountain where Germans, under orders from Governor General Hans Frank, blew up the magnificent bronze statue of Frederick Chopin, a victim of the Third Reich's policy to destroy Polish culture. An army truck came to a halt in the square. Alex pulled his son into the shadows.

An SS officer spoke through a bullhorn. "All males over the age of sixteen report to the square immediately, by order of the commander, Warsaw District."

"Upstairs to the roof," Alex ordered. They clambered up six floors and peered over a parapet.

No one responded below. The Waffen-SS bashed doors and broke windows, driving men into the square. Frightened, anxious families followed, held back by baton-wielding armed troops. SS stood at attention, rifles ready.

"Attacks have been made on soldiers of the Third Reich by members of renegade partisan groups. Men have been killed, supplies looted. These illegal acts must be halted and paid for," stated the officer.

Men in the square shouted him down. Machine gun fire burst over their heads. The officer continued without emotion. "Form a straight line. Every fifth man step forward."

Guards prodded them, gun-butting those who refused. "The rest, clear the area," commanded the officer. They scattered.

At a nod from their commander, guards opened fire. Bodies jerked and spasmed. Women rushed from buildings to the executed men. Troops walked among them, prodding, poking, firing point-blank at any sign of life.

"Now I know why you helped the Jewish Fighting Organization. They may have lost the war, but they didn't lose their dignity," said Jurek.

"My son is braver and wiser than his father. Don't say a word about this to Mama."

The death squad drove out of the square, leaving behind bodies sprawled in pools of blood. Weeping, keening wives, mothers, fathers, brothers, sisters, sons, and daughters gently carried them away.

"If there is a hell, it looks like this," Alex said, anger in his voice.

"Our scoutmaster warned us they slaughter to terrify, to make us afraid. If they succeed, the world will crumble beneath our feet."

"The future will take care of these monsters," Alex sighed. "We have to deal with the here and now. Mama's waiting."

Mela stared through a broken window in a grimy room. Walls were cracked and stained with uneven green veins of mold turning black. Water dripped through the ceiling. Muddy, fetid torrents overflowed streets. A festering, malodourous courtyard with an ancient well, the only source of water, loomed out of sodden weeds. "I can't live like this!" she cried.

Alex tried to take her in his arms. "We'll manage. We always have."

She pushed him away. "I don't want to manage. I'm not noble like you. So wonderful. Helping others. What about me? Our children? I'm tired, Alex!" Mela yelled with feral fury. "It would be better if I went to the Germans and told them everything."

She ran out, leaving Alex shocked. Jurek grabbed his father's arm. "Papa . . ."

Marisia ran to follow her mother. Alex stopped her. "Stay here. Your mother's my responsibility."

He ran along cold, rain-swept streets, through narrow lanes, past the rubble of a hundred bomb blasts and vast areas leveled by air raids, until he came to a large square with avenues and streets stretching in every direction. It was the first time he consciously acknowledged a sense of loss, in time and space. Mela's cry, 'What about me?' hit with ferocity.

From a more peaceful time, he remembered the petite, shy girl with blue eyes and blonde hair in braids. Her father's cherry and apple orchards grew to the edge of the Roslan wheat fields on Białystok's outskirts. They hiked verdant Pietrasze Forest, swam in the Biała River, picnicked under the green canopy of Knyszyńska Woods overlooking slow-moving Supraśl bubbling along reed-covered banks.

"Farming is not what I want to do." Alex opened a drawing pad with sketches of buildings, designs of interiors, carefully colored landscapes. "One of these days I'm going to be an architect."

"Can you do that in Białystok?" asked a credulous Mela.

"The city has a good library, but not as good as those in Warsaw. I also need a tutor. Three days a week I work part-time doing accounts for Noah Teitelbaum at his textile mill. All around me, Jews work machines, create designs, and talk and yell in Yiddish. I learned the language to get along in the factory. I was the goalie on their soccer team. The captain, manager of the factory, listed my name on the roster as Alex Ornstein. Mr. Teitelbaum has a friend, Bohdan Lachert, on faculty at the Warsaw University of Technology Architecture Department.

He made arrangements for me to see him every Sunday in the city. He'll teach what I need for university entrance exams."

"You can't afford tuition!" exclaimed Mela.

"Mr. Teitelbaum's paying for me."

"A Jew paying? What does he want?"

"It would make him happy to see me succeed. Once I pass exams, I'll go to school. After graduation, I'll come back and we'll get married."

"If Teitelbaum believes in you, so do I."

Lachert, a master of modern, avant-garde architecture, introduced Alex to the work of Swiss architect Charles-Édouard Jeannere, known professionally as Le Corbusier, a pioneer of modern architecture. Lachert encouraged Alex to experiment with form and material.

Under the Nazi occupation years later, Bohdan Lachert and his wife, Irena, organized the Jewish Military Union with the Polish resistance working side by side with former officers of the Polish army to aid Jewish children in hiding or incarcerated in the Warsaw Ghetto.

Thirteen years before the unthinkable invasion of Poland, over two hundred aspiring students crammed University of Warsaw exam rooms the spring of 1926. With his affinity for mathematics and tutoring from Lachert, Alex swept through the tests.

Mela, her face lined with grief, met him at the rail terminal. "Your father had a heart attack while you were gone."

Alex's distraught mother stood next to the coffin laid out in the living room. "My husband dead. My son going off to university."

"University can wait. I'll take care of you."

Although Alex's aspirations to a professional career felt out of reach, Mela insisted he needed to fulfill his dream. "You can reapply after the harvest. I'll wait. "

A year later, his mother married a friend of Alex's father. With Bohdan Lachert's recommendation, the university permitted him to retake the exam. He spent two weeks in Warsaw absorbing theater, music, and art.

A Jewish theater company from Lithuania presented a drama that changed the face of theatrical history. *Between Two Worlds: The Dybbuk*, an Expressionist play by Sol An-Ski, who died before it opened, cast new light on possession real or imagined. The drama reinforced the atheism of Alex's late father. If there was a god, how could there be bloody wars? How could the wealthy, pretending piety, receive privileges denied the lower classes?

Alex joined students protesting the Soviet Union persecuting dissidents, authors, composers, artists, and anyone else seen as an enemy of the state. Uplifted with moral courage and a sense of righteousness, he returned home.

Dismayed, he found crops unharvested, fruit rotting on trees, and the impeccable farmhouse his father built in a state of disrepair. The man his mother had married, the trusted friend of his father, lay in an alcoholic stupor. His mother, grown thin and worn, explained away the bruises on her arms and legs as the result of falls. Alex demanded his mother tell the truth. Shaking with fear, she admitted her husband beat her. Driving his stepfather off the land, Alex threatened to break every bone in his body if he returned. He promised his mother he would rebuild the house, restore the farm, and give her security. His dream to build a new world vanished. Alex hired a trusted manager for the farm. After bringing it back to life, he acquiesced to Mela and they married in a church.

With the farm in good hands, Alex returned to work at the Teitelbaum factory, where he met other mill owners in Białystok and Łódź, the center of the textile industry. With his innate logistical talents, he soon became assistant manager under Isaac Weiss of Łódź Fine Textiles, a company owned by a dynamic woman, Ludmila Sobansky.

Mills and textile companies depended on the newest fashions to survive. At the end of the season, Ludmila had yards of unsold material. Alex suggested he take her bolt ends and sell fabric in the town square at a discount. Within a short time, his part-time job brought in a healthy income.

Isaac and Ludmila recommended Alex to other fabric merchants. He and Mela opened a small shop in Warsaw. Warehouses provided bolt ends for a fifty-fifty split of sales.

Mela's brother, Vladek, traveled from Kaminsk, a farming village south of Warsaw, for his annual Easter visit. She proudly bombarded him with her husband's success. Despising comparisons to Alex, he focused on depleting the Roslan liquor cabinet. For the sake of keeping peace in the house, Alex held back his abiding distaste for Vladek during his short stay in Warsaw.

Nineteen thirty-nine the world witnessed the sudden, brutal invasion of Poland, turning the world of blossoming sunflowers, and the hope of future prosperity, to darkness and subjugation. Alex failed to appreciate how Mela quietly steered the ship, keeping a steady course through good and bad times. The burden she carried, caring for the children, keeping them safe under perilous conditions, drove her to escape a world gone mad. Nature wept with Alex, raining harder and harder, soaking clothes, blinding eyes.

A German patrol marched by, ignoring the drenched Pole. They continued past scorched buildings where Mela hid behind a collapsed brick wall. Her conscience would not permit giving herself up to these persecutors. A crack of thunder preceded drenching rain and freezing sleet. She crouched beneath shattered wood benches and tables for protection.

Alex entered the flat facing the children waiting for news, good or bad. The look on their father's face told the story.

"Where's Mama?" Jurek yelled.

Alex sat on a chair streaked with mold. "She'll come back," he sighed through tight lips.

"You heard what she said. The Gestapo! The police!" Marisia cried.

Alex slammed his hand on the worn, gouged table. "Mama will return. I know her. She will want us to do what's necessary."

David knelt before him. "Geniek. What about Geniek?"

"Tomorrow we bring him home."

Morning broke over the ruins hiding Mela. She stumbled through pieces of marble and masonry, torn and charred Hebrew books. She knew the place. As a final act of destruction after the revolt by the Warsaw Ghetto fighters, SS Gruppenführer Jürgen Stroop personally pushed the plunger that dynamited the Great Synagogue. He exulted in its destruction as the last bastion of Jewish life in the city. "The Jewish resistance was assisted by partisans. I want them broken. I want the arm of the Polish government-in-exile, Armia Krajowa, destroyed. Break the back of Communist Armia Ludowa," ordered Stroop.

Despondent and forlorn, Mela desperately wanted to go home. An orange ball, bright as the sun, unexpectedly bounced through the debris. A girl no older than six or seven, dressed in rags, her face red from the cold, hesitantly walked in the rain toward Mela.

"What is your name?" Mela asked.

"Benedykta."

"A beautiful name for a pretty child. It means "blessing." You must be a blessing for your mother and father."

She stared at the broken tile beneath her feet. "They went away. My brother said they fight for us."

The innocent girl's words touched Mela's soul. "You have given me something very special, Benedykta: courage."

Mela handed the ball to the girl in rags, touching her fingers. She snatched it, darting away. In the most difficult times, thought Mela, children play, dream, and hope tomorrow will be different. She stood straight and strong and walked the long road home.

Alex, consumed with worry about his wife, anxious to bring Jacob home, met Masurik at the hospital. They laid Jacob, his head bandaged, in the bottom of the couch. The physician tucked a bag with medicine next to the boy and gave Alex a sheet of paper with instructions for the patient's care.

"If he misses a dose, don't double up. Start fresh. Move him and take the couch. Nurses keep asking why I want that piece of junk."

Jurek and Alex maneuvered the sofa on their shoulders down the hall. The nurse who complained when they brought it in, looked askance. "Where are you going now?"

Alex smiled. "Dr. Masurik changed his mind."

"Get it out of here," she ordered imperiously.

They loaded the couch onto the cart and traveled slowly through muddy streets with water-filled potholes. Wary armed soldiers stood on every corner, on guard against a sudden partisan attack.

Marisia and David ran down when the horse and cart pull up to the building entrance. They helped carry the old sofa up to their flat. David didn't wait. He tore away the cushions.

Jurek helped Jacob to his feet when Mela threw open the door. She rushed to him, kissing his forehead, tracing fingers along the bandage. "Does it hurt?" she asked.

"Not anymore. Maybe a little sore."

Alex stood back. She acted as if nothing happened. "I looked for you. Where have you been?"

"Hiding. In the ruins of the Great Synagogue." She pulled out a worn, rain-spotted, slim, and smoke-stained leather book. "I found this book of Psalms. Tadek, Geniek, it's part of your history, your tradition. Listen." She opened it and read: "Though I walk through the valley of the shadow of death, I fear no harm, for you are with me . . ." She kissed both boys. "I walked through the valley of shadows and came home."

Chapter Four

Escape

Rain seeping through the ceiling woke Alex in the middle of the night. He slipped away from Mela, sleeping under a thin blanket on a palette in a corner of the flat. The children slept soundly after the turmoil and worry about their mother. He lit a candle scribbling notes on the back of an old newspaper.

"If you don't want to sleep with me, I understand. I don't know what I was thinking," Mela whispered.

He held her in his arms. "I'm the one to say sorry for everything I put you through."

"We're together. One day we'll look back and tell stories no one will believe."

Alex tapped his notes. "Here's one story needs fixing. What will we do when the Hetman money disappears? We need food, healthy food for Geniek and the others."

"You always find a way. No need to worry about me."

"I told the children you would come back."

"Did you believe it?" asked Mela.

"With all my heart. Together, we're unbeatable." He picked up his notes. "We have only enough merchandise to last a few weeks. I hid most of the fabric under the shop floorboards. Jurek and I will take out a little at a time and store it in the cellar."

"You're not going to the black market. Germans cracked down, arresting people, sending them to camps."

"You know me. Slick as an eel."

"Listen, Mr. Eel, don't get caught in one of their nets."

For a week, Alex and Jurek trotted the horse and cart back and forth from building to shop. Their early morning excursions made them almost invisible to German guards and patrols. On one occasion a Waffen-SS trooper stroked the horse's muzzle. "We had a plow horse looked just like him. Makes me feel sad."

"I hope you see your farm again," said Alex, thinking the young man used his rifle to cut down innocent civilians.

In time, Alex located relatively safe pop-up markets in areas with multiple escape routes for a fast retreat in case of a raid. At the end of each foray, Jacob counted the earnings and wrote them in a ledger he made from a 1938 calendar with a circle David drew around his birthday: March 17.

Armia Krajowa partisans hid in forests to the north bordering train tracks running into the city. The unit commander Dariusz Marek raised his fist signaling the attack. A team leaped down the embankment planting explosives on the rails. A supply train rumbled into view. Wehrmacht squads stood guard on a flat car. Another unit manned machine guns. Marek pushed the plunger. A massive explosion sent flaming clouds into the atmosphere, blowing the engine off the tracks. Rail cars collided, steel screeched, glass shattered, sending shards flying in the air. Bloodied troops littered the embankment. Partisans fired furiously, cutting down soldiers in shock from the explosion. They cracked open the freight cars, capturing arms and ammunition.

News of the partisan raid raced through the city and became a topic of excited conversation at the black market where Alex set up shop.

"You're out of the arms business, Roslan," said a voice behind him.

Alex turned to face Marek. "What the hell are you doing here?"

"On a search for my wife and who do I find? Alex Roslan, gunrunner for Jews. Too bad your customers are dead."

"You didn't believe they'd fight."

"Lose is lose and dead is dead," smirked Marek. He picked up a piece of cloth. "My wife will like it."

"Take it and leave."

Marek tipped his hat, folded the cloth, and slipped it under his jacket. "We do the dirty work and you profit. Learn from your Jewish friends?"

Mela knew something was wrong the moment Alex walked into the flat. "The look on your face. Like you could kill."

"Marek, one of Armia Krajowa's commanders, saw me at the market. He's an asshole. I never liked him."

"The one who gave you guns for the JFO?"

"The one who took the last piece of silver and gold Jews kept as a remembrance of their old lives. Weapons purchased with blood. God, I hope I never seen him again."

"Is that a prayer or a wish?"

"A slip of the tongue." He handed a small package to Mela. "I traded a pair of pants and a jacket for some real coffee."

"We need to boil more water. Geniek, Tadek!" she yelled.

David ran in. "Geniek's helping Marisia with arithmetic."

"We need water to make soup and coffee. Go to the well in the courtyard and come right back. Take a jacket, it's starting to rain again."

The old well had a rusty crank and frayed rope pulleys, and a cracked wooden bucket sealed with tar, making it heavier.

David hooked the bucket to one end of the rope and lowered it with a creaking iron handle. It splashed into the water. Using every bit of his strength, David strained to pull up the bucket. He lost his grip on the wet handle. It spun around, cracking against his forehead. He fell in the mud, blood gushing from the wound. Staggering to his feet, he wiped his face and froze when he saw his hands streaked bright red.

Lurching into the flat, David fell on the floor. Alex lifted him onto a table. Mela pressed a cloth to his forehead to staunch the bleeding. Jacob, Marisia, and Jurek stopped in their tracks when they saw bloodied David on the table.

Jacob and Jurek helped him onto a blanket. "We should give you a medal for being wounded in the war," said Jacob.

David glared at him. "You're not funny. Go step on a nail."

"Geniek, keep quiet. Tadek will be fine. Jurek, go to the hospital and find your uncle, Dr. Galler. Tell him what happened."

Twenty minutes later Galler arrived. "Not too bad. Needs a few stitches. May leave a scar. Tadek, I'm going to give you an injection to prevent pain. After the stitches, we'll place a bandage on your head." He turned to Mela. "You can remove it in three days."

Galler worked swiftly. "You're an excellent patient. There's nothing more to do." He handed a bottle of aspirin to Alex. "No more than two a day if he has any pain."

Alex bent down to David. "Next time be careful. No more accidents." He pulled Jacob close. "Make up with each other."

Reluctantly the boys shook hands. All of a sudden, David reached up and hugged his brother. "I didn't mean what I said."

Rain did not discourage black markets from flourishing across the city. It had the opposite effect. Fewer squads patrolled during inclement weather, although vendors assigned teenagers to watch from rooftops for possible armed incursions. At first sight of troop movements, they blew whistles. Within minutes, stalls faded from the area.

A black market slowly emerged in an alley off Cesta. Alex found a spot close to the intersection, giving him an immediate escape track. He erected a canvas tarpaulin next to a peddler selling shoes made from discarded tires.

"Hear what happened yesterday?" the peddler whispered. "A collaborator tipped off the Gestapo partisans planned an attack on a truck caravan. The Germans were ready. They captured the commander: Marek." Alex grabbed one end of the tarpaulin. Marek may have been an antisemite, but he once said, "All I care about is killing Nazis."

News of Dariusz Marek in Gestapo hands filled Alex with trepidation. The commander had valuable information about partisan plans and Poles who undertook anti-Nazi action. He could do nothing except continue trading fabric for a few zlotys and groschen. Returning to the apartment building, he pushed aside the chest of drawers. The lock on the cabinet door dangled from the hasp. Basement lights flickered on. Gestapo agents threw Alex to the floor.

"Get him to his feet," ordered Oberscharführer Koch.

Pounding on the door interrupted Mela preparing a modest meal for the family. "Mrs. Roslan, Mrs. Roslan," a woman's voice she recognized called out. Gray-haired Mrs. Kalina, her face pale, took her hand. "Your husband. The Gestapo."

Mela ran to the window. Officers dragged Alex into a car. She ran into the street, yelling, "Alex! Alex!" trying valiantly against all odds to stop the car.

Guards restrained her. "Get back inside if you don't want to join him," ordered a black-uniformed SS officer.

Archives maintained by the SS, discovered after the war, methodically recorded the capture of "Armia Krajowa unit commander Marek, Dariusz. Interrogated, July 22, 1944. Provided name: Roslan, Alexander, assisting Jewish Fighting Organization, Warsaw Ghetto. Disposition of prisoner Marek: Executed by order Oberscharführer Koch, July 23, 1944."

Foreboding, ancient, built of great stone blocks, Pawiak Prison stood as a stark reminder of more than one hundred years during which imperial Russia incarcerated, tortured, and executed Poles. Nazi's operated it as a base for assaults on Jews and partisans. Polish police officers, many of them accomplices of the Gestapo, used the prison to violently act out their hatred of Jews, Roma, and homosexuals.

Handcuffed and shackled, Alex, in striped prisoner's pajamas, sat on a stool in a narrow, austere interrogation room with a switched off floodlight next to a desk with a typewriter. On the wall, the Nazi national symbol, a brass eagle clutching a laurel wreath surrounding a swastika.

Oberscharführer Koch and a lance corporal entered. Koch sat in a comfortable upholstered chair. He snapped his fingers. The corporal switched on the light, blinding Alex. The noncom returned to his desk and inserted a sheet of paper into the typewriter. "Date: July 28, 1944," he typed.

Koch nodded and looked up at Alex. "You understand what brought you here?"

"Dealing on the black market."

Pounding the table, Koch laughed. "If we arrested everyone who sells shit on the black market, we would run out of prison cells. You are accused of treason against the Third Reich. For several months prior to the destruction of the Warsaw Ghetto, you engaged in illicit trade providing weapons to the so-called Jewish Fighting Organization."

"My business is textiles, not guns," said Alex.

"We know all about you. A merchant of textiles becomes a merchant of death. Do not play games. Your friend Darius Marek confessed, implicating one Alexander Roslan who owns—or once owned—a shop on Jerozolinskie and bartered with his Armia Krajowa unit to obtain arms and ammunition stolen from the Reich."

The corporal efficiently struck every word on the typewriter keyboard. "Herr Oberscharführer: disposition of the prisoner?"

"Noon, Wednesday, August the second, you will be summarily executed by firing squad."

Fire lit within Alex. He looked directly into Oberscharführer Koch's eyes. "The Russians are massed across the river. The Allies are swiftly closing in. You will go down with the rest of the Nazi criminals," he said with steel in his voice.

Koch abruptly stood, pulling out his pistol. "I could take care of you now. But I'd rather see you sweat waiting for bullets to rip you apart. Take him to his cell." He took a deep breath. His voice calmed. "We are not monsters. Permission has been given for your wife to visit. A last goodbye."

Holed up in his narrow confines, Alex steeled himself, considering his slim options. A door in the corridor clanged opened. Alex peered through his cell's barred window. Five blindfolded prisoners were tied to stakes driven into the earth. The SS officer in charge called out an order Alex couldn't hear but understood. A squad set up a machine gun. The officer went down the line of prisoners, inspecting their bonds. He stepped aside.

"Feuer!" he shouted.

Bullets riddled prisoners; their bodies jolting and buckling under the onslaught. Smoke cleared. The dead sagged against bonds dripping with blood. The officer removed his pistol and shot each of the prisoners in the head.

For an unknown reason, the Gestapo did not arrest the Roslan family. It was a reprise for Jacob and David, who expected to be dragged off, sent away, murdered like thousands of other victims of the Nazi's sadistic antisemitism.

"The authorities said I can visit Papa," Mela told the children. They packed a bag with sandwiches and an apple scrounged from a black market.

Jurek shook his head. "No one's ever come out of the prison alive."

"Never let me hear you say that again," demanded Mela.

David broke down in tears. His brother held him fast. "Papa always has a plan."

"I don't believe you."

"Geniek's right. Every time we thought the worst, Papa found a way out," said Marisia.

"Jurek, you're in charge. Anyone comes to the door, don't answer. All of you, keep very, very quiet," said Mela. She kissed them, picked up her coat and package, and began the long walk to Pawiak.

Prison guards dived into Mela's bag, scattering food across the table. When they finished, they ordered her to clean everything up and follow them. Corridors lit by stark, white ceiling lights in arched ceilings led past one steel door after another. A guard slid a heavy bolt and opened Alex's cell.

"Fifteen minutes," grunted the guard.

The door slammed shut. Mela ran into Alex's arms. "What surprises did you bring?"

Mela laid out food and clothes. She stopped sobbing. "I'm sorry the way it looks. They threw it down. Even examined the apple to see if it had an explosive inside. I'm scared."

"We've had a good life. It's not going to end. Not now. Not here."

"I don't know what to do," said Mela.

"There is a way to free me before August the second. They let us out for five minutes every day. You know I speak German. Nervous guards report rumors the Russians on the east bank of the Vistula River are ready to attack."

"What good will it do if they kill you?"

"When the Soviets invade, they'll accuse the Polish prison secretary of aiding and abetting the execution of innocent Poles and Russian prisoners of war. His life will be worth zero. He'll need someone to vouch he was not responsible. He saves me, he saves his own life. Get the money box. Geniek knows I have American dollars in a hidden compartment. Demand to speak to the weasel on your way out. Tell him what I said about saving his life and give him one hundred American to get me out of here."

"He can be bribed?" asked Mela.

"That frightened little man will jump at the chance."

Mrs. Kalina stopped Mela on the way up to her flat. "There's a rumor the Russians will invade any time. We need to pray. We all need to pray it's true. God bless you and your husband."

Worry and fear filled Jacob waiting for Mela to show up. He ran into her arms. "You have to stop them. After all your warnings, Marisia and Tadek went outside. Suppose someone suspects? Suppose we're reported. We'll be killed."

Her heart sank. David and Marisia played on the street with a small dog. They dived behind a concrete wall as an army truck blaring a klaxon rounded the corner.

"Outlawed Armia Krajowa attacked valiant soldiers of the Third Reich. They claim to represent citizens of Poland. We will not tolerate sabotage and will retaliate, life for life," a burly Oberfeldwebel, master sergeant, bellowed through a bullhorn.

He raised his arm. Troops fired indiscriminately at innocent people. A woman pushing a baby carriage was cut down. A man trying to take cover killed by a shot in the back. Others ran for their lives, but not before machine-gun fire blasted into them. The scrawny dog scampered to safety. Army trucks squealed away through pools of blood.

Mela ran down, grabbed her daughter and David, dragging them upstairs. "You believe they won't kill you because you're children? What in the world were you thinking? How many times have we told you. Never go out without me or Papa. We know when it's safe."

David, shaking uncontrollably, clung to Marisia. "I didn't mean it. I didn't mean it," he repeated over and over.

"What possessed you, Marisia?" Mela asked.

"The sun was shining. It looked like an ordinary day before the war. We just wanted to have a little fun."

"How do you think I feel? I'm smart enough to obey rules," snapped Jacob.

David stamped his foot on the ground. "It wasn't fun."

"Dead isn't fun!" shouted Jacob.

"I don't want to be dead!" David cried.

"Just dumb. Nobody as stupid as you could be my brother."

"Stop it!" shouted Mela.

"You're a dumb, stupid little kid," snarled Jacob.

"Stop this instant," Mela commanded.

Completely out of control, David kicked the wall flinging himself on a mattress. "I hope the Gestapo gets you." Pounding on the door interrupted his tantrum.

"Now you bothered our neighbors. Get into the cupboard, Geniek."

He ran into the kitchen and curled under the sink. The door burst open. Gestapo agents and German-controlled armed Polish General Government police officers pushed Mela aside. David and Marisia clung to her skirt.

"Where are the Jews?" demanded a Gestapo agent.

Mela summoned up a hidden core of courage. "You want Jews? We have them hidden inside the walls, closets. Fifty, a hundred."

"Search," the agent ordered. Police pounded on walls with their gun butts. Bayonets sliced into ragged furniture, spilling stuffing on the floor.

Mela rushed them, hitting their chests and shoulders. "You ruin everything. Leave us alone."

David, horrified, pushed himself against the kitchen cabinet. Inside, Jacob held his breath.

"Get away from there," a police officer ordered. He yanked open one door, finding a jumble of plumbing and dirty rags. He slammed it closed. David fell to his knees. The agent looked down at his pale face, blue eyes, light-brown hair. "Lovely child. The other your daughter? Their papers." Mela handed them over, hands shaking. He scanned the documents. "Your nephew?" Mela nodded. As quickly as they came, they left.

Twenty-four hours passed since Mela paid off the prison secretary to free Alex. His death sentence had been signed, his execution scheduled. Ever the atheist, Alex turned down an offer to have a priest say prayers over him.

The cell door flew opened. The prison secretary, face coated with perspiration and hands trembling, entered.

"Good news?" asked Alex.

The secretary shoved a handful of American dollars at him. "Take it back. I can't release you. It's impossible to get your records."

Alex threw the simpering man into a corner, staring unblinking into his eyes. "I warn you: kill a fellow Pole and partisans will hang you by your feet." He dragged the secretary to the door. "Get me out of here or I swear my children will have your blood." The little man ran, feeling Alex's wrath chasing him down the corridor.

August 1, church bells resounded across Warsaw. Alex looked out on the courtyard. German troops darted back and forth in disarray. Officers shouted for them to march in order. Instead, they crashed through heavy doors leading outside. A partisan unit raced down the corridor. The bolt on the cell door slid open. Their commander shouted, "Get the hell out of here!" Alex dashed into the street. Partisans on motorcycles flying the Polish flag roared through the city. Banners with Polish colors unfurled from windows. Snipers hiding in buildings, on rooftops, were taken down by Polish militia.

Alex surprised everyone when he showed up in striped prisoner pajamas. A building exploded in a ball of fire. "Gestapo headquarters!" Jurek shouted.

Partisan squads swept through streets, wiping out German enclaves. Behind the squads, units created tank traps, ripping up pavement and cement sidewalks. Ordinary citizens fired on fleeing German vehicles and troops. Panzer tanks were caught in makeshift snares. Partisans dropped hand grenades through hatches. Tank crews flung themselves, burning, on the ground, left to die.

In a moment of exuberance, Jurek put on his scout uniform. "You're not going anywhere. It's too dangerous," warned Alex.

"We have them on the run. All my comrades are parading in the streets." He dashed outside.

"Stop him, Alex!" shouted Mela.

Jurek joined a milling crowd of uniformed armed teenagers singing the national anthem "Poland Is Not Yet Lost." Alex searched the growing celebrating mass. Joy filled the air. Youngsters believed they achieved freedom from their oppressors, when gunshots suddenly rained down from an apartment building.

Scattering behind walls, inside stores, behind a monument in the plaza, scouts fired back blindly. Machine guns sprayed the square, wounding boys and girls. Partisans in an armored truck sped in. Gunfire flashed from a terrace. Several more scouts fell. Armia Krajowa fired rifle grenades, blasting the machine-gun nest off a balcony. German bodies landed with ominous thuds.

Alex found Jurek on the ground. Blood spread across the boy's chest. "We did good, Papa," he coughed.

"An ambulance! Get an ambulance!" Alex yelled.

Partisans lifted Jurek into an armored personnel carrier. Alex held his hand. "Stay with me. We'll get help."

The boy smiled. "Take care of my brothers, Geniek and Tadek. Say goodbye to Mama and Marisia." He coughed up blood. "If Mama's right, I'll be sitting next to God." His hand went limp.

"He's gone, Mr. Roslan. We'll take him to headquarters," said the driver.

Alex walked through the apartment door, his body stiff, face gray. "Jurek's dead," said Mela, falling into his arms.

"He gave me a message. He said take care of his brothers, Geniek and Tadek."

She sobbed. Jurek died a hero. They had to live up to his bravery. "We'll bury him like every hero—with honor, with prayer, with hope in life everlasting."

Scouts placed Jurek, still wearing his uniform, in a crate. Partisans drove to the closest cemetery, Cmentarz Żydowski, a desecrated Jewish burial site near the center of Warsaw. Alex, David, and Jacob dug his grave, placing it between two fallen headstones.

Alex wrote down names on the gravestones and drew a rough map of the area. "We will return when the war is over."

Following SS Chief Heinrich Himmler's announcement that "The city must completely disappear from the surface of the earth," German High Command, bitter and embarrassed about their withdrawal from Warsaw, unleashed a massive land and air invasion. German bombers retaliated on courageous, underequipped, outmanned Polish partisans, cutting short the Roslans' grieving. Unremitting bombing raids continued day and night for two months in the fall of 1944, creating firestorms incinerating innocent men, women, and children.

Faced with flamethrowers and massive fire power, Polish fighters perished under the grinding wheels of Germany's war machine. Death squads gunned down civilians in streets, alleys, and throughout the countryside. Torrential rain swamped streets. Sewers overflowed, hindering the SS's relentless murder spree.

Alex knew back alleys, forgotten lanes, hidden basements, and areas where the Wehrmacht did not have outposts or watch towers. "We're getting out of this hell," he told Mela. "Clouds rolling in from the north. Soon we'll have a major storm."

"Since when are you a weatherman? The rain will let up."

"I was five when a monster storm hit Poland and Czechoslovakia. It frightened everyone. Dropped five hundred millimeters of rain in a few hours. Cities, towns, villages flooded. Families drowned in their homes. Rivers overflowed. It won't be bad. It will be perfect."

"What do you mean 'perfect'? Perfect if we drown?"

"We're leaving Warsaw the minute the brunt of the storm hits. It's our best chance to avoid being seen."

"This is one of your crazy schemes. Where will we go?"

"Vladek's farm in Kaminsk."

"You and my brother never got along."

"This is not the time to worry about small disagreements."

"How will we manage the children in the middle of nowhere?" worried Mela.

"Stop throwing obstacles in our way. We stay, we end up in a camp, or worse. Marisia and Jacob are tough. If necessary, I'll carry David."

Mela couldn't change his mind. Death by hanging or death in a flood. The difference was choice. They had to take a chance if they were to live to tell the tale.

Alex clambered down to the basement. He gathered up heavy jackets, coats, and stripped German uniforms from the closet, wrapping them in a canvas tarpaulin he used in the black market. Mela threw blankets, old fleece jackets, and scarves in an old rucksack and duffel bags. They collected the children and told them the plan. "You must be brave little soldiers. We will protect you every step of the way. No matter what happens, trust Mama and me. Do as we say. Stick together," warned Alex.

"We leave when Papa says. He knows secret ways out of the city. No crying. No complaining. I pray God watches over us," said Mela.

With a loud crack of thunder and lightning, skies erupted. A storm of apocalyptic proportions pounded the city. Alex and Mela bundled up their family. Alex carried the rucksack. Duffels were divided between Mela, Jacob, Marisia, and David.

Bombers roared overhead. Explosions shook the earth. They crawled through twisted steel, charred bricks, shattered glass. Streets turned into muddy swamps. A barbed wire fence stretched for miles in either direction. Alex warned Mela and the children to wait while he scouted the barrier. He found a small break.

"One at a time. Go slow," he cautioned.

Alex went through first, assisting the others into a broad, rain-soaked field where plows left furrows they used for cover. A watchtower a few yards away swung its searchlight across the landscape.

"Stay. Don't move," Alex said.

Searchlights picked up fleeing refugees. Machine guns cut them down. Festering odor of death hovered over the bleak countryside. Unremitting rain swept away topsoil from shallow graves, exposing bodies of children murdered by Nazis or dead from ravages of disease. Determined the same fate would not befall Marisia, David, and Jacob, Mela and David sheltered them under abandoned bales of hay and in bombed-out warrens.

In desperation, Alex dug into mud barrows, creating small caves where they huddled in tattered blankets sleeping fitfully. Alex and Mela took turns staying awake to warn of danger.

A glimmer of light peeked through clouds. "The storm will pass tonight. Then we move," said Alex.

A pallid moon shone in the black sky. Alex and Mela woke the children. They trudged, boots mired in mud, a slow, circuitous trek through war-torn, bomb-blasted forests. "I'm scared," David whispered to Jacob.

"Me too. But we're lucky. Papa Alex always gets us out of trouble. He got me to hospital and saved my life. Look at the way he escaped prison. We'll make it."

They crawled, scrambled, and walked when it was safe enough through devastated woodlands, settling down at dawn.

Alex pointed into the distance at the silhouette of a two-story barn. "As soon as it's dark, we'll head for shelter."

"German soldiers might be in the barn. What then?" wondered Mela.

"I looked around while you were asleep. No sign of trucks, motorcycles, any vehicles. Footprints, yes, but not from army boots."

"How do you know?"

"Hobnails. Their boots have hobnails that leave distinctive marks."

In the middle of the night, Mela and Alex awakened the children. David, bleary-eyed and tired, could barely stand. Alex carried him to the barn with wood partitions originally housing cows and horses.

Inside the battered building they joined refugees groaning, coughing, talking in their sleep, screaming unconsciously. Many stared blankly into space, weeping about a stark future of never-ending dread. A mother, tears flowing down cheeks blackened by smoke, tended her sick infant. An elderly, care-worn, wrinkled woman with a kerchief over her head held a Bible and rosary in gnarled hands, repeating the same prayer over and over: "Lift up those who have fallen . . ."

Alex moved to the far end of the barn searching for a way into the loft. He yanked open a slatted door. A ladder beam poked out of a moldy hay pile. He propped it against the hayloft's edge. With David clinging to his shoulders, he climbed up and placed him on a dry bale of hay. Mela covered him with a ragged blanket. Jacob and Marisia held onto one another, glad to be far from the tangle of people below.

"We're all in the same battle," Alex told them.

Rain beat down relentlessly. Mela gathered the children. "When I was your age and felt sad and lonely, my mother sang an old Polish lullaby."

Marisia leaned her head against Mela's shoulder. "Do you still remember it?"

"I'll try." Mela closed her eyes, trying to hear her mother singing a long time ago.

> Two little kittens,
> Both speckled gray,
> Do nothing at all,
> But play all day.
>
> Two little kittens
> Both speckled gray,
> Frolic and rollick
> Baby all day.
>
> Two little kittens,
> Both speckled gray,

> First one gray and white,
> Second white and gray,
> Hide under a chair.
>
> Two little kittens,
> Both speckled gray,
> If there was one
> It would drink milk with care.

They nodded off until planes roared overhead releasing lethal bombs on Warsaw. The barn became silent as the battered city, exhausted under the siege, entered its final death throes. Refugees drifted away from their haven, daring to trek far into the country during daylight hours.

"Risking their lives. Maybe some will survive. I will not place any of you in danger," said Alex, refusing to move until nightfall.

Storms continued to roll across the country, providing an opportunity to move. David promised he would walk on his own. Alex shook his hand. "You're growing up."

"To be like you."

A mortar exploded, sending shrapnel tearing through barren trees, churning up the earth, showering thick clods of mud over the Roslans. Alex and Mela dived to cover the children. Jacob clamped David's mouth, keeping him from screaming. "Be brave."

Boots tramped within inches, then retreated. Alex listened for another incoming shell. Silence settled over fields; interrupted by unnerving thunder. Heavy rain sluiced through clouds, pounding the earth.

Alex carved barrows with his hands in the mud for the children. "Rest. Tomorrow we'll find the train to Kaminsk." He and Mela huddled under the canvas tarp.

In the morning, rain turned to snow falling gently over fields, softening battle-scarred forests and meadows, filling bomb craters, draping stark trees with icicles. Ash from Warsaw fires drifted in, turning hills, ridges, and surrounding forests, gray.

Mela pulled jackets, sweaters, and scarves once worn by the enemy out of their packs. "Into warmer clothes," she ordered.

The children followed Alex and Mela like ducklings trailing a drake and hen. Dry nettles tore clothes. Brittle branches scratched faces.

Alex halted, put a finger to his lips and pointed ahead. A water tower loomed above trees. "Wait until you hear my call . . ." He slipped through pines and oaks.

Hunkering out of sight on the snow, they waited. A fast, high-pitched series of bird screeches pierced the icy air. "It's Papa. Hold hands," said Mela.

They plodded through ankle-deep snow to the tree line. An old steam engine pulling wooden boxcars took on water. Pushing aside the water chute, an engineer mounted the train. Alex slid open a freight car door, hoisting the children and Mela inside, leaving the door slightly ajar.

The engine hissed to life, lurching forward. Through the slats they watched a somber panorama of bleakness roll by. Smoke rose from farms and villages turned to cinders by the Nazi scorched-earth program. Men and women strung up from electric poles lined the tracks, a silent, barbaric warning the same fate awaited anyone who opposed the occupation.

The train approached a water stop on the outskirts of Kaminsk. Alex opened the door, leaped out, helping Mela and the children onto a rocky path paralleling the rails.

Poor, destitute, impoverished Kaminsk survived in a forgotten, discarded cocoon. A few forlorn houses, a bakery with half its walls shattered, a grain silo leaning at a perilous angle, strung out along a muddy road. Mela plodded to a rundown, two-story, half-timbered house with a slate roof and hammered on the door.

Mela's brother Vladek, his wife Basia behind him, opened it. They were shocked and surprised by the sudden appearance of Alex, Mela, and Marisia with two strange boys. "You look as if mad dogs of hell are after you. Get inside," said Vladek.

The fireplace, kept alive with dry branches and grass, barely warmed the interior. The children huddled close to the meager flames. Basia poured tea into cracked cups. "They came, destroyed, deported, or killed every Jew in town, and left, God willing, forever," she sighed.

You'll bring them back if they find out," whispered Vladek, hands shaking, eyes darting into the dark.

"No one's going to find out," Alex interrupted. "As far as you or anyone else in Kaminsk is concerned, Geniek and Tadek are our nephews."

"For Christ's sake, you're asking for trouble," grumbled Vladek. "What the hell do we need with a couple of Jewish brats? The Germans will kill us. Send them on their way."

"I took care of you when you almost drank yourself to death. I protected you from our parents who wanted nothing to do with you, with your gambling," snapped Mela. She grabbed Vladek by his shirt. "Geniek and Tadek are our sons. They have seen the worst of evil. Let them stay, or I go."

Basia pushed her husband aside. "Your family is our family. What do you need?"

"Food and clothing," answered Mela.

"How is clever Alex Roslan going to pay for food and clothing?" smirked Vladek.

"The village is a wreck. Every brick I lay, every nail I hammer, every repair I make is worth bread, maybe milk from your skinny cows; a piece of cheese, a chicken or duck to roast," said Alex.

"Goddamn it, no one knows you," groused Vladek.

"How long have you lived here?" asked Mela.

"Ever since Basia and I married—maybe twelve years."

"Fourteen. But who's counting," said Basia.

"Call a town meeting. Introduce me as your brother-in-law—a mason, carpenter, electrician, and plumber ready to help Kaminsk," said Alex.

"What about the kids?" asked Vladek.

"You have a school?" asked Mela.

"A shack with two rooms," said Basia.

"They'll go to school with Kaminsk students," said Mela.

"I'll repair it and make it into a proper place to teach," announced Alex.

Over the next few months, Alex made himself indispensable. He and Jacob restored cottages, fences, and walls. Scouring the countryside, they hauled pieces of abandoned trucks and wood from blasted barns, renovating the small school.

"Once we're finished, you'll take classes with Marisia and Tadek. No arguments," said Alex.

Peter Sawicki, son of the town baker, begged Alex to fix his brick hearth. He had to make do baking bread in his fireplace, and everyone complained. "You'd think a loaf of bread, even one baked on an open fire, would be appreciated," he groused.

"Geniek and I will have it up and running in no time."

They scoured the village for bricks, piled them in a hand-cart, tore down the old hearth, and built a new one. Peter fired it up with oak branches, pressed his hand against it, and felt bricks heating up. While waiting he mixed a large batch of dough. The hearth's warmth doubled it. He punched it down, rolled it out, braided five loaves, and put them on the hearth.

"You really believe the Russians will invade? It's already January. Rumors have been floating for months," said Peter.

"To be honest, I have no trust in the Soviet Union or Communists. All I can do is hope they'll drive out the Germans so we can bring back Władysław Raczkiewicz our president-in-exile and rebuild our lives," replied Alex.

An hour later, Peter shoved a bread paddle into the hearth and retrieved golden brown loaves. Alex and Jacob applauded his artistry.

"Better than the old oven! What will you take for the work?" asked Peter.

"A loaf of bread."

"Good. We have no money." He handed Alex two loaves. "One is not enough." They shook hands. "To better days."

An agitated Vladek, bottle of vodka in hand, waited outside the house. "Trouble, Alex," he slurred. "You're accused of being a Jew."

Enraged, Alex snatched the bottle from his brother-in-law and tossed it away.

"Is this true, or vodka talking?"

"I swear on my mother's grave, it's true. A member of the village council is spreading the story."

Alex thrust the bread into Jacob's hand. "Inside." He dragged Vladek yelling and kicking down the street. "Take me to your doctor."

The doctor's office and home, a small cottage pocked with bullet holes, sat between a bomb-damaged church with half its steeple gone and the school Alex rehabilitated. He pushed Vladek into the office. The staggering drunk startled, then angered, the doctor.

"Get the hell out of here, Vladek. You don't need a doctor; you need a cold bath."

"Not me, Dr. Grosz."

Alex stepped in. "Take a good look." He unbuttoned his trousers.

"You're ill?" asked Grosz.

"Sick to death of idiots. I need a certificate proving I'm not Jewish." Alex dropped his pants to the floor.

Flustered, the doctor sat down. "From the looks of your . . ."—he tried to find the word—". . . shall we say, endowment, my diagnosis is you are definitely not Jewish."

Alex held onto Vladek, who was staggering under the influence of alcohol, to keep him from falling down as they walked back to the house. He waved the certificate in his brother-in-law's face. "Report back to your council I have proof. Next time, they, their family, or friends may be accused."

War news filtered into Kaminsk. The Roslans gathered daily with the sparse community around the only operating radio, in Dr. Grosz's office, listening to reports. For months, the village anxiously waited, praying for the expected onslaught against the beleaguered Nazi forces as the Allies closed in from the west. In Yugoslavia, by July 1944, facing Russian, Yugoslav, Montenegro, and Bosnian armies, as well as partisans, a number of Wehrmacht units broke ranks. A few units surrendered. Others, fearing the Russians would take revenge for the siege of Stalingrad, headed west to reunite with the German army.

Russian forces massed on the Eastern front, giving hope to the long-suffering Polish they would be free of Nazi rule. Despair, disappointment, hopelessness tore at the heart of the nation as months passed with no sign of movement. Friday, January 12, 1945, the Vistula-Oder two-pronged offensive began. Over 2 million infantry, 4,500 tanks, 2,500 assault guns, and almost 2,200 multiple rocket launchers smashed across the front.

Artillery rounds and rockets screamed into the sky, lighting up battle lines as if a million flashbulbs ignited at once. Soviet tanks, large weapons, trucks, and mobile rocket units softened up German entrenchments. The Russian infantry advanced, routing remnants of the Wehrmacht, leaving German corpses and destroyed equipment in their wake.

Disorganized, demoralized, panicking German units fled south on the fastest route possible, straight through Kaminsk. Soviet rockets rained havoc on frozen farm fields. Salvos blasted the countryside into a surreal landscape of twisted charred trees and bomb craters.

Thin, frightened, David tunneled under a threadbare blanket on the second-floor bedroom in an attempt to block out the fiery uproar. Russian military units swarmed through the village rooting out German soldiers left behind.

"The Russians are driving back the Germans!" yelled Alex.

Jacob ran upstairs yanking the blanket off David. "Tadek, the war's over. We're free. We're finally free."

Marisia, leaped onto the bed. Jumping and bouncing, the children screamed, "We're free! We're free!"

Mattress springs creaked and squealed. With a loud crack and snap, the bed frame broke. They fell laughing and giggling on the floor. Sprinting down splintered stairs, they ran outside coming face-to-face with a tall, bespectacled Russian soldier wearing a brown quilted jacket, high black boots, and a backpack and rifle slung over his shoulder. "You look a little like one of my sons. He's very handsome," he said to David, ruffling his curly hair. He carried him to the front step of the house. The soldier's scarred and calloused fingers wrapped gently around David's hand. "What's your name, little man?"

"Tadek. My name is Tadek. Where is your son?"

"My wife and I divorced. He was eight-years-old and went to live with my mother. The Nazis murdered almost all the Jews in town. I heard my son escaped. I hope we'll be reunited."

"That's a sad story," said David.

"For me, perhaps. For you and your family, a time to celebrate. We're on the offensive. We'll win this war and maybe bring peace to the world." He touched the jagged scar on David's forehead. "A war wound?"

David shook his head. "Just a scar. We needed water from a well. When I pulled up the bucket, the handle slipped and hit me in the head."

"I'll give you a heroic story. Once there was a great swordsman and poet, Cyrano de Bergerac. He fought a hundred scoundrels who tried to kill him. Guess what happened?"

Wide-eyed, David guessed, "He died fighting."

"He battled them, one by one, until they fell, mortally wounded. A hundred against one. Is it true? Who knows? That's the way he told it. Let everyone know you fought off ten, twenty Nazis. They slashed you with a bayonet. You grabbed a rifle and bang! Got them all."

"That's lying," said David.

"Nothing like a good war story to win the girls."

David blushed. "I don't like girls."

The soldier cleaned his eyeglasses. "It's all the way you look at it. In a few years you'll change your mind. Now, what's the first thing you want?"

For a moment David's mind went blank. Then he remembered, with food in short supply, adults dreamed of vodka and kielbasa. "Vodka and kielbasa!" David exclaimed.

The trooper took a sausage wrapped in cloth from his backpack. "Surprise! Kielbasa." He also retrieved a small bottle. "Let's celebrate our victory with vodka."

"I'll have some of that," said David, pointing to the sausage. "Then I'll have vodka."

"You're sure?"

"One time in Warsaw the Polish and German police came to our apartment looking for my brother. They left us alone after Papa gave them a drink," David said, biting off a piece of sausage. He gulped the vodka just as Alex and Mela came outside. David held up the bottle. "I just had sausage and . . ." His face turned deep red. He clutched his stomach and threw up.

"Vodka?" Alex glared at the soldier. "You gave a six-year-old boy vodka?!"

He laughed. "Everyone has to learn sooner or later. He won't take another drink for a long time. If I offended you, I apologize."

A squad of soldiers trotted down the road. One of the men whistled and shouted, "Grossman, stop playing house! Get your ass over here. We have a war to win. You have a story to write for the *Red Star*."

He shook Alex's hand. "One day your son will have a good laugh over vodka." He reached into his jacket and gave David a tattered book. "I wrote this before the war. You'll like one of

the stories, 'In the Town of Berdichev,' when you grow older."
He wrote a note in Russian and his name, Vasily Semyonovich
Grossman, inside the front cover, marching into the mist with
his squadron.

"How can anyone drink that stuff? It tastes like kerosene,"
sputtered David.

Jacob laughed. "You always get in trouble because you
don't think about what could happen."

In a fury, David leaped at his brother. Alex pulled them
apart. "No time to fight. Shake hands and give each other
a big hug."

"I don't want a hug from him," said David crossing his arms
over his chest.

"Poland is free. Be happy," said Mela.

Reluctantly, David and Jacob embraced. David burst into
tears. "I'm sorry."

Cold winter rain pelted the village. Everyone scurried inside. Vladek prodded a log burning in the fireplace, warming
the room. Basia gave David a mug of warm goat's milk. "This
will settle your stomach. Vodka is not for little boys."

David clutched his aching head. "I'll never go near it again,"
he moaned.

The blazing log popped, sending red sparks flickering
across the room. "If those were fireflies it would be a sign of
good luck. We're going back to Warsaw to find our store," Alex
announced.

"Stay in Kaminsk," Vladek urged. "You helped so many of
our villagers. They'll miss you."

"After they found out I wasn't Jewish," Alex said derisively.
"All I've done is lay bricks and patch roofs. I need to get back
in business."

"You want to sell fabric to people more interested in food and shelter?"

"With peace come dreams for a normal life. We're picking up the pieces in Warsaw."

"Maybe we'll find Aunt Hanka, Aunt Devorah, and our grandmother!" shouted Jacob.

Mela took the boys in her arms. "We'll look for them."

"Warsaw's sixty kilometers away. The railroads are unreliable. You'll freeze to death," said Vladek.

"We'll get to Warsaw one way or the other." Alex held Mela and the children in his arms. "What do you say?"

"Back home," said David.

"I wonder what it's like?" asked Jacob.

"My little shop might have survived," hoped Alex.

Mela smiled. "Only one way to find out. We have to return."

Chapter Five

Words are More Important than Bullets

Rain turned to gentle snow cloaking the scattered remains of weapons, backpacks, and helmets thrown aside by fleeing German troops. Mela wrapped a shawl around her shoulders and stood in the open doorway. Snow-covered discards of war cropped up, stark tombstones created by a nation under the thrall of a madman tumbling into the abyss of hell.

David, Jacob, and Marisia thumped and banged into the kitchen. Her children had survived. For the first time in years, their only concern to keep their bellies filled and playing in the snow. Late at night while everyone slept, a neighbor knocked on the door asking for Alex's help.

He prodded Mela. "Someone needs help to fix a tractor. Don't wait up for me."

"This time of the night? It's freezing outside."

"He's been trying to make it run for hours and gave up. It may take a few hours. Go back to sleep." He kissed her and pulled on his jacket and gloves disappearing in the dark.

"Where's Papa Alex?" David asked in the morning, diving into a bowl of hot porridge.

"He went out in the middle of the night. I begged him not to go. He insisted he had to take care of something very important," said Mela. "When he makes up his mind there's no way to stop him. "

"He takes off and expects all of us to sit around and wait for him to miraculously return. You married a daredevil," grumbled Vladek.

"He'll come back and surprise all of us!" shouted David.

Alex stomped in, rushing to the fireplace, holding his grease-stained hands over the heat. "We're off to Warsaw."

"It's a hell of a long walk," said a skeptical Vladek.

Alex opened the door. A blast of cold air surged into the room. A farm wagon and tired-looking horse with a frost-coated blanket draped over its back stood in front of the house. "We're riding all the way," said Alex.

"It must have cost every zloty we have," complained Mela.

"A farmer traded me the wagon and horse for repairing his tractor with some leftover parts from a damaged German truck."

"You won't get past Grójce with that old bag of bones," laughed Vladek.

Alex clapped Vladek on the back. "I'll talk her into it." The children applauded.

"Alex can do anything when he's determined," said Mela.

The family stashed their few belongings in the back of the wagon. Basia handed old blankets to Alex and Mela. "Children shouldn't ride on bare wooden planks. Go with God," she whispered.

Vladek shook Alex's hand. "You have more courage than anyone I know."

Alex responded stoically, "Not courage: survival."

With a flick of the reins, the horse gave a snort, and they ambled on their slow journey toward Warsaw. Jacob and Marisia huddled together under a blanket. Feeling abandoned and excluded, David threw himself onto a pile of pillows in a corner of the wagon and clasped his arms around his chest, rocking back and forth. One day he would prove he was smart and clever.

Alex and Mela's faith in him kept anger at his brother and Marisia at bay. David treasured something neither Marisia nor David ever dreamed of having—a book written by a Russian soldier. Even if it was written in a language he understood but spoke haltingly and could not read. On the night they left Kaminsk, David asked Alex to translate the sentiment Vasily Grossman wrote in the book. They sat by the fading fireplace light.

Alex traced his fingers over the inscription. "'A soldier and a scholar. Wars enlist even artists.'"

"What did Vasily write, Papa?"

"'To Tadek, words are more powerful than bullets. Your Friend on the Battlefield, Vasily Semyonovich Grossman.'"

David always carried the sentiment in his heart. He fell asleep dreaming Cyrano de Bergerac battling one hundred swordsmen and winning. In his dreams the one hundred were evil, gray-clad German soldiers swept away by brave Tadek Roslan.

Howling winds sounded like calls from giant wolves roaming the countryside. Leafless trees stretched out their twisted branches—talons clawing at him. Lightning flashed, throwing bolts of fire in David's path.

The wagon hit ruts, waking him to the sight of straggling refugees trudging with pitiable belongings over their shoulders, hollow-eyed children struggling through mud, carts loaded with the detritus of lives pitched over in water-filled bomb craters. A clanging bell eerily echoed across hazy, forsaken fields.

A black steam engine belching smoke loomed out of the thick mist screeching to a halt. Husky men wearing waxed canvas jackets over coveralls tossed unbroken rusty rails off flatbeds. With picks and sledgehammers they ripped damaged tracks off snow-covered ties, casting them aside. Oxidized, unbroken rails took their place.

Alex plodded through a soggy field to the foreman barking orders at his crew. "Any problem taking the train to Warsaw?"

"What Warsaw? The city's leveled. The goddamn bastards destroyed anything the Russians or we could use," said the foreman. "Find another destination, my friend."

"Warsaw is my home. Where I worked and raised my family," Alex said.

"I can't stop you from going."

"Can we take the train to the city?"

"We don't carry passengers. In two or three days, trains might take you from here to hell," said the foreman, ordering his crew off the tracks.

Alex trudged to Mela and the children. "They repaired most of the line to Warsaw. We just have to wait."

"The children aren't sleeping outdoors again. We have to find shelter tonight," Mela insisted.

Alex snapped the reins. The horse jerked the wagon forward. David pulled a blanket over his shoulders. He closed his eyes, listening to the squeal of rusty axles as the wagon jolted over the road.

"The old horse will take days to get us to Warsaw," said Jacob.

Marisia tugged on her father's sleeve. "What's the horse's name, Papa?"

"She's a horse. Let's call her what she is: Horse."

"Horse needs a real name," insisted Marisia. "I want to call her Roza." She turned to David and Jacob. "Everyone who agrees raise your hand."

"We want Roza!" they yelled.

Alex smiled. "All right, Roza, let's see if giving you a name helps get us to Warsaw faster." Debris-filled earth exploded into the air. The horse stopped in its tracks. "Everyone under the wagon!" shouted Alex.

Refugees on the road crouched beneath dry, brittle bushes. Machine-gun fire cut through the air. A Russian infantry squad advanced slowly across the field. A soldier raised a long tube to his shoulder and fired a missile. The troops advanced. A Russian captain drove up. "Where are you going?"

"Warsaw," Alex replied.

"It's a hellhole. Everyone else is going in the opposite direction."

"I have to see with my own eyes!" exclaimed Alex.

"Be careful. We came through so fast we missed a few German emplacements. We're mopping up." The captain made a U-turn and sped away.

Mela grabbed Alex's arm. "Vladek was right. Think of the children. Let's go back to Kaminsk."

"I don't trust Russians. Maybe they want to keep us away from the city while they loot and ransack." He placed his arm around her shoulders. "I promise at the first sign of danger we'll turn around."

Roza pushed her muzzle into the earth, yanking out roots. She chewed each piece slowly and carefully, savoring each bite.

"She's hungry," Marisia called out, "and so are we."

Alex pulled a burlap sack from under the wagon seat. "The farmer who gave me the horse and wagon provided for the animal."

"Her name's Roza," said David.

"A fine name for a tired old horse." Alex sifted oats through his fingers. "Help me feed Her Highness Roza."

The children poured grain into the feedbag. Alex looped straps over Roza's neck, securing her while she contentedly munched. Mela placed a jug of water in the back of the wagon, along with a loaf of hard black bread.

"The bread Peter Sawicki gave us," remembered Jacob.

Alex raised it over his head. "The last loaf he gave us for rebuilding his oven. Better than money."

Mela sliced a slab of dry cheese. "Along with this."

The children gobbled up bread and cheese. "This is the best food I ever had, except for the Russian sausage," said David.

"Thank goodness we don't have vodka," winked Alex.

At sunset they turned up a dirt path to a barn on an abandoned farm. Doors swung on broken hinges. Water dripped through ragged holes in the roof. "Over here," called Alex. Dry hay bales lay heaped in a corner.

Mela threw down blankets. David slept between Alex and Mela. Jacob and Marisia, side by side.

Night fell rapidly. Stars twinkled through shell-pierced holes; rain fell, followed by hail clattering against the walls. Rattling changed to sporadic gunfire and shouting. A squad of Russians herded exhausted, frightened German soldiers across a field.

"The great Wehrmacht—scared out of their skins, hoping to have their lives spared. Let it be a lesson. Strength doesn't come from guns and bullets. It comes from your head and heart," said Alex.

It reminded David of the note Vasily Grossman wrote to him in his book: "More powerful than bullets are words."

Alex hailed the sergeant in command. "I need to get to Warsaw and learn what happened to my shop."

"The city's a cemetery, comrade," the sergeant reported.

"It's important for the sake of my family."

"We're returning to Warsaw in about an hour. You can come with us. But I warn you, German snipers are still holed up there. Don't hold us responsible if anything happens." The sergeant waved at Mela and the children standing outside the barn. "Have enough to eat?"

"A little bread and cheese."

"We'll drop off some rations."

Alex walked back to the barn. "The sergeant's taking me to Warsaw. He promised food for you and the children."

Jacob tugged at his sleeve. "You said you didn't like Russians."

Alex smiled. "There are good ones, like the soldiers who came to Kaminsk."

A Jeep roared to the barn door. A corporal unloaded two baskets of food. "Comrade sergeant sends this with his compliments."

To their delight, they found black bread, hard cheese, sausages, cans of beans, tins of sardines, and eggs wrapped in straw bundles. "Real food!" shouted David.

"Been a long time, yes?" asked the soldier.

"A very long time," said David.

Jacob poked him in the shoulder. "No vodka."

"I'll be back tomorrow or the next day," said Alex, stepping into the Jeep. "There's work to be done while I'm gone. Princess Roza needs to be groomed and fed." He placed a container of grease on the ground. "Lubricate the wagon axles. Wipe down the leather traces and reins to keep them from cracking. Everyone clean up. Don't leave anything behind we may need in the city. And last, behave and listen to Mama."

The driver handed Alex a helmet. "You have to wear it. Orders. We're driving through an area that may have snipers left behind." Gears ground and they took off for Warsaw.

Mela hoisted buckets off a shelf. "Time to wash. Use the water pump outside."

"We'll only get dirty again," Jacob grumbled.

"Easier to wash off one day's dust than dirt from seven days," said Mela, building a fire with hay. A pot bubbled on the flames. "No drinking from the pump. Only boiled water. The rest is for washing. "

David splashed cold water on his face. "It's freezing."

"Don't be a baby," Jacob scolded. David threw a handful of water at his brother, who yelped from the sudden frigid onslaught.

"Now who's the baby?" smirked David.

"Stop it!" yelled Marisia.

"Afraid I'll hurt your boyfriend?" laughed David.

"I'm not her boyfriend," Jacob growled.

"All cuddled up with Marisia last night!" yelled David.

"We didn't cuddle. We were keeping warm," said Marisia.

"Enough," ordered Mela. "We don't need a war in our family. Sit down and eat. Build up your strength."

Russian guards prodded crushed, desolate German prisoners through the field. A German, face blackened with soot, wearing a torn smoke-stained uniform, stumbled and fell. He stared at David and Jacob, abject fear in his eyes betraying the ideology ingrained in his soul. A grizzled German officer yanked the soldier to his feet and slapped his face. "Sie ein Mann. Sie sind ein Krieger des Dritten Reiches."

With gut-wrenching primal screams, the trooper pulled himself away running across the scarred landscape. A Russian sergeant yelled: "Anhalten! Anhalten!" A shot rang out. The young soldier spun around, falling to the ground. His eyes, begging for mercy, turned to David standing in front of the barn. With a final cough, the soldier spewed blood from his mouth. Quaking with shock, David ran inside.

Jacob grabbed him by the collar. "What's wrong with you?"

"You're almost the same age."

"A year ago, he would have looked at you with disgust and killed you."

"Take away their guns and they're frightened, weak men. Papa always said one day we would see the real faces of our enemy. Take care of the horse and wagon," said Mela.

David washed and brushed Roza. With each stroke across her back, he tried to understand how ordinary people became monsters murdering innocent men, women, and children. He and Jacob greased axles and wheels, spending hours going over straps and traces until the leather gleamed. The work helped David forget for a brief time the dread those uncompromising men and boys in gray tattered uniforms forced on him and his family.

A very disappointed Alex returned. The Russian driver shook his hand. "Good luck, comrade."

Alex sat on a hay bale. "I hardly knew the city, except for a few broken signs."

"What are we going to do?" asked Jacob.

"I worked with a woman, Ludmila Sobansky, who manufactured textiles in Łódź, south of here. The Russians told me it isn't as badly damaged as Warsaw. If she's still alive, she might help us find a place to stay."

A lone, brick railway station, its paint peeling, doors hanging on loose hinges, windows shattered, stood next to rusted railroad tracks. An unshaven old man wearing small spectacles sat behind a plank placed across sawhorses. His moth-eaten uniform bore the Polish National Railway silver eagle patch.

"When do you expect the next train to Łódź?" Alex asked.

The old man peered over the top of his glasses. "The Russians tell me it starts running tomorrow morning from Warsaw to Łódź and from Łódź to Warsaw in the afternoon. If you're lucky it might happen, if not I suggest you feed your horse and keep on riding."

"How much for tickets?"

"No one's given me orders to collect fares. As far as I'm concerned, you have a free ride courtesy of the Soviet Union."

"We'll stay inside the station until the train arrives," Alex said to Mela and the children.

"We can't take Roza on the train," cried Marisia.

On the other side of the tracks a farmer repaired a hole in the side of his house. Alex crossed over. "Bring the horse and wagon," he told the children. They led Roza over rails and waited as Alex talked to the weary farmer.

At first, the two men stood apart; then they shook hands and slapped each other on the back.

"Come over and meet Mr. Wójcik," Alex called to the children.

The farmer opened Roza's mouth and examined her teeth. He ran his fingers over the greased axles and wheels. "It's a deal," he said, giving Alex a handful of zlotys. "I don't know if they're worth anything, but it's all I have."

"Good enough," said Alex.

David patted Roza's velvety muzzle. "She wants to go with us."

"I didn't know you spoke Horse," said Alex.

"Papa, please let's ride the wagon to Łódź," Marisia pleaded.

"In the city, your wonderful horse will be forced to haul heavy loads day after day until she wears out," said Alex. "On the farm she'll pull a cart, maybe a plow. Out here there's fresh air, plenty of grass to eat, and a meadow. The old princess can roam free. Liberated just like us."

"We'll take good care of her, young lady. She'll grow fat and happy," promised Wójcik.

At sunset, David, Jacob, and Marisia sat on the station platform with Alex and Mela. The dark-blue heavens slowly gave way to an ebony sky pierced with glittering diamonds.

"I miss Roza," said Marisia.

"Whenever you miss the old lady, look up," said Alex taking her on his lap. He cupped her chin and directed her eyes at the northern sky. "The orange star is the muzzle of Pegasus, the flying horse belonging to the muses of memory, arts, and science. The goddess of wisdom gave the steed to a great warrior to defeat his enemies. The warrior ended up believing he was a god."

"Papa, you're making this up," said Marisia.

"The Greeks tell the story to their children; but I'm not finished. This human who thought he was a god, tried to force Pegasus to fly him to heaven. The great horse threw him off and galloped into the sky, where he remains. Someday Princess Roza might join him, and you can watch them run and play. Time to sleep. We have a long day ahead."

The children climbed onto benches inside the ticket station. Mela and Alex kissed them goodnight and sat together as darkness closed in. David dreamed about stars circling the sky, wondering if worlds in far galaxies warred or enjoyed peace.

A clanking train woke them early in the morning. Travelers surrounded by battered suitcases and overflowing canvas bags sat, stood, and crouched on rough floors in ancient carriages. Grit-streaked, passengers clutching handholds and each other perched precariously atop cars. Apprehension and fear flickered in the eyes of children clinging to parents.

Alex and Mela pushed through the mass of people. They found space in a corner.

Steam hissed and the train rocked forward. David sat back, chewing a crust of bread. A tall, thin boy, black circles around his eyes, a shabby blanket thrown over his shoulders, tried to snatch the bread. Alex took hold of the boy's shirt collar. "Do that again and you'll be sorry."

The boy's father pushed through to Alex. "Don't manhandle my son. Isn't it bad enough we had Germans, now Russians?"

"He can ask if he wants bread. My children share. They don't need threats," warned Alex.

The father yanked his son back. "You hear, Volya? Keep your hands to yourself. Ask nice."

Volya stared at the floor. "A piece of bread?" he muttered.

Alex handed him the crust. The boy stuffed it hungrily into his mouth and slinked back into the crowd. His father wiped away tears. "You're a good man, thank you."

"Papa, it was our last piece" David said.

"For us it was the last. For the boy it might have been his first."

Guards held back passengers pushing against doors hoping to start a new life in Łódź. "Serious injury may occur if any attempt is made to disembark while the train is in motion.

Stay where you are until the train stops," they repeated over and over.

Elongated icicles—primeval, translucent spears—hung from steel beams buckled by bombs in Łódź Fabryczna, the city's oldest and largest rail terminal. The train's reverberating iron wheels broke them loose and they crashed onto debris-covered floors. Conductors slid open carriage doors. Passengers rushed out. Bags, tattered suitcases, threadbare rucksacks lay in piles on gray snow heaped in drifts inside the rail station.

The Roslans dragged their bags across pools of frozen water scattered between the rails. A large sign outside read: 'Welcome to Litzmannstadt.'

"I thought we were going to Łódź," Jacob said.

A laborer clambered up a ladder and ripped down the placard. He nailed a new one in its place: "Welcome to Łódź."

"Almost back to normal," said Alex.

Blocks of undamaged buildings and stores backed up against demolished structures in the center of the city. The unexpected clang of a bell sounded as a battered trolley wobbled along buckled tracks of Zachodnia Street's median.

Refugees and citizens in ragged, soiled clothes scurried along sidewalks. Weeds poked out of a broken grand piano abandoned in the middle of a boulevard. Buildings with fronts sheared off by cannon fire revealed a maze of decimated apartments exposed to weather. Armed Russian soldiers stood at every intersection.

"What are we looking for?" Jacob called out.

"Ogradowa Avenue." Alex pointed down a street. "This way."

Buildings reduced to rubble flanked a brick warehouse with a broken sign: "Łódź Fine Textiles."

"Found it!" Alex announced.

A woman threw open the shutters on the second-floor window. "Go away. I have a gun. Break in, I'll shoot."

Alex raised his hands. "Ludmila, don't you recognize your old friend?"

She leaned further out the window. "Alex, Alex Roslan!" A door opened on the ground floor. A woman in her mid-forties, salt-and-pepper hair pulled under a Polish cavalry cap, wearing khaki army pants and a flower-patterned fleece jacket, burst out embracing Mela. "You haven't aged a year since Alex worked for me."

"Always a good liar, Ludmila."

"Better a lie than half a truth. Your family's grown. Two sons . . ."

"Nephews. We took them in for safety," interrupted Alex.

"This beauty must be Marisia you bragged about when you came here after setting up shop in Warsaw. Where's your oldest—Jurek?"

"Killed during the uprising in Warsaw," whispered Mela. "He was only fourteen."

"So young. What can one say? Warsaw's a cemetery. Łódź barely survived. Over half our population perished."

"At least your warehouse stands. And Isaac Weiss, your foreman?" asked Alex.

"Thrown in the ghetto with his family. He escaped and came to me, all skin and bones. I hid him in the warehouse, fed him until he regained his strength. He grew a beautiful red beard. Dyed his hair blonde. He needed papers, so we gave him a new name: Alex Malinowsky. We got married to complete the disguise. Ludmila Sobansky became Mrs. Ludmila Malinowsky."

Mela stepped back, surprised. "Alex?"

"We used to call your husband Alexander the Great. Isaac always worried someone would give him away. If the Germans found him, I should tell them he would kill me if I opened my mouth. It lasted two years. He was sold out to the Gestapo for a tin of coffee and a carton of cigarettes. They dragged him to right where you're standing and put a bullet in the back of his head."

She turned away, shoulders shaking. Her story was eerily familiar to Mela and Alex. Rumors they harbored Jews forced them to move over and over again until, suspicious of strangers, they ended up in a war-scarred, dank tenement.

"Everyone has terrible stories. Our son, a brave fighter. Your innocent Isaac," said Mela.

"It's been a long time since we watched the sunset from the veranda of your home overlooking magnificent Nad Jasien Pond," Alex reminisced.

"Gone. Nothing left but a big hole in the ground." She pointed to the high window. "I live in the attic. Germans employed slave labor in my factory to make uniforms. Hundreds starved to death. They forced more and more to work in the most unspeakable conditions, treating them like tools wearing out, discarding in ditches three, four deep, bulldozed to hide their crimes. I tried to help the children. Young ones bludgeoned, tossed away. Stronger boys and girls, forced to fill impossible quotas, died of exhaustion, while I stood by powerless, hoping the Russians would save us. When they surrounded Łódź, the goddamned Nazis destroyed all my machines. I'm lucky they didn't pull down the building."

"Nothing left?" asked Alex.

"They planned to burn down the factory, every bolt of fabric. The Russians arrived just in time." She laughed. "In time for what? Who's going to buy? I can't manufacture until I have machines. No one's giving them away."

"How much do you have in the warehouse?" Alex asked.

Mela elbowed her husband aside. "Already talking business? Ludmila, we need a place to live. Can the children play on the rolls of cloth for a bit?"

"They can make them their playground. It's the only thing they're good for," the woman lamented.

Ludmila pushed open large sliding doors, flooding the interior with sunlight. Rolls and bolts of fabric and textiles crowded the warehouse. The children bounced and jumped, raising clouds of dust. They snorted, sneezed, and laughed.

"Enough to last maybe two, three years. It's a waste to leave them here," marveled Alex.

"The gears in your head are spinning. You have a plan?" asked Ludmila.

"Not a plan," he smiled. "An idea that could become a plan. But Mela's right. We need a safe place for our family."

Ludmila wrote an address on a scrap of paper with the stub of a pencil. "The old building's a bit shabby. It was once quite elegant. Tell the concierge you're a friend."

They trudged several city blocks to a war-damaged four-story apartment house with ornamental arches over boarded-up broken windows. Dark stains ran like tears from the windowsills. Eager customers formed a line in front of a dilapidated motion picture theater across the street. The marquee announced, with several letters missing, the Russian film of the week: *Two Soldiers.*

"A war story. Can we go?" Jacob asked hopefully.

"We'll talk about it later," said Alex.

"I haven't seen a film since I was five. *The Wizard of Oz.* I loved it," said Jacob.

A soccer ball bounced out of a grove of bare-branched trees, chased by a boy David's age. David kicked it back, sending it soaring into the air. "Nice kick. You know how to play soccer?" the boy asked.

"A little," answered David.

"We have a team from our apartment house and another team down the street. We need one more player. What's your name?"

Hesitantly, he answered, "Tadek."

Alex stepped between the boys. "Tadek Roslan."

"I'm Shimon."

Another boy emerged from out of the trees. "We have a game to play!"

"Join my team after you settle in."

Shimon rushed back to his friends.

Jacob punched David in the chest. "The great athlete's going to show those kids how to kick a ball."

David pushed Jacob away. "I can play soccer."

A short, stout woman, with a wrinkled face, stringy gray hair tucked beneath a faded scarf, poked her head out a door. "Who are you and what do you want?" she rasped.

Alex handed her the scrap of paper. "Ludmila Sobanski sent us." "This way." She pushed open a cardboard-patched door with broken stained-glass windowpanes and led them up a cracked marble staircase with loose railings rattling the walls. "Be careful, we don't want accidents." The caretaker unlocked the door of an apartment on the third floor. "Because it's Ludmila, I'm giving you the grand suite. Bedroom, living room, kitchen. Your own bathroom. Most places have to share.

Sometimes the plumbing works, sometimes it doesn't. Don't call me. I can't fix it. No electricity. Kerosene lamps in the basement; also old beds. Russians give out food at a canteen around the corner. Don't let them catch you throwing any away. Makes them very angry. Rent due first of each month." She held out the keys to Alex. "First the money." He handed her several bills and she shoved them in the pocket of her apron. "My name is Anka. I'm old and cranky. I go to sleep at eight o'clock. No one's allowed to wake me unless it's a life and death emergency." She abruptly hobbled down the stairs.

They entered a dingy, dusty apartment with one window boarded, the other covered with grime. Mela shook her head. "If this is the grand suite, I hate to think what the other apartments look like."

"At least it's not the back of a wagon," Alex sighed.

He and the boys hauled old brass bedsteads and a sofa with stuffing jutting from seams into the apartment.

"Better than sleeping on floors. Marisia and I are going to the Russian food kitchen. I need to think about feeding everyone," sighed Mela.

"Come on, boys. We'll scout the neighborhood," Alex said.

Snow piled against curbs and sides of buildings. A few yards from the apartment house a long queue waited in front of a store with a sign: "The Central Committee of Polish Jews— Jewish Agency."

"What's going on?" Alex called out.

A woman in patched clothes, wearing a scarf over her head, responded: "We're trying to locate our families. The committee has records."

"What kind of records?"

"Official papers, lists of those who immigrated to Palestine, letters from relatives. You never know what they'll find."

Alex joined the line. "Could be the first step to locating your family."

"Think they'll find our father?" asked Jacob.

"The worst that can happen is nothing. The best? We'll find him alive and well."

Haggard officials sat at desks and stood behind counters, attempting to answer questions coming at them in a barrage of Polish, German, Russian, and Yiddish. Boxes heaped against walls overflowed with files and papers containing names of fathers, mothers, sons, daughters, near and distant relatives.

During lonely nights hiding in Warsaw, Jacob told stories about the Gutgeld family. His father and grandfather owned apartment houses and shops in the city. Jacob vaguely remembered riding in the front seat of his grandfather's big, black American car next to the Gutgeld chauffeur Stasiek, dressed in an olive-colored uniform with bright brass buttons.

David had no connection to stories of gilded pleasures. Memories of living in fear were etched into his young mind. Cruel, stern, armed search parties herding Jews behind ghetto walls. Executing innocents in retribution for partisan raids. The foul smell of death creeping through Warsaw.

Jacob pushed David forward. "Keep moving."

A weary man dressed in a shabby suit looked up from a pile of papers on his desk with tired eyes through wire-rimmed glasses. "Your name?"

"The boys are Jacob and David Gutgeld from Warsaw," replied Alex. David and Jacob jolted. Alex warned them never to say or think those names.

"How can we help?" asked the representative.

"A woman in one of the lines said you have records, notices about families, relatives still living. This is true?"

"Quite correct, Mr. Gutgeld."

"No. Alex Roslan, also from Warsaw. We're looking for their father."

"I don't understand. You're not the father. Relative? Friend?"

"Their father and grandfather left Poland when Germany invaded. In 1943, my wife and I managed to bring Jacob and David out of the ghetto. We want to know if anyone in their family still lives."

The official took off his glasses. "Excuse me, the children have been with you four years?" he asked incredulously.

"With my daughter. We all escaped Warsaw."

"Difficult to believe," said the official.

"You want someone to vouch for me? Tadek, Geniek, tell him."

Jacob leaned forward. "Papa Alex and Mama Mela rescued us from the Nazis. Without them we would be dead."

"Anything else?" asked Alex.

"Nothing else needs saying." The official grasped Alex's hand. "Isaac Feldsheim, investigator with the agency. Give me the children's full names again."

"David and Jacob Gutgeld."

Feldsheim turned to the boys. "Your father's name?"

"Nachum Gutgeld," said Jacob. "Our grandfather is Wolf—Wolf Gutgeld."

"Very good, young man."

"What's next?" asked Alex.

Feldsheim pointed to piles of boxes. "You see these? Each one contains at least a hundred documents. More come in every day. We search through them for information. They include official records retrieved from Nazi files. We receive letters every day from people searching for family. If you're fortunate, one of those documents or letters will hold the answer you want."

"Before we leave, I need information about schools for the boys and my daughter," said Alex.

Feldsheim handed a sheet of paper to Alex. "A few schools are open. Write down your address and we'll contact you if we find anything about their father."

"We're in the apartment house on the corner—third floor, number two."

"I won't have to traipse all over the city to find you."

"You won't have to, Mr. Feldsheim. We'll come every day."

"It won't be necessary."

"Very necessary," said Alex. He turned to the boys. "Now, let's see what Mama created from Russian handouts."

Cold air blew into the apartment through an open window, clearing out the smoke from the wood-burning stove. Mela and Marisia scraped potatoes and peeled cabbage in the small kitchen. Bits of sausage floated in hot water, mixing a spicy aroma with the smell of charred wood.

"Tomorrow, we go back to the Jewish Committee and see if they have news for us. Then it's off to school with all of you," said Alex.

"I can't wait!" yelled David.

"They'll probably put you in the dummy class," snorted Jacob.

"You think you're so smart because Marisia shared school-work with you. I'll do better in school than anyone."

"Listen to the arguing! You're both smart. You'll do alright," Mela assured them.

"Do I have to go to school right away?" pleaded Marisia, leaning against Alex's shoulder.

"First we had a horse for a princess and now the two-legged princess speaks up. Without an education you'll have a hard life. I would have given anything to go to university and become an architect. But I had to take care of my family's farm after my father died. Then Mama and I married . . ."

Mela glared at him. "Placing blame on me won't work, Alex Roslan. You wanted to marry me ever since we were children. Don't deny it."

"How could I resist the most beautiful girl in Białystok? Even so, I had this idea in the back of my head I might return to school. But Hitler and his Nazis had other plans. If I hadn't been in Warsaw, if my friend Stasiek had not been your grandfather's driver, I never would have known about you boys. Who knows what would have happened?"

"It was the will of God. It was His plan," said Mela.

Alex's smile vanished. "He wrote invasion plans for the Germans. Was it God's plan to kill innocents? Sorry, not my kind of god. If there is a god, he wants us to help ourselves and others."

Mela crossed herself. "I'm praying God loves you."

"Good. Then I can avoid all the hocus-pocus."

He reached over and kissed her.

"Not in front of the children!" said Mela.

"Everyone who thinks a kiss is bad raise their hand." No one stirred. "We have approval."

Chapter Six

Friends

Faded, tattered posters hanging on school walls depicted giant insects oozing from thick, crusted lips of crude Jewish caricatures with the vicious caption: "Jews are lice. They cause typhus." Another poster in German and Polish, left over from Nazi occupation, read: "Reward for information regarding hidden Jews. Report information to office of Jewish Affairs Deutsche Gestatzpolizei, Commander, Sicherheitz Polizei SD, Łódź District." Furious, Alex ripped them down. An exhausted young woman stared at him from a doorway. "Mr. Roslan, is something wrong?"

"Children will believe these despicable posters because they're in a school," said Alex angrily.

"We're doing everything possible to remove all traces of the Nazi occupation. It's only been a few weeks."

"Waiting even one hour is too long to get rid of hate."

Alex balled up the remnants of the posters, tossing them in a wastebasket. The woman offered her hand. "I promise we'll be more diligent. I'm the school registrar, Kasia Ulinski."

"Next time, no more garbage."

"You have my word. Right now, your daughter and sons are my concern."

"My concern also. These spiteful lies . . ."—he searched for the right words—

". . . pollute the air we breathe."

The registrar turned pale in the face of Alex's indignation. "Everything will be taken care of by the time Marisia starts school."

"And Geniek and Tadek?"

"They haven't attended classes for a long time and must be on a level with other children before we can place them."

"They're smart. They'll learn fast."

"Every father wants to believe his son or daughter is the best scholar. They scored very high in mathematics. They need help with language, history, and geography. I have no doubt a few months of intense tutoring will bring them up to our standards."

"If the school provides such services, let's do it."

"The city has to conserve resources in order to repair water supplies, electricity, gas. It's necessary to rebuild roads and bridges. You will have to find and pay for a tutor."

Alex jammed his hands in his pockets. "Don't worry. I'll take care of it."

Marisia bounced out of a classroom and ran to her father. "I can start right way, Papa. All I need are paper and pencils." He kissed her on the forehead.

"They don't want us," muttered David.

Jacob glared at Miss Ulinski. "This isn't fair. History? Geography? What about math and science?"

"Rules are rules."

"Enough complaining. We'll do what's necessary," Alex promised.

Straggling lines of men and women hauled furniture, clothing, boxes filled with copper pots, pans, and dishes from store to store, anxious to trade for food, shoes, clothes. or cigarettes. Women waited outside S. Baranski Tailor, clamoring for service. He peered out with a weary look on his face. "All I can do is repair. I have no fabric. I can't make anything for anyone," he said to disappointed customers.

A dim light inside the Central Committee office illuminated Isaac Feldsheim leafing through stacks of paper. Alex rapped on the window. The investigator ignored him. Alex knocked harder. "We're closed," said Feldstein.

"Remember me from yesterday?"

He adjusted his spectacles and looked closer. "Roslan. You rescued the boys." Feldsheim looked down the street. "Quickly, come in." He locked the door and pulled down the shade. "We keep our doors closed for at least two hours a day, so we can review files. With hundreds of requests, we don't have enough hours in the day. You're here about the boys' father?"

"Not today. The school insists they need a teacher to bring them up to speed."

"A qualified tutor," said Feldsheim, flipping through the pages of a notebook, running fingers over a list of names. "The Joint Distribution Committee provides funds for that purpose. Here we are. The perfect person. Ella Rosenberg, a well-educated young woman recently arrived from Palestine. Studied at the Hebrew University of Jerusalem. An excellent match for your boys. She's staying at a nearby hostel."

"Sometimes we find treasure right in front of our eyes," said Alex. "What do I have to do?"

Feldstein handed Alex a form. "Your name, wife's name, address. Names of the boys. Place of birth if known. Names of relatives who may still be alive. We'll telegraph the information to the agency in Jerusalem. Once approved, they'll arrange Miss Rosenberg's schedule. The process will take approximately fourteen days. In the meantime, I'll contact her. She may want to meet Jacob and David ahead of time. I believe this will make an excellent *shidduch*. Excuse me, an excellent—"

"—match. I learned Yiddish a long time ago," said Alex.

They ran into Shimon and his team playing in the park. "Tadek, we need a goalie."

"I want a promise. When this teacher, Miss Rosenberg, comes, you'll pay attention and work hard," demanded Alex.

"We don't need to catch up!" shouted Jacob.

"You'll do what the school wants."

"Okay with me," said David, eager to join the other boys.

"Go on, enjoy yourself," said Alex.

David bolted into the street feeling exhilarated; soon he was running, kicking, and shouting with his new teammates.

An older man, dressed in a worn-out suit and wearing a soiled tie, excitedly accosted Alex and Jacob at the top of the stairway. "Did you hear the news?" he gleefully shouted, grabbing Alex by the hand. "Dov Lazik. And you?"

"Alex Roslan. What news?"

"The Allies making a push for Berlin. It's on the radio." He motioned Alex to his apartment. "Come in, come in." A slight woman with a lined face and gray hair, carefully twisted a dial on a wooden cathedral-style radio with a domed top. Static-punctuated noise came out of the speaker. "Ida, we have guests, neighbors."

She shook hands with Alex. "You must meet my grandson, Shimon."

"The soccer player? He just recruited my other son, Tadek, for his team," said Alex. "Marisia, Geniek, ask Mama to join me. Go downstairs and watch Tadek."

"He's playing soccer. I'm not a referee," complained Jacob.

"I'll go," volunteered Marisia. "Geniek can sit alone in the apartment."

"Okay, okay. Maybe I can show them a few tricks," mumbled Jacob.

"The master athlete has spoken," remarked Alex.

Mela hesitantly entered the Lazik apartment. Ida gave her a hug. "You're always welcome in our home. I'm Ida. This is my husband, Dov."

"Let's celebrate our new friendship!" Dov opened a bottle of liquor and poured three glasses. "From your accent, you don't come from Warsaw."

"Originally Białystok. We moved to Warsaw when we married."

"What they did to that beautiful city is tragic."

"At least Łódź survived almost intact," said Alex.

"If you call the decimation of the Jewish community and destruction of most infrastructure 'intact.' Don't get me wrong. There's no better or worst story. Warsaw reduced to ashes. Ghettoes in both cities ending up as way stations to death camps." Tears welled in Dov's eyes. "Ida's family, my family, murdered."

"How did you survive?" asked Mela, reliving her own doubts and fears.

"Łódź was our home until Dov gained a teaching position at the University of Warsaw. Then the invasion. We escaped with the help of fellow teachers. They carted us by hay wagon to a farm. The family hid us and fed us until the Russians drove out the Nazis," said Ida.

"We had friends in Warsaw who ended up in the ghetto. Let's hope no one ever has to go through that pain again," said Mela.

"Poland should have welcomed us back," Dov stated.

"My husband was a university professor. He received awards as Faculty Extraordinaire," Ida said with pride.

"It meant nothing after all the anguish, torture, and death we encountered. We met the future on February 2, a date inscribed on the calendar of our life. Ida and I had a small cottage near the Vistula. A neighbor we counted on as a friend took it over. After Russia routed the Germans, we returned to thank him. He pointed a rifle at us and ordered us to leave or he would kill us," said Dov.

"It was your property. What right did he have?" asked Alex.

Dov laughed. "What right? I'm a Jew. A nobody. An outcast."

The Lasiks and Roslans felt the haunting truth. The enemy, dedicated to murdering every Jew in Europe, was headed toward defeat. Bigotry and hatred lurking beneath the surface took its place.

"The police or courts wouldn't help?"

"With bribes. After all, every Jew, beggar, or teacher has diamonds, gold, and silver hidden in secret places."

Alex shook his head. "What did we fight for?"

"Freedom. At least we're alive, healthy, good neighbors, and have our grandson."

"And Shimon's mother and father?" asked Alex.

"We begged them to come with us when we left Warsaw. They joined the Jewish partisans in the forests. The agency is trying to locate them." Dov raised his glass. "Hope for the best."

Alex took a sip and choked. "Kicks like a mule!"

"I make it myself. One of these days I'll get the formula right." He raised his glass to Alex. "Your health." The radio crackled. "BBC news," Dov announced. "Sometimes we receive speeches by British prime minister Winston Churchill. A moral leader in the fight against Hitler. He gives us hope."

Dov turned the radio dial until three bells rang out, followed by the first notes of Beethoven's Fifth Symphony, emulating the Morse code for the letter "V" for victory. A clipped British voice with no emotion announced: "American Third Army troops are reported inside the city of Koblenz today, and the First Army bridgehead across the Rhine has been expanded by almost a mile."

"All I understand is Koblenz. What's happening?" asked Alex.

"I'll translate," offered Dov, turning up the volume:

> "Supreme Headquarters says American forces have driven to the crossing point at Remagen. The bridgehead is under German military fire. Berlin says American troops have made another crossing at the Rhine and troops have joined the main bridgehead, but there's no confirmation. There is a report the Russians are fighting in the southern suburb of Danzig. The Germans say fighting is going on in the Central front before Berlin."

Dov took a deep breath. "Haven't translated in a very long time. It's good to know I can still do it. A few teachers from Warsaw faculty are talking about starting a college or university here."

"I'm amazed how you always find Jews," Mela said when they returned to their apartment.

"A miracle from your god," Alex replied.

"Heretic. It's a good thing I love you or I'd turn your atheist soul over to the Church."

"I'm trembling with fear."

"What about school?" Mela asked, ignoring his sarcasm.

Marisia and Jacob stomped up the stairs. Anka opened her door. "What is that, a herd of cows?"

They ran into the apartment laughing. "Mama asked about school. I was just about to tell her you start tomorrow, Marisia."

"Tadek and I will be stuck here with some old lady to teach us," said Jacob, throwing himself on a chair. "We don't need special help."

"Schools have rules and regulations. Follow them," ordered Alex.

Mela's face went white. "Where's Tadek? Why isn't he with you?"

"Last time we saw him, he and the other kids were busy pretending to be great athletes," said Jacob.

Mela peered at the street below. David played soccer with Shimon and his friends. "I have difficulty believing the nightmare's over. Geniek, go outside. Find some friends. Enjoy yourself."

"I'd really like to go to a movie. Maybe Marisia can go with me?"

"Papa, can I please go?" Marisa pleaded.

"All right." He handed Jacob coins for tickets. "Come home immediately after it's over."

The children dashed out. Mela glanced at Alex with fire in her eyes. "Very nice, giving them money we could use for a tutor."

"Money's no problem, my doubting wife. Jewish organizations provide and pay for teachers. The investigator, Isaac Feldsheim, is contacting a young woman who will help us." He leaned out the window expecting to see a game in action.

There was no sign of David, Shimon, or the other boys. Alex and Marisa ran out of the building. A tram rolled through the intersection.

"He's gone. We should never let him go out on his own!" cried Mela.

Anka poked her head out of a window. "What's all the fuss about?"

"Tadek was playing football a while ago. Now there's no one!" shouted Alex.

A tram bell rang. "Such a worrier. Boys always get into mischief. Sometimes they ride all over town on the streetcar."

"He doesn't have money for the fare."

The concierge shrugged her shoulders. "They jump on board while it's moving. When the conductor collects tickets, they jump off and wait for the next car."

A trolley carrying the boys clattered through Łódź along warped rails. They passed block after block of ruins left behind by retreating German forces. A cracked granite slab etched with Hebrew letters lay among scattered marble and brick columns.

"Germans blew up every synagogue in the city. They packed Jews into the ghetto. We lived in Warsaw. When they forced friends and neighbors out of their homes, we escaped. You're not Jewish. You wouldn't understand."

The back of David's neck tightened. He and his brother experienced the same agitation. Guns at their heads. Men, women, children whipped with rifle butts. Executing innocents not moving fast enough, too argumentative, or attempting to escape. He understood.

The tram stopped near the entrance of a large park. "Come on," shouted Shimon. They trekked through rubble. Collapsed walls revealed broken furniture and piles of paper on cracked wood floors. David picked up envelopes with stamps. A few had postage from other parts of Europe, America. He shoved them under his shirt and followed Shimon running up a gravel path to a frozen pond littered with leaves glittering under the sun.

A marble arbor with part of its dome blasted off leaned forlornly at the far end. Columns pocked by bullet holes tilted at the edge of a shell hole. Shimon skipped flat stones across the ice. Ravages of war added mystery to stark, bare trees and glistening firs with rainbow-shimmering icicles clinging to branches.

"My grandmother used to come here as a young girl in the spring," said Shimon. "Later she came with my grandfather and mother. She said it was the most beautiful place in Poland until the Germans smashed everything."

They crossed a small bridge over a canal. Bombs had twisted wrought iron railings into surrealistic tangled metal loops. On the other side of the canal the boys jumped over boulders in a dry meadow. A sign on the path read: "Poniatowski Park."

"Poniatowski's a funny name," said David.

"Every kid knows Prince Josef Poniatowski. He was the nephew of the last king of Poland. He led an army to fight the Russians."

"I must have been sick the day they taught that in school." David felt uneasy telling a lie, but afraid of being discovered.

"At least you went to school. I was lucky my grandfather was a university professor. He taught me history and English on the farm."

"Tell me more about the prince."

"One of Poniatowski's friends was Tadeusz Kosciusko, a Polish officer who went to America before the battle with the Russians. He joined the American general George Washington to train his soldiers. When Kosciusko returned to Poland, he and the prince fought side by side."

"I'll read up on their adventures," said David.

Shimon swung back and forth from a tree branch. "I'll lend you one of my schoolbooks."

Long shadows stretched across the park, painting the snow gray and purple. "Getting late. I have to go home," David said.

"We have plenty of time. My grandfather and grandmother let me go out every day."

"You're lucky. Mama and Papa always worry."

"I'm staying."

"This is my first time in the city. I don't know my way."

Shimon dropped from the tree. "Let's go. No sense getting in trouble." They hopped a trolley and traveled back to the apartment house.

Stern and concerned Alex waited for them. "Shimon took you on a tour of Łódź?"

"We went to a park named after a famous Polish prince. It had trees and a big pond," said David.

"Mr. and Mrs. Lazik told me you like to hop on and off trams. You're asking for trouble," Alex said to Shimon.

"All we want is a good time," Shimon protested.

"Next time, I need to know where Tadek's going. I don't want him hurt in an accident." Alex waited until Shimon joined his grandparents. "Congratulations. Maybe one day you'll be a scientist studying ponds and forests. Wait. To be a scientist you have to go to school. The only way you're going to school is by having someone teach you to qualify. Your teacher's waiting upstairs."

A slight, attractive, dark-haired young woman in a plain dress and sensible flat-heeled shoes sat on the sofa with Jacob and Marisia. David slipped into the room. "Tadek also needs help," announced Alex.

Mela rushed to David. "We were so worried. Don't ever wander off again."

"You should've come to the movies with us. It was wonderful," said Marisia.

"It was awful," groused Jacob. "In between battles, soldiers and girls hugged and kissed. One of them even sang a love song."

"Miss Rosenberg isn't here to talk movies. She's here to plan your education," said Alex.

"Mr. and Mrs. Roslan told me you're very good in math. It's not my best subject, so you can teach me," said Ella Rosenberg. "We can have fun learning about history and geography. What do you know about the history of Poland?"

David's arm shot up. "A little."

"Very little. You don't know anything about Polish history," griped Jacob.

"I know all about Prince Josef Poniatowski. He was the nephew of the last king of Poland and fought against the Russians, who tried to take over our country."

"Very good," said Ella. "One of his best friends was Kosciusko. Not only was he a military officer in Poland, he went to America and helped win their war against the British." Ella shook David's hand. "Seems we have a scholar in our midst."

"I told you they were smart," smiled Mela, every bit amazed as Jacob.

Alex took Ella aside before she left. "Only you and Isaac Feldsheim know Tadek and Geniek are Jewish. Everyone else, including our Jewish neighbors, believe we're related."

"Why keep up the subterfuge? The war is almost over," said Ella.

"There's still a strong current of Jew-hate in Poland. I need to protect my boys. Promise me," entreated Alex.

"No one will know."

"When will you begin lessons?"

"Officially? When they approve your application. Unofficially, I can start right away. Your boys are exceptional."

Ella came fully equipped with books, pens, bottles of ink, pencils, and paper tablets. Class ran from nine in the morning until noon, three days a week. Jacob studied two hours, David for one. Their tutor challenged them with math and science problems. They engaged in lengthy discussions after each session. On the third week, Ella brought approval from the agency, formalizing her position.

As time went on, it became increasingly apparent Jacob's math and science skills were remarkable for a child wrenched from school when he was nine. Never schooled, David had a remarkable facility for arithmetic and fluency with reading beyond his years.

"I had to learn by myself. Every time I asked Geniek for help he refused. He wanted to keep me ignorant. I fooled him. I asked him to read stories to me slowly and repeat the same lines over and over again. I connected sounds to words on the page."

"How clever. You invented your own learning system. Perhaps one day you'll be a teacher," Ella said.

After lessons, she briefed Alex and Mela on their progress. "Tadek and Geniek are very bright children. Geniek's grasp of subjects is overwhelming. Both boys have astonishing ability. Watch out for Tadek. He's intelligent and very good-looking. Girls will run after him."

David dived into his studies. He loved reading history and folktales about the youngest and poorest boys or girls accomplishing heroic deeds. One story, "Red Riding Hood," had a disturbing moral in the form of a sonnet at the end of the tale.

> "I say the wolf, for every wolf that roams
> Is not the same.
> Some, in appearance tame.
> Gentle, well mannered, affable, and gay,
> Trotting beside them in the friendliest way . . .
> Alas, how many to their cost do find
> These plausible wolves are the most dangerous kind."

"I know those wolves." David's voice trembled with apprehension. "They walk on two feet, hunting us.

Penetrating insight by a seven-year-old into the metaphor of a simple story about a girl fooled by a hungry animal astonished Ella. She folded David in her arms and held him until his anxiety dwindled away. "They can't hurt you any longer. Hitler, and everything he represents, is being destroyed. Write about your feelings. We'll make it part of your lesson."

David's emotionally bitter essay imagined swastika-adorned, slavering wolves wielding knives, hovering over cowering children rescued by a man and woman who destroyed the beasts with fire.

Ella carefully wrote the last line of the "Red Riding Hood" sonnet on his paper: "Alas, how many to their cost do find, / These plausible wolves are the most dangerous kind." In place of a grade, she presented him with a book from her own collection. "*Uncle Tom's Cabin* is very important. Harriet Beecher

Stowe, an American, wrote the book. It's translated into many languages, including Polish. It influenced Abraham Lincoln, president of the United States, who freed the slaves. When you finish reading it write a paper about what it means to you."

David read by the light of a kerosene lamp. The story painted a picture of noble, brave, self-sacrificing men and women surviving as slaves in the face of unspeakable brutality. Uncle Tom, Eliza, and George, three black slaves in America's South before the civil war, escaped from their masters. Uncle Tom was torn away from his family and sold to a pitiless slave owner who murdered him.

David's essay compared the tragic events in the novel with his experience under Nazi violence. Ella wept after she read his essay and wrote "A+" on the paper. "Remarkable," she said.

"I wrote how I felt," David said quietly. "I have something I want to show you." He went to the bedroom and returned holding the book given to him by the Russian soldier. "Tell me what this book means."

Ella looked at the cover. "Vasily Grossman? How did you get it?"

"He gave it to me when we were in Kaminsk."

"This is overwhelming. Vasily Grossman's a famous Russian author. Most of his books are banned in Russia. At university in Palestine, we read them translated into Hebrew. This has one of the first stories he published." She opened it and stopped. "My God, he signed it. 'To Tadek, words are more important than bullets. Vasily Grossman.'"

"I don't understand," said David.

Seeing the sad, serious look on David's face, Alex asked, "Anything wrong?"

"Nothing's wrong, Mr. Roslan." Ella showed him David's grade.

"It's what I expect. If he's finished with his studies for the day, I'm taking him on an errand."

Before she left, Ella sat down with David. "We'll talk about Grossman's book next time."

Alex and David met Ludmila Sobanski at her warehouse. "It's time Tadek learned something about business."

"Shame on you putting the little boy to work."

"It's important for him to understand money doesn't grow on trees."

"I know money doesn't grow on trees," David said. "What are we doing here?"

"In the story of Rumpelstiltskin, a princess made gold out of straw. We're going to make money out of cloth."

"It's a fairy tale."

"Sometimes fairy tales tell the truth."

"You're opening a shop in Łódź," said Ludmila.

"I don't need a shop for both of us to benefit. All one has to do is observe and listen how people want nothing more than a return to normal life. I can provide a bit of dignity with your cloth. Remember the time I made a deal with you and your compatriots to sell out-of-date fabrics? You and I can do it again. With your approval, I plan to set up in the town square and sell your stock at a major discount."

"My inventory's not doing any good sitting in the dark. Take what you think you can sell. We'll split it fifty-fifty."

"Tadek, you're our witness," said Alex.

They loaded a four-wheeled cart with bolts of patterned cloth, navy blue and powder blue textiles, a bolt of blue serge, and one roll of lace-edged fabric.

"Good selection. Some of my best goods. You really believe hungry people, living in misery, will actually purchase nonessential fabric?"

"We're selling dreams, not textiles. Dreams of another time. Dreams of bright summer days, winter nights under the stars. A sane world where our concerns centered on warm, spicy apple *szarlotka* served with steaming hot coffee and cream at a local café." He held up a piece of cloth. "This is magic."

"Wave your wand and make me plenty of money."

Alex picked up an old, wood panel. "This is my wand. A sign announcing: 'Roslan & Son. Fine Fabric for Women and Men. Reduced 60%.'"

"That's below what it cost to manufacture," complained Ludmila.

"You said it's not doing any good sitting in the dark."

She sat on a bale. "You're right. Take it; make me rich."

"You won't get rich, but you won't starve," said Alex, wheeling the cart out of the warehouse.

The town square stood at the edge of a burned and gutted area of the city. Skeletons of brick buildings, half-timbered homes rose over vacant streets. Rusty barbed wire stretched across broken cobblestone avenues. Weeds struggled to break into sunlight.

The sight looked eerily familiar. David felt the shudder of mortars pounding the earth. He heard screams echoing, felt strong arms grabbing his hands and legs, tossing him over a wall into blackness. A stranger rushing him into the night.

"Warsaw," stuttered David.

"Łódź Ghetto. The Germans destroyed it as they retreated," said Alex.

"Is that what the Warsaw Ghetto looks like now?"

"I didn't go there when the Russians took me to what was left of the city."

"What happened to Aunt Hanka and Devorah, and my grandmother?"

"Let's hope they escaped."

"Maybe they found a way to get out and we'll see them again."

Alex didn't know how to tell what might be a terrible truth. "Come along. We're setting up for business." He pointed to a post. "Put the sign up there." He handed David a small box. "When we make a sale, the money goes in here."

"Suppose no one wants to buy anything."

"A good salesman doesn't sell—he lets the customer sell to herself."

"Papa, I don't understand how it works."

Alex winked. "Watch and learn."

A woman carrying a shopping bag wended her way through vendors in the square. Alex broke into a broad smile. "Welcome, madam, I see you're a woman of great taste. I have the best prewar fabric saved just for you."

The woman held up the powder blue yardage. "You're a good liar."

"The color matches your beautiful eyes," said Alex, appraising her. "I see an elegant dress on a graceful lady."

"I need a dress, not elegance."

"Drape it over your shoulders," suggested Alex. Other women clustered around the cart.

"I'll take ten yards," the woman said.

"Excellent choice. Give the money to my partner, Tadek," said Alex, pointing to David. "He's in charge of all financial transactions."

She tousled David's hair. "Such a cute little boy. You look like your father."

David held Alex's hand, confirming the woman's judgment. The small group of women grew into a crowd, and in a short time, Alex ran out of merchandise, except for the lace. He trundled out of the square with David sitting in the cart. "Show me the park where you and Shimon played," said Alex.

"It's not too far." David pointed south. "See those trees?"

They walked to the pond slowly thawing under the sun. A rooster crowed and strutted out of dense bushes, pecking in the grass.

"Our lucky day. Where there's a rooster, we'll find hens," whispered Alex. "Keep very quiet."

They crouched in the undergrowth. Three clucking hens marched into the clearing scratching for food. Alex snatched one of the birds, holding it firmly under one arm. The hen squawked and tried to peck him.

"What are you going to do with the chicken?" asked David.

"She'll make an excellent roast."

David's eyes opened wide in alarm. "You're going to kill and eat it?"

Alex wrapped it in a piece of cloth and placed it in the cart. "They don't pluck their own feathers and jump into a roasting pan. This one's nice and plump."

"You stole it!" exclaimed Mela.

"We caught it in a park. They're running wild," said David.

"Dinner will be special," said Mela. It never occurred to David how chickens and roosters went from pen to oven.

Alex dumped his earnings on the dining room table. "Just the beginning."

"You could sell ice to Eskimos," Mela said.

"I wasn't only me. Tadek made the sign. Women in the square made a fuss over him. Tomorrow will be even better when today's customers tell their friends."

Jacob came in from the bedroom. "Want me to help with your accounts like I did when we were in Warsaw?"

"Tadek has more time. Study for school."

"I know numbers better than Tadek," Jacob complained.

"Concentrate on your schoolwork. It's more important."

David, five years younger than his brother, insisted on doing his part. He recorded their day's earnings in a workbook and counted out the money, placing it in two stacks—one for Alex, the other for Ludmila. It crossed his mind she might suspect Alex took a bit more for himself. To ensure she could not accuse him, David peeled a zloty out of Alex's earnings and added it to Ludmila's. If a question came up, he could show she received more than fifty percent.

Jacob dropped a large loose-leaf book on the table. "I don't care if you help Papa Alex. I have better things to do. Take a look at this album I found in the basement filled with a lot of old stamps. I'm starting my own collection."

David peered over Jacob's shoulder. "I'll help you."

"I don't need help. Go back to counting money," groused Jacob.

David placed envelopes he found next to Jacob's album. "These were in bombed-out apartments near Poniatowski Park."

Jacob resentfully examined the stamps. "I don't have any of these."

"They're yours."

"All right," Jacob said grudgingly. "We're partners, but be careful. Some of these stamps are worth a lot of money." He closed the album and placed it on a shelf when they heard banging on the door.

"Roslan, come out!" shouted Dov from next door.

"What's the emergency?"

"An important broadcast's coming in a few minutes. Bring your wife and children."

They crowded into the Lazik apartment. The radio played patriotic British music. It stopped on the hour with the familiar BBC chimes, followed by:

> "This is the BBC. The battle to clear the Rhineland has gone well. Good steady progress all along the front. The bridgehead over the Rhine is fourteen miles long and seven miles deep. American and French troops have taken several villages. This is a squeeze play by the Third and Seventh Armies. They are pushing the legs of the triangle together and, as they do so, clearing the Rhine banks both north and south. Two thousand eight hundred men have been taken prisoner. German forces are severely weakened by the daily total loss in killed and wounded troops. For the moment, Russians appear to be clearing up pockets of German resistance along the Baltic shore. Marshall Stalin has just announced the capture of the important Baltic port of Kolberg, an operation in which the Polish First Army participated."

Everyone applauded when they heard news of the Polish army. The newscast continued:

> "Russians attacked the bridgehead which the Germans still hold on the east side of the Oder Estuary. This improves Russia's military position for the major drive to Berlin and cuts off the German supply lines."

"We're squeezing Germans tighter and tighter. Soon Europe will see the end of tyranny," Dov observed.

Alex hugged the boys. "I told you we would make it."

Feldsheim waited at the door of their apartment. "Good news about the war. Germans are making their last stand," reported Alex.

"I heard. In the meantime, I have something else to celebrate." Feldsheim opened a folder. "We found a notice from a Nahum Gutgeld searching for his sons Jacob, Shalom, and David." The mention of Shalom cast a pall over the boys. "Did I say something to upset you?"

"Shalom died in Warsaw a few weeks after we brought him to live with us," said Alex.

Feldsheim placed his hands on Jacob and David's shoulders. "I'm not a religious person, but there is a blessing for mourners. "HaMakom yenachem etchem betoch sha'ar aveylei Tziyon v'Yerushalayim," he said in Hebrew and then translated: "May God comfort you among the other mourners of Zion and Jerusalem."

"We did everything in our power to save him," said Alex.

Jacob regained his composure. "The letter from our father."

"We have to verify it. Apparently Nahum Gutgeld from Warsaw left with his brothers and their father Wolf Gutgeld in 1939, when the Germans invaded."

"No need to verify it," said Alex. "Where is he?"

"Tel Aviv, Palestine. They made their way east to Russia, traveling through Turkey."

David's phantom father rose miraculously out of ashes, untouched by war. The father he never knew; the father who abandoned him to the ghetto lived safely in another country while he, his brothers, aunts, and grandmother suffered the Nazi terror.

"Write and let him know Jacob and David are safe and healthy. When the war ends, Mela and I will bring them to their father," said Alex.

"Mail takes a long time to travel these days. We may not hear for two or three months."

"Use the telegraph," suggested Alex.

"It's only for official business, not for personal messages. We'll keep channels of communication open with the Gutgelds through the agency."

Marisia prepared tea and placed biscuits on the table. "Tadek and Geniek are so lucky to have found their family," said Mela.

They aren't my family, thought David. Real families do not leave their children to monsters, wolves "trotting . . . into homes," waiting to kill.

"I have a secret for you," Alex said to the boys. "Mama and I decided if we found your family, we would personally take you to them. I promised your aunt Hanka you would survive and never forget who you are. Write your father, Jacob. To receive a letter from his son after all these years. Proof you and David are alive and well."

Leaving Alex and Mela for someone he didn't know, agitated and confused David. He slipped out and slouched against a tree. Light flickered in the room where Jacob and Ella hunched over the dining room table writing a letter bringing him nearer and nearer to losing those closest to him.

"What should I write?" Jacob asked Ella.

"How you feel. What it's like living with the Roslans. The truth."

Jacob took another sheet of paper, penned the date on top, and wrote:

> "Dear Papa:
>
> David and I are safe and living in Łódź with our protectors, Alex and Mela Roslan, who have been like a mother and father to us. I have sad news. Shalom became very sick in Warsaw and died. It was terrible for us all. We are safe and taking lessons from a very smart lady, Ella Rosenberg. We are preparing to go to school in September. It's been very nice ever since the Germans left. Sometimes I go to the movies. David likes to walk around the city. We have been eating as good as possible. I hope when you receive this letter you will write back. Alex and Mela are the most wonderful people. Aunt Hanka made a very good decision when she decided we should live with them. I hope we will see you soon.
>
> Your son, Jacob."

Feldsheim promised to send the letter off immediately. Rushing to connect with an insubstantial shadow passing through his life made no sense to David. Alex and Mela stood as tall barricades, protecting and nurturing him. Their presence, concrete evidence of love born out of tragedy.

He said nothing, trailing Alex to the square, worried it could be the last time he would see the sign "Roslan & Son." A gaggle of women pounced on the cart; pulling out bolts of cloth, draping them over their shoulders, asking others for opinions. Alex cajoled, flattered, and advised customers. By mid-morning they had a box crammed full of zlotys, rubles, and several American dollars. The cart stood empty, except for one roll of blue serge and the expensive lace-edged fabric.

They prepared to leave when a young woman dressed in a skirt and blouse, patched jacket, shoes run down at the heels, blonde hair covered with a kerchief, rushed toward Alex. "You're the one who's selling all those wonderful fabrics," she said with a strong Russian accent.

"I'll have less expensive material tomorrow," Alex assured her.

She picked up the lace. "No. This is what I want. It's beautiful. How much is it?"

Alex took David aside. "The lady wants it so bad. I think we should sell it to her at a price she can afford. How do you feel about it?"

David peeked under Alex's arm at the woman caressing the cloth as if it was gold lamé. "Ludmila said it doesn't do any good sitting in the warehouse."

"Smart boy." Alex turned to the young lady. "You can have it at an eighty percent discount."

Her eyes widened. "Your sign says sixty." She paused. "Is it stolen?"

"Madam, everything I sell is legal. Check with Ludmila Sobanski at Łódź Fine Textiles on Ogradowa Avenue."

She handed him a roll of money. "Thank you . . ." She looked at the sign, ". . . Mr. Roslan."

"And Son . . ." added Alex.

Chapter Seven

The Russians Are Coming

The delightful aroma of Mela's cooking greeted Alex and David, who whooped, hollered, and hugged her. "What's come over you?" she asked.

Jacob looked up from his homework. "The little boy needs his mama."

"Don't make fun of your brother. Even you need Mama," said Alex.

David spilled bills and coins on the table. "This is what came over me. We made a fortune."

"Not a fortune. Tomorrow, maybe. Mama, we're hungry and the stove calls. After dinner, homework."

Marisia put down her pencil. "You two are so lucky. I have to go to school five days a week. Your teacher only comes three days."

"Not so lucky. Ella gives us enough work for a full week. We take quizzes, write reports, read maps. I have to learn the history of Poland with kings, princes, grand dukes marching to war. I bet you didn't know Nicolaus Copernicus, a Polish astronomer in the sixteenth century, used mathematics and his telescope to show planets revolved around the sun. A lot of people didn't like the idea our Earth wasn't the center of the universe. I'm going to be like him," said Jacob.

"Excellent goal. The world needs dreamers," said Alex.

"My dream is to always stay with you and Mama," David said.

"Who knows what the future will bring? Do you enjoy working with Papa?" Mela asked.

"We almost gave away our most expensive cloth to a nice poor lady."

"He wanted to do a good deed. So we earned a little less to make her happy," said Alex.

Jacob folded his arms over his chest. "It's not Tadek's merchandise. I'm surprised he didn't ask you to give it away."

"We have an obligation to help those less fortunate." Alex said. "Tomorrow is Wednesday. Ella Rosenberg will not be here. Suppose I take you to the town square. You'll learn there's more to life than making a big profit."

"I helped with your accounts in Warsaw, remember?" Jacob reminded Alex.

"And did a very good job. Now it's Tadek's turn. Łódź is different. The women who buy from me search for reminders of life before the war. So, are you coming with us?"

"There's a new movie I want to see, *Ivan the Terrible*, all about armies and a king who's very brave."

"Then it's David and me again," said Alex, scooping up the money.

"Everyone clear the table," ordered Mela. She placed a basket of bread and a platter of roast chicken on the table.

David couldn't look at the roast. He remembered the unsuspecting hen pecking in the grass. "I'm not very hungry."

"Eat what you can," said Mela. "We'll pray first."

"Silently," said Alex.

"Not all of us need to pray, but we need to eat." Mela crossed herself and held Alex's hand. "I'm praying for you as well."

"Silently," he repeated.

David lost his appetite at the sight of the roasted, basted, chicken. He stuffed bread in his mouth and drank a glass of water.

After dinner Jacob spread a pocketful of stamps on the table. "I took your advice and walked through ruined buildings and found envelopes." He held up a pale-red stamp with the image of Adolf Hitler in a heavy overcoat, wearing an officer's cap. A swastika emblazoned the background with the words "Deutches Reich," German Empire, beneath the picture. "It celebrates Hitler's fiftieth birthday in 1939," stated Jacob proudly.

"How can you bring horrible things in here? Tear it up and throw it away," yelled David.

"Stamps with terrible people are worth a lot." Jacob snapped the album closed. "Don't you dare go near it."

"I wouldn't touch it if it was worth all the money in the world," David shot back.

"Enough about stamps. Word is spreading throughout Łódź we have the best merchandise in the city. Tomorrow's going to be busy. Schoolwork and bed," ordered Alex. He held Mela in his arms, listening to the gentle breathing of children no longer living in fear.

"I don't know how we managed to walk out of hell into this new world," murmured Mela, loosening her braids, letting her blonde hair fall around neck.

"I haven't told you how much I love you. Without you none of this would have been possible," Alex whispered.

"We did it together. No matter what happens, Tadek and Geniek will be our children as much as Marisia. We're tied to one another by stronger bonds than blood. We're tied by love." They settled back as the moon hovered over a dark horizon.

Rapid raps on the door broke the brief interlude. Dov Lazik stood in the doorway. "The president of the United States is going to speak on the BBC about plans for after the war."

"The children are in bed," whispered Mela.

"So is Shimon. We're right next door. If you don't feel comfortable I'll tell you about the speech tomorrow."

"Something big is going on. I want to hear this Roosevelt," said Alex.

Ida prepared tea and biscuits. The radio crackled, then a voice introduced the broadcast:

> "This is Alistair Cooke, BBC, broadcasting from Washington, DC. President Franklin Roosevelt is addressing the Congress of the United States about the results of the Yalta Conference that was held with Prime Minister Winston Churchill and Soviet Marshal Josef Stalin."

Due to weariness after his long trip, Roosevelt spoke in careful cadences:

> "I come from the Crimean Conference with a firm belief that we have made a good start on the road to a world of peace. There were two main purposes at the Crimean Conference. The first was to bring defeat to Germany with the greatest possible speed and with the smallest possible loss of Allied men. That purpose is now being carried out in great force. The German Army and the German people are feeling the ever-increasing might of our fighting men and of the Allied armies. And every hour gives us added pride in the heroic evidence of the heroic advance of our troops over German soil toward a meeting with the gallant Red Army.

"Hitler has failed. Never before have the major Allies been more closely united—not only in their war aims, but also in their peace aims. And they are determined to continue to be united—to be united with each other and with all peace-loving nations, so that the ideal of lasting world peace will become a reality.

"The German people, as well as the German soldier, must realize that the sooner they give up and surrender by groups or as individuals the sooner their present agony will be over. They must realize that only with complete surrender can they begin to reestablish themselves as people whom the world might accept as decent neighbors.

"We made it clear at Yalta and now I repeat—that unconditional surrender does not mean the destruction or enslavement of the German people. The Nazi leaders seek to convince the people of Germany that the Yalta declaration means slavery and destruction for them, for that is how the Nazis hope to save their skins, to deceive their people into continued and useless resistance. Unconditional surrender means the end of Nazism and of all its barbaric laws and institutions . . . It means for the Nazi war criminals a punishment that is speedy and just and severe. Our objective in handling Germany is simple. It is to secure the peace of the rest of the world now and in the future . . ."

Tears welled up in Alex's eyes. "Thank you, Dov. May our children be beneficiaries of peace in the world."

Dov raised his cup. "L'chaim." He closed his eyes and chanted in Hebrew, "Oseh shalom bimromav. Hu ya'aseh shalom aleinu. V'al kol Yisrael." Let me translate. 'They who make peace in their high places, may they bring peace upon us, and upon all Israel.'"

Early next morning Alex and David pushed the cart through a light fog that hung over the square. At the far end, a youthful Russian officer and the woman who bought the lace waited for them. She set a trap, thought Alex. A snare to catch him doing business without Russian permission. "Tadek, go home," he ordered.

"What's wrong?"

"Don't argue, just go," said Alex, clenching his jaw.

"Roslan. I want to meet you and your son," called the officer.

Alex placed a hand on David's shoulder. "Too late." He waited until they approached. "Madam, you don't need to bring protection. I have permission from the mill owner to sell goods."

"This has nothing to do with legalities. I am Major Nikolai Grishen. My wife Kristina informed me you gave her a large discount yesterday."

"I did nothing wrong," said Alex, expecting the worst.

"Of course not. I came to thank you personally for your generosity. Very little of it goes around these days."

Alex composed himself. "Your wife has very good taste in cloth and her choice of husband."

Grishen smiled. "You must have been very successful before the war. What business were you in?"

"Textiles, in Warsaw. You saw what happened to the city."

"Broken stone and burned buildings."

"Some of my goods came from a warehouse in Łódź. I decided to pick up where I left off."

"Your sign says 'Roslan & Son.' Is this your boy?"

"Tadek's my youngest."

"Did you suffer much from the war?" asked Grishen.

"My oldest son was killed during the uprising. We survived by not giving up or giving in."

The major shook Alex's hand. "Perhaps there's a way I can repay your kindness to Kristina."

After the major and his wife left, David tugged at Alex's sleeve. "You always complain about Russians. The soldier who gave me his book, the one who took you to Warsaw, and the major are nice."

"Sometimes we paint people with too broad a brush. Not every Russian is bad. Playing fair usually pays off in the long run. If I cheated Ludmila before the war, she would never allow me to sell her goods. Where would we be? We're saving money and one of these days I'll have my store back."

David rattled off the story to Mela and Jacob about the Russian officer and his wife. "He congratulated us for being kind."

Alex shook his head. "The major's only one person. The Soviet Union believes everything belongs to the government."

Loud pounding on the door jolted them. It was a reminder of harsh days in Warsaw when the Gestapo and Polish police arrived unexpectedly with guns and rifles. Jacob and David jumped to their feet, fright on their faces. Mela took Jacob's hand. "Sit down. You too, Tadek. Those days are over."

A Russian sergeant and private stood in the doorway. "Mr. Roslan?" asked the sergeant.

"I am Alex Roslan."

"Major Grishen requests we escort you to his office."

"What's this all about?" asked Alex suspiciously.

"We have orders. We suggest you comply."

Mela rushed to his side. "You said you didn't know what he had on his mind."

"I have to go with them." He turned to the sergeant. "Inform my wife if anything happens to me."

The soldiers escorted him to an army car. They drove to the Russian garrison. It was a replay of the day in Warsaw when the Gestapo threw Alex in Pawiak Prison for selling goods on the black market. The sergeant ushered Alex into a meeting room. Major Grishen sat with a group of officers lounging with jackets off and collars unbuttoned. The scene made no sense to Alex, expecting the worse. Grishen vigorously shook Alex's hand. "Good to see you again."

"What was so important you pulled me away from my family?"

"My fellow officers want to meet you. Most of their wives and girlfriends are in Russia. Our wives here, as well as our women back home, need their spirits lifted. We have music. Even cinema to help morale, but nothing can take the place of a beautiful dress or coat."

A steady source of income loomed before Alex. "I would be delighted to help whatever way I can."

"Of course, they expect to get the same discount you gave my Kristina," said the major.

A potential disaster suddenly turned into financial advantage. "It's the least I can do for the men who freed Poland from Germany. You and your wives come to the square. Let me know what you're looking for. If I don't have it, I'll find it."

Grishen poured a glass of wine for Alex. "A toast to our good fortune."

The other officers raised their glasses. "Vashe zdorov'ye!" they shouted.

Alex leaned over to Grishen. "How did you know where I live?"

"Everyone in Poland must be registered. When you rented your apartment, the concierge wrote your name and the names of everyone in your family in a ledger. Each week we collect the lists and compare them with names of those who collaborated with the enemy. You were not on the list, but Roslan with a son named Tadek lives in number two on the third floor of your apartment building. I apologize for my method. I had to make it look like an official inquiry or else I could get into trouble with my superiors."

Alex checked his anger. His wife and children were frightened they would never see him again. "I would like to join your party, but my wife will be worried."

"Stay a few minutes." Grishen poured Alex another glass of wine. "You don't have a Warsaw accent. Did you always live in the city?"

"My wife and I come from Białystok."

"I traveled with my father and mother to Białystok for Jewish theater and music. I asked why they were so interested. They told me they wanted to study Jewish influence on Russian and Polish culture."

"The city was exciting," Alex reminisced. "I stood in back of theaters, music halls, operas. Writers and poets, mostly Jews, gave talks and read from their books. They published their own newspaper, the *Voice of Byalistok*. Textile workers organized an association to raise wages. Białystok became a center of industry. Some people would never associate with Jews. My father had no problem. We brought our wheat to a Jewish-owned flour mill. A Jew repaired our shoes,"

"The Nazis made a fatal error when they went on a murder spree to wipe out an entire population." The young major filled Alex's glass. His eyes narrowed. "We liberated the Łódź Ghetto in January and found eight hundred out of twenty thousand barely alive. The Nazi *Führerprinzip*, their top priority, forced the Jewish council to become slavish figureheads. If you think the Warsaw Ghetto was the ultimate misery, Łódź Ghetto was a monstrous abomination. Warsaw fought back. The Jewish leaders in Łódź gave up believing they could escape slaughter." He shook his head. "I was one of the first into the ghetto. I will never forget."

"The world needs witnesses or else it will be forgotten," said Alex.

The major handed him a box filled with cakes, cookies, and a bottle of wine. "In return for taking you away from your family under false pretenses. Give them my regards, especially little Tadek."

The weight Alex carried on his back when he left Mela melted the moment he walked into the apartment. She rushed into his arms. "Thank God you're back."

"Tadek had more to do with it than God. He pushed me to sell to a woman he thought was poor." He handed the box to David. "The major gave me sweets."

David took a cookie and sat down with a serious scowl on his face. "The major's wife should have given us more money. She could afford to pay the regular price."

"I'm cloth merchant to Major Grishen and his officers because we made her happy. Tailors will have work. Businesses will grow. A small act of kindness resulted in the unexpected. Your grandfather's driver asked me to help you and your brothers. A Polish policeman who wouldn't do dirty work for the Germans warned me when storm troopers ransacked my store in Warsaw."

"It was so dangerous," said David.

"Dangerous, but necessary. I will never forget how neighbor turned against neighbor or how close we came to being discovered," said Alex.

"Why did you do it?" asked David.

Alex smiled. "One day someone else will ask me the same question. I will answer: when I saw you and your brothers, I pictured all the children of the ghetto. If I could save only three, my life would be complete."

Chapter Eight

Girl in the Ghetto

Increased business due to Alex's reputation among women of modest means to wives and mistresses of entrepreneurs and Russian officers, caught the attention of businessmen with vacant properties. They flattered Alex, praising his acumen at a time when others failed or would not take chances, offering him shops on Piotrkowska Street, the main artery of the city.

After consulting with Ludmila and making the case paying rent and a percentage of sales would require raising their low prices, they agreed their major discounts were the reason customers preferred his modest kiosk on the square.

"It's time I became the architect I always wanted to be," Alex confidently informed Mela. Gathering colored pencils, pens, a drawing pad from Ella Rosenberg's school supplies, he sketched a picture of his old kiosk drawing a curtained dressing room and a small booth with room for a tailor and sewing machine.

Alex laid out the specifications for Stanislav Baranski. "It's time to make good use of your talent by expanding my kiosk on the square to include space for your talents. One day a week you help customers choose fabric, measure them, creating custom garments for a percentage of sales. Everyone wins."

Baranski peered skeptically over his spectacles. "What makes you believe customers will come?"

"I have a contract with an officer in the Soviet garrison to supply their women here and in Russia. Women in Łódź will want clothes as soon as possible. I'll send samples of fabric to those in Moscow and Stalingrad. They choose what they want, along with the style, and provide their measurements. Once you finish, the Russians pay and the officer will arrange to have them sent by military transport across the border. No questions. No inspections. We're talking a steady source of income."

"Roslan, you're either crazy or a genius."

"Neither. Just good business. Deal?" They shook hands on the arrangement.

Jacob and David helped Alex expand his space on the square with wood gathered from ruins, paint supplied by Ludmila, and mirrors found in abandoned shops. The new sign read: "Roslan & Sons. High Quality/Low Prices/Tailor on Premises." Local women and Russian officers' wives and mistresses flocked to the reopened stall. On weekends David and Jacob sorted, packed, and greeted customers.

Life settled into a comfortable routine. Marisia attended school. David and Jacob studied with Ella Rosenberg three days a week, giving them time to explore parks and forests surrounding the city. They joined volunteers replanting flowers and tending trees ravaged in battle; they watched artisans renovating impressive villas and restoring palaces containing ancient artifacts hidden by partisans.

During one of David's study sessions, he placed Vasily Grossman's book on the table. "You promised to tell me about his story 'In the Town of Berdichev.'"

"It's not for children. When you grow up it will make sense to you," said Ella.

"Please tell me about it," pleaded David.

Ella decided David's remarkably adult emotional responses to "Red Riding Hood" and *Uncle Tom's Cabin* deserved respect.

"The book is filled with love, compassion, and adventure. A tough Bolshevik commissar, who's a woman, becomes pregnant during the Russian Civil War. She's sent to live with a poor Jewish family in the town of Berdichev until she gives birth. When the enemy approaches, she decides to stay with her little son, Alyosha, rather than join her regiment. At the last minute, workers march toward the enemy. Determined to defend her comrades, she runs out of the house, following them to their deaths; the Jewish family raises Alyosha as their own."

"Like Mama and Papa Roslan."

David's simple reaction stirred Ella. "How do you see beyond words into the heart of stories?" The young boy had no answer.

March rain fell on the windows, streaming silver against gray clouds. David saw patterns, formations, intersecting images. He was Alyosha in Berdichev , whose mother died and father abandoned him and his brother, finding safety in the arms of Mela and Alex.

A few days later on March 25, 1945, the BBC aired a special report:

> "Robert Barr from the BBC on the Western front. The Germans are flying in confusion from the Rhine. For the first time we're getting the real feeling of conquest. The end can't be far off. Our tanks and guns are rolling through the countryside unmolested through the enemy's country. This afternoon Prime Minister Winston Churchill crossed the Rhine on an American landing craft in the Ninth Army beachhead sector and spent a quarter of an hour inspecting the eastern bank. He also made a short cruise along the river, his first cruise on the Rhine since World War One. The sound of machine-gun fire and bombs could be heard clearly."

"Who would have imagined Prime Minister Churchill walking on German territory? We should celebrate!" said Alex, dashing out of the Lazik apartment. He returned with a bottle of wine. "Courtesy of the Russian army." Alex raised his glass. "To the coming victory."

Spring arrived, snow melted, days turned warmer. With their income growing due to word of mouth, Alex and Mela refurbished the apartment, repaired windows, and installed furniture stored in a warehouse near Ludmila's factory.

Mela relished cooking fresh vegetables from farms around Łódź. Ella Rosenberg, David, and Jacob studied in idyllic Sienkiewicz Park, surrounded by bright yellow larches, evergreen pines, and one-hundred-year-old spruce trees.

An extraordinary rapport grew between the merchant and major. They often met at Grishen's favorite café to talk about the future. He let slip his concern about the Soviet Union's intentions in Poland and Eastern Europe. Grishen hoped his country would emerge from its centuries-old xenophobia.

"I'm fully aware it's dangerous to talk like this, Mr. Roslan."

"It goes no further. I never favored autocracies or dictatorships."

"For a dealer in textiles, you have unique insight into geopolitics," remarked Grishen.

"Alex Roslan's an accidental merchant. I would have gone to university. Personal problems reared their heads."

Grishen raised his coffee cup. "Here's to continued success in Łódź."

Before doing anything Mela might disapprove of, Alex asked her permission to invite the major and his wife to dinner.

"Why not? Instead of shooting you, he helped make us more comfortable. I'd like to meet his wife. She must be very good-looking to have made you almost gave away your merchandise."

To Alex's pleasant surprise they accepted. The officer and his wife, Kristina, brought wine and pastries for dessert. David stared in awe at the major's navy blue dress uniform with its double row of gold buttons, gold epaulets, and wide gold-colored belt. Multiple rows of war ribbons stretched across his chest. Kristina Grishen wore a dress tailored from lace she bought from Alex.

"You look beautiful," Alex said.

"I have you and Tadek to thank."

David had done nothing but watch Alex lower the price, thinking she was a poor soldier's wife. Now the major sat in their living room. He didn't resemble fierce Russian soldiers who liberated Kaminsk, or fighting in fields along the road to Łódź.

"Your children seem to be dealing with difficult times," said Grishen.

"Schoolwork takes young minds off their troubles. We have to move forward," said Alex.

"Tadek looks a lot like you. Who does Geniek take after?"

"Mela's father. We lived near each other as children. Even then I knew Mela was something special. It took a while, but we married in 1928 and eventually moved to Warsaw."

"You're a romantic."

"Hard as nails on the outside, soft as potato bread inside. Dinner's ready," Mela announced. "Nothing fancy. These days we use what's available. Alex has always been good at finding the one thing to make a meal special. First, we have our guests, Major and Mrs. Grishen. Second, you brought a delicious dessert. Third, Alex found fresh cauliflower and I used it to make soup from a recipe my mother taught me."

"What news of Berlin?" Alex asked Grishen.

"Capturing German soldiers left behind. Important bridge-heads over the Oder. Their army collapsing and running as fast as it can, destroying almost everything left behind."

"When the war's over I hope we stay in Łódź," said David.

"What's the best thing about living here?" asked Kristina.

"Being with my family and freedom to do whatever I like without feeling afraid."

"My brother thinks Nazis hide behind every corner," said Jacob.

"I do not," scowled David.

"He's not wrong," warned Grishen. "They're out there. We'll bring them to justice."

"What will happen once they're caught?" asked Marisia.

"After the surrender—and I hope it's soon—the Soviet Union, America, Great Britain, and France have agreed to hold special trials. The leaders of Hitler's Germany will face judges and juries. The Nazis committed crimes against humanity. They did horrible, terrible things and must be held accountable."

"The children shouldn't hear this," said Kristina.

"They need to know, Mrs. Grishen. Everyone must remember," said Mela.

"I'm afraid we haven't seen the last of Nazi cruelty. We suspect unspeakable things will crop up. They're beginning to surface in Poland," said the major.

On April 1, 1945, the BBC confirmed Major Grishen's prediction:

"Edward Ward with the BBC. I entered the town of Weimar with the US Eighty-Ninth Infantry Division that led us to the Buchenwald concentration camp. This report is an eyewitness to the barbarism and cruelty of the Nazi regime. In Buchenwald more than 20,000 famished prisoners still watch their numbers dwindle.

"Let me tell the story of Buchenwald as I see it. When I passed through this frightful monument to Nazism, I found myself in a vast compound. Just inside the gates was a large open space where prisoners were mustered for roll call. It was crowded with men and boys, mostly Jewish. Most of them dressed in a travesty of pajamas. Most looked like emaciated scarecrows. In the huts were hundreds of people who could not move or talk. They were living skeletons."

Ida Lazik snapped off the radio. "Send the children outside."

"Everyone needs truth," said Alex. "The report comes from someone who is there, facing evil. Evil created by people with nothing but hate in their hearts."

Dov switched on the radio. His voice strained and cracked with emotion as he translated:

"They have been freed from Buchenwald, but they have not been freed from slow starvation. Each day takes its toll on human life. In January there were 61,000 men in the camp. In January 6, 477 died or were butchered. In February there were 62,000. Five thousand six hundred and fourteen died. In March the number had risen to 82,000, of which 5,479 died. Between April 3 and 10, 915 had died. "As the Allies rolled into Germany, the SS, who ran this camp, made mass deportations further into Germany. When the Americans overran it, there were a mere 20,000 left.

> One man said that what happened here was 'scientific murder.' He was forced to give blood to the German army and Germans injured in the bombings. They were forced to sleep naked in the dead of winter. His eyes filled with tears. 'Thank God the Americans came. In a few hours they planned to machine-gun all of us and blow up the camp. We've been saved and can go home again.'"

They sat silent after the broadcast ended. Stark, terrifying words confirmed to David Nazi wolves prowled in dark recesses of German nights with the precise intent of destroying every Jew in Europe. The nightmare did not come true. The Jewish committee in Łódź demonstrated the strength of a stubborn people fighting its way out of blast furnaces of war.

David pushed away his dark thoughts by reading a book of folk tales Ella gave him. "Hansel and Gretl," "Cinderella," "Snow White" fascinated him. In stories, fathers remarried after their wives died. Wicked, jealous stepmothers treated children with abject cruelty. They sent them off to perish, but in the end the stepmothers were defeated. David secretly enjoyed tales of youngest sons or daughters winning a gold ring, box of treasure, marrying the king's son or daughter.

"We all have stories about survival," said Ella. "They're different and at the same time they're the same. I can't imagine what you went through living under Nazi occupation. My parents left for Palestine when I was a child. It's difficult having the British control everything, but they're civilized, and one of these days we'll have a country to call our own. Refugees like you and Geniek will make the new Israel strong. It's the reason I volunteered to come back and teach."

"What's it like living in Palestine?" asked David.

"Beautiful. We swim in the ocean. Hike in mountains where ancient synagogues stand exposed to the elements. Like us, they survive against all odds. Sometimes we visit date and olive farms. Summers are warm. Everyone has a vegetable garden. Some of the girls date British soldiers. As I grew older and attended university, I began to understand real freedom means the right to have a say in how we live."

"Were you afraid?" asked David.

"British patrols rumbling down our street frightened me."

"The British fought Hitler and Germany. How could they be your enemy?"

"Don't get me wrong. England is our ally in the war against the Nazis. On the other hand, they have quotas, a limit on how many Jews can immigrate to Palestine. Only fifteen hundred Jews per month escaping from Nazi persecution are allowed into the Mandate."

"Why would they stop them?"

"Oil. Egypt and Saudi Arabia demanded Britain limit Jewish immigration or they would turn off oil supplies to Great Britain. One of these days it will change." She unfolded a map of the world and drew a circle around a sliver of land on the eastern shore of the Mediterranean Sea. "My home. Soon, your home."

Nations with strange names—Saudi Arabia, Syria, Lebanon, Transjordan, Egypt—surrounded the British Mandate for Palestine. David tried to imagine his grandfather and father living in a country so different from Poland. He hoped when they realized how Alex and Mela cared for him and his brother, they would shower them with gratitude.

A fox hunting rabbits raced past David in a forest on the outskirts of Łódź. Birds sang in sun-dappled meadows. He could not imagine thick forests of green pine, white and black birch, linden trees anywhere else in the world. Bombed-out ruins of the ghetto on the northeast edge of the city stood as dark silhouettes against an incongruously peaceful blue sky scattered with clouds. David crossed a broken bridge entering deserted rubble-filled streets lined with shattered trees. Scarred, burned buildings stood empty. Walls tumbled to the ground. Glass crunched under his shoes. He pushed through a door hanging by one hinge and found a child's cracked shoe without laces in a corner. A table set with broken china waited forlornly for phantoms to sit and eat.

David picked up empty envelopes with stamps from America, Great Britain, Switzerland, and one from Mexico on the floors of empty, desolate apartments. Beneath a cabinet he found a small sheet of green ten-zloty stamps with an image of a middle-aged man with gray hair wearing wire-rimmed glasses. Under the picture, the name of the chairman of the Łódź Jewish Council of Elders, Mordechai Chaim Rumkowski, and the words "Juden Post, Litzmannstadt Getto."

Beneath a moldy mattress he discovered a small prayer book with a white leather cover streaked with soot. David flipped through brittle pages with Hebrew on one side and the Polish translation on the other. "O, Lord, strive with my adversaries, give battle to my foe . . . and come to my defense; ready the spear and the javelin against my pursuers . . . they hid a net to trap me; without reason they dug a pit for me . . . but the net they hid caught them . . . they fell into it when disaster strikes . . ." The net spread as American, British, and Russian troops advanced into Berlin for the final battle.

Grime-filtered sunlight illuminated dust on broken stairs leading to a room with one wall blown away, open to the elements. Tell-tale marks made by hobnailed military boots tracked across cracked linoleum floors. A pair of weathered woman's leather gloves might have been Mela's. A small doll still dressed in a faded red polka-dot dress could have belonged to Marisia. A cryptic note tacked to a doorpost read: "Searching for grandfather."

Sun glinted on a tin box protruding behind torn, faded, water-spotted wallpaper. David pried open the lid decorated with delicate pink flowers. Inside, he found a photograph with the year 1938 written on the back. A dark-bearded father, wearing a black cap, dressed in suit and tie sat stiffly in a chair. His wife, hair braided and coiled, dressed in an ankle-length dress, stood to his right. A small girl in a lacy white blouse and long skirt, sat between them, smiling into the camera. David carefully unfolded a note beneath the photos written in neat, clear script: "I don't know if anyone will ever read my letter. We have been in the ghetto for two years. Most of my friends have died or been taken away and never seen again. This morning we were told to pack up and prepare to travel east where we will be settled on a farm. No one believes the Germans. There are no farms. Unless we run away, our family will go up in ashes. If someone is reading my letter, please remember my name. Rebekah Landau, 1942."

David's stomach ached. So many girls and boys; so many families disappeared. A false move one moment too soon or late made the difference between life and death. He tucked the letter beneath the photograph and pushed the box back in the wall. Perhaps Rebekah Landau survived and would return for the precious memento. David shoved the sheet of stamps under his shirt and ran into the street to get away from anxiety and suffering radiating from the ruins.

A diffuse image wavered in the bright sunlight, gently clearing. The girl in the photograph stood on the refuse-cluttered cobblestone street. Dumbstruck, David stared, without moving. The vision faded. Rebekah Landau's oppressors ordered her family to leave. She knew it was a death sentence.

Clang of a tram bell broke the spell. David jumped aboard, his heart racing, perspiration blinding his eyes. He repeated over and over to himself, "Take me home. Take me home." He waited to calm down in the shade of birch trees surrounding the makeshift soccer field before facing the Roslans and Jacob. Stamps retrieved from the ghetto were real, substantial. His mind played tricks. The secret of the tin box, the photograph, her fleeting image, remained with him.

He handed the stamps to Alex. "From the ghetto. Walking through, I expected to find someone behind a door. Nothing. All I felt was pain." Tears welled up.

"Survivors of the Łódź Ghetto will return and meet old friends. They'll remember streets and neighbors. They won't permit anyone to forget," Alex said, hoping he could relieve David's anxiety.

Church bells rang throughout the city without warning on April 12, 1945. The Roslans and Laziks gathered in the hall, wondering what set off the alarms. "Let's get to the radio," said Dov.

BBC correspondent Alistair Cooke in Washington, DC, broke into a broadcast with a special report.

> "This afternoon in Warm Springs, Georgia, Franklin Delano Roosevelt, the thirty-second president of the United States died during his fourth term in office. His last words were, 'I have a terrific headache.' Vice President Harry S. Truman was sworn in as the

thirty-third president of the United States. Until today Republicans feared President Roosevelt was im-
mortal. Now they know he is."

Former Missouri senator, Vice President Harry Truman,
stepped up to challenges in world affairs that would destroy
anyone who did not have his indomitable will. Sworn in as
president, he faced major decisions as the war in Europe came
to a close and war in the Pacific raged.

Chapter Nine

A New Day

Angst-ridden Łódź huddled around radios, in cafés, restaurants, and bistros, anticipating the unknown. Children, freed from fear of hostilities, went to school, parks, and cinemas.

Jacob leaped from behind the sofa, aiming a broomstick at David. "Pow! Pow! You're dead. I just watched a movie called *The Ural Front*. Russians killed all the Nazis. The only thing wrong was another dumb love story right in the middle."

Marisia pushed aside her homework. "All you think about is movies. Someday you're going to be an actor."

"Ella gave me a book about famous scientists. Cinemas are all right for adventure, but I want to be Albert Einstein."

"You already look like him, except for his moustache—and brains," laughed David.

Mela thumped a plate of vegetables on the table. "You'll have plenty of time to battle once we get to Palestine. Time for supper."

The inevitable bubbled up again, pulling David down a road into an unrecognizable future. "I don't want to eat. I'm tired."

Mela placed her lips against his forehead. "No fever. Eat dinner."

"I want to lie down." He threw himself on the bed and pulled a pillow over his eyes, trying to shut out images of Rebekah Landau.

Mela stroked his hair. "Tell me about it."

"People pray to God. God doesn't care. He lets horrible things happen. Papa doesn't believe. He never goes to church. Maybe he's right."

"My father always said praying can't hurt. I prayed one day I would marry Papa, and it came true. You're too young to worry about such things. Be happy Papa's earning good money. Soon you'll be in a real school. You'll meet friends, have a good time."

"My accountant can't be sick. He has to enter our earnings in the ledger," Alex said, holding up the cash box.

"He's sick in his heart. He thinks God doesn't care about us," Mela lamented.

Alex sat on the bed. "Mama believes with all her heart and soul there's a god up in heaven who watches over us."

"What do you believe?"

"If you want answers, look in your heart. Don't look to the sky."

"We have answers?"

"More questions than answers. We found Ludmila. How did she survive? The major's wife found us. We made her happy. The Russians want to please their wives and girlfriends."

"I still believe God helped turn a piece of lace into a business," remarked Mela.

"God waved his hand, poof, lace into money. When Ludmila and I went into business together I told you the story about Rumpelstiltskin and the girl who spun straw into gold. A troll gave her power. Without you, my little troll, by my side, we wouldn't have succeeded."

"What did I do?" asked David.

"Gave women hope. Major Grishen thinks you're a good kid. Which reminds me: he and his wife will visit May 1. A big holiday in the Soviet Union. We need to prepare something special."

Mela closed her eyes in exasperation. "Instead of trying to turn everyone into a heretic, find me a steak or piece of fish. You're the one who makes things appear like magic."

"Mama's made of tough stuff. She orders me around. I'll fool her and we'll eat, if not like kings, then princes and princesses. Now, get in the kitchen and have your dinner. We're getting up early tomorrow morning."

A pale cloud-covered moon rising over the horizon joined the sun behind heavy mist. Street cleaners clanked steel-wheeled carts, picking up the night's rubbish, work done during the occupation by prisoners punished if they left a scrap of paper or cigarette stub on the sidewalk.

Alex woke Jacob and David. "Get dressed. We're going to find Mama something to cook tonight for the major and his wife."

"It's too early," said Jacob, blinking sleep from his eyes.

"Best time for catching fish," Alex said.

David pushed off his blanket. "I never fished."

"It's time you learned," said Alex. "What do you say? The three of us on an adventure?"

Without another word, David jumped out of bed and dressed. "Come on, Geniek, let's go fishing."

"I have a lot of studying. When you reach seventh grade, it won't be all reading and geography. You have to work hard."

"My brilliant scholar. It's David and me. I hope you won't be too sleepy to enjoy the celebration in the town square. It's Russia's International Workers' Day. Every worker bee in the Soviet Union is praised, unless he says something the government doesn't like; then it's off to Siberia."

"What's Siberia?" David asked.

"A prison with no walls. Freezing cold in winter, a stretch of mud in summer."

With a sigh of relief, Jacob fell back on his pillow and closed his eyes. "We're not in prison and I'm not freezing. Say hello to the fish. See you in the square."

Alex ransacked the basement and found two cracked bamboo poles and a dented tin pail. "Good enough. Find some string." David rolled a ball of twine across the floor. "Like magic. 'Seek and ye shall find.' Don't tell Mama I quoted from her precious Bible."

Churches with gargoyles around their steeples, floated in the mist, unanchored from land. David wondered if those strange creatures would leap down from towers, ravaging the countryside.

Rushing water roused him from daydreams. On the eastern side of Łódź, a narrow stream flowed down a steep slope past the remains of clattering broken water wheels.

"Fish are usually hungry," said Alex, pushing fingers into soft earth and coming up with a handful of wriggling worms. "Place one on your hook."

David made a face. "They're slimy."

"When Mama has nice fresh fish for dinner, you'll be her hero."

David squeezed his eyes closed and grabbed a squirming worm. Alex coiled it around the hook until it held fast. Holding his breath, David did the same. With a flick of his wrist, Alex's fishing line flew into the water.

"It's your turn," said Alex.

David dropped his line in the pond. "Now what?"

"We wait. While we wait, we have a little breakfast." Alex opened his backpack, took out a jar of coffee for himself and a jar of milk for David, along with cheese and black bread.

"How long before we catch a fish?"

"It's up to the fish. Sometimes they're cagey. Most times curious. They'll take the bait when they're ready. Keep an eye on your line. When you see it pulled tight, you have your catch." Alex sat against a tree and closed his eyes.

He had gone through the war without giving up, without being crushed. David made an oath he would live the same way. Dozing off, he dreamed of life with the Roslans. "Your line," Alex whispered.

It shot straight across the water. A fish leaped and splashed. The bamboo rod skittered across the grass. David grabbed the pole before the fish tugged it into the stream. "Pull in slowly." Alex placed David's hand on the line. In a few moments the writhing, floundering fish flopped on the earth. "Congratulations. You're a fisherman. This is a big one. If I'm lucky we'll have a fine dinner tonight," he said, dropping fish in the water-filled pail.

David yelled as Alex's line became taut. Alex dived for his rod and yanked out another large fish. "Shopping's finished, and it didn't cost one zloty."

Mid-morning crowds gathered in the town square for the May Day celebrations. A choir sang patriotic Polish and Russian songs. Men, women, and children bought blinis, small pancakes filled with cheese or fruit, pickled cucumbers, and wild mushrooms gathered from the nearby forest.

"Can't we stay?" asked David."

"We have to get our catch in the bathtub at home," said Alex.

Mela examined the fish. "Looks as if they just came out of a river."

"I did it, Mama. I caught the first fish. I never went fishing before and on my first day I caught one," David said proudly.

When the major comes we'll have a fine dinner," said Mela."

"Where are Geniek and Marisia?" Alex asked.

They dashed into the apartment. "We're ready for the celebration!"

"Twenty-five groschen for each of you. Don't spend it all at once. There's food, games, concerts, plenty of things to do."

Polish and Russian flags fluttered over crowded food stalls. A bishop in a corner of the square held a service. "You go, Mela, I'll watch the children," Alex said.

They ran from one kiosk to another, buying cookies, blinis, kompot, fruit drinks. Voices of a church choir soared overhead. David wandered along the edge of the square, searching for the girl in the photograph. He wanted to tell her he found the tin box and would never forget. Shimon Lazik dragged David to a coin toss game. The winner won a teddy bear suffering the ravages of war, with a cross-stitched smile and one eye missing. Every coin Shimon tossed fell to the ground.

"Let's find something easier."

"I'm going to get Mama the bear."

"The guy running the game cheats," whispered Shimon.

"He's in for a surprise."

David squinted at the glass containers, tilting slightly to one side. A coin thrown directly at them had no chance of dropping in. He calculated the arc the coin had to make. He carefully flipped. The coin traveled a path David mapped in his mind, rolled halfway around a jar's edge, and dropped in with a resounding clink.

"We have a winner on his first try!" the barker shouted, handing over the bear. "A first-time lucky winner!"

"All you have to do is figure it out," David said, tossing the bear up and down.

"How did you do it?" asked an amazed Shimon.

"Easy. Mathematics."

Mela placed the teddy bear on a shelf over the stove. "You gave our horse a name. the bear needs a name as well. 'Happy Bear.'"

She stirred sauce made from local herbs and tomatoes. Delicate aromas floated through the apartment. The fish simmered. Potatoes boiled. Bright-green flat beans stewed with mushrooms bubbled on the stove.

Major Grishen brought wine and vodka, along with a fruit tart for dessert. "From our army baker. I asked him to make it for a special friend."

Alex showed the vodka to David. "Like to try again?"

David made a face. "It's terrible and makes me sick."

"I said the same thing at first," said Grishen. "It's an acquired taste. In other words, you get used to it."

"Never," said David firmly.

"Time will tell." The major poured a glass for Alex and himself. "Here's to friendship between your family and mine; between the Polish and Russian peoples. I'm not supposed to believe in God, only the state, but let's say a prayer for peace." They clinked glasses and drank vodka in one hearty swig.

A knock on the door interrupted them. "I'm sorry to intrude," said Dov. "The BBC has an important bulletin coming on the air in five minutes." Mela lowered the fire. A bell chimed four times on the Lazik radio.

"Adolf Hitler has been killed at the Reich Chancery in Berlin, according to Hamburg radio. At 22:30 local time, a newsreader announced that reports from the Fuhrer's headquarters said Hitler had 'fallen at his command post in the Reich Chancery fighting to the last breath against Bolshevism and for Germany.' It said he had appointed Grand Admiral Donitz as his successor. There followed an announcement by Admiral Donitz in which he called on the German people to mourn their Führer, who, he said, died the death of a hero in the capital of the Reich."

Dov's face flushed red with joy. "I'll translate."

"No need. I learned English in officer cadet school. According to the BBC, Hitler is dead. Expect surrender, but not before they mount a major offensive," said Grishen.

"Time for a feast," said Mela. "I want the Laziks to join us. We have plenty for all."

Cheering crowds raced through streets. Fireworks exploded over the town square. Shouts and laughter rang across the city. A yoke lifted off the neck of the world.

"Thank God for this day. May it all be over very soon," Mela prayed.

"I pray the same," said Kristina Grishen.

"Let's hope May Day will have another meaning for us all," said a skeptical Grishen.

Hitler's death overshadowed May Day celebrations. The strange little man with piercing eyes and Charlie Chaplin moustache ranted his empire would last a thousand years. It collapsed after twelve years on May 1, 1945, leaving behind the slaughter of over eleven million innocent human beings in death camps, including six million Jewish men, women, and children.

David tossed and turned, haunted by the brutal dictator's image in Jacob's album. The face of a man who turned he world upside down, conquering and devastating nations and people he believed inferior to his imagined master race.

He slipped out of bed and pulled the album off the shelf. Using a thick, red crayon, he scrawled a heavy X across the stamp and returned to sleep, satisfied he demolished his enemy.

Excited and tired, Ella arrived in the morning. "I was up late last night partying. Rumors spread Hitler was so afraid of the Russians, he killed himself."

"Papa said German soldiers were only tough when they had guns and bullets," said David.

"Your papa's a very astute individual." David looked quizzically at her.

"Another lesson: 'astute' means clever. You may want to use the word someday."

"I can use it right now." He stood: "I'm very astute."

Ella held up an old book with a bent spine. She flipped to a portrait of a king with flowing white hair and a large gray moustache. "He also was very astute. Wladyslaw the Elbow-high was very short, probably shorter than you. In the fourteenth century he defeated the Teutonic Knights and was crowned king of Poland."

"Excuse me for interrupting your lesson. I'm going out to look for more stamps," said Jacob.

"Be back in one hour," warned Ella.

David put his finger on the picture of the Polish king. "I never heard of Teutonic Knights."

"Germany's first terrorists. Cruel barbarians murdering their way across Europe."

"Wolves. They rip and kill everything in sight," David suddenly spit out, remembering "Red Riding Hood."

Ella sat back surprised at his sudden burst of adult imagery. "Teutonic Knights were wolves. They hunted us when Germany adopted them as their ideal. Jews lived in Germany for thousands of years, but were always seen as the other, as enemies. King Wladyslaw did something brave and significant. He wrote a legal code assuring our safety and freedom, placing us on an equal footing with Christians."

Jacob returned with old envelopes shoved in his pockets. He opened his album. The *X* scrawled by David an ugly red scar across his precious collection. He lunged at his brother. "You ruined my collection." David ran into the bedroom and slammed the door. Ella held Jacob back. "I'm going to make you pay for this, you little rat! You had no right to destroy my property."

"Hitler doesn't belong in our house. Burn the stamp."

"I'll get you for this," snapped Jacob.

David edged out of the bedroom and ran into streets strewn with trash from the nightlong celebrations. He jumped on a trolley and rode as far as he could from Jacob's threats.

A tree-lined lane led to a tall gate. He climbed an old oak, crawling out on a thick branch growing over a wall. Tendrils of creeping grass sprouted through cracks in a brick drive curving up to a large two-story house surrounded by a garden grown wild with roses, bilberry bushes, raspberry shrubs, and hazel plants. Ivy clung to a dry, fractured circular fountain in the shape of a tree. Windows covered with decorative iron latticework looked into a villa filled with lavish furniture and statues lining hallways.

An armed Russian soldier crashed through the under-growth. "Get out of here, little boy."

David scrambled to the grass. "I only want to look."

"You had your look—now, on your way."

"Who lives here?"

"No one. Go, before I arrest you."

"I'm only seven years old," said David defiantly.

"I don't care if you're a hundred and seven," said the soldier. "Move your skinny legs as fast as possible or I'll take you to my commanding officer. He's not as nice as me. He'll throw you in a box filled with rats."

"My papa will come after you. He's strong and beats up bad people."

The soldier burst out laughing. "Some papa. I'm not afraid."

Folding his arms over his chest, David stared into the guard's eyes. "He's a friend of Major Grishen."

The soldiers face whitened. He coughed and cleared his throat. "All right. It was a joke." He paused. "Don't tell the major."

"I won't if you tell me who lived here."

"You'll leave if I tell you?"

"Right away." "

"Won't say a word?"

"Promise."

"Germans used the house as one of their headquarters. It's under guard because we're looking for evidence we can use when they surrender. They stole paintings from the villa, but left almost everything else in place."

"Who lived here before?" asked David.

"You had your question answered; now leave."

"You only answered half a question. Someone lived here before the Germans took over."

"You're a clever little chap. The family of a wealthy Jewish merchant owned the villa. When the Germans invaded, they escaped to Vilnius in Lithuania. It didn't help. They were rounded up and sent to a ghetto. I hope their ghosts haunt the Nazis for the rest of their lives. Enough history. Now get out of here before I get in trouble," ordered the soldier.

The Roslans were gathered in the Lazik apartment when David returned home. Dov fiddled with the tuning dial until a Russian broadcast announced: "News from Moscow. Berlin has fallen. Marshall Stalin has announced the complete capture of the capital of Germany; the center of German imperialism; and the cradle of German aggression. The Berlin garrison laid down their arms this afternoon. More than seventy thousand prisoners have been rounded up so far today."

"Surrender can't be far off, unless the Germans have something up their sleeve," said Alex. "I can't understand why the British and Americans permitted Russians to take Berlin."

"Politics, Roslan," said Dov. "Who knows what kind of deals they made? For now, who cares? The Nazi Empire has vanished into the pages of history."

Łódź received the news about Berlin's fall with strange quiet on its streets. It seemed almost unbelievable Germany's unbeatable war machine ceased to exist. Perhaps it was a dream, thought David. When he woke he would be hiding once more in the small, bombed-out shell of an apartment building in Warsaw.

Jacob slammed open the door and glared at David. "My stamp would have been worth a lot more with Hitler dead."

"I don't care. All I want is to get back to my studies," said David.

"I won't forget. I'll make you pay for what you did."

"I can't forget how we hid from the Germans. I won't forget the people who helped us when they didn't have to. Your stamp is only a small piece of paper, something to collect. There's always another to take its place."

"I'm not finished with you." Jacob ran outside, banging the door as hard as he could.

Alex burst in. "What's all the noise?"

"Nothing," David said.

"Doesn't look like nothing to me. Tell the truth."

"The Hitler stamp. Geniek shouldn't keep anything like that."

"What did you do?"

"I ruined it," David said defiantly.

"You feel good after destroying Jacob's property?" asked Alex.

"We agreed to work together on the album. It's half mine. When I put a big, red X on it, I erased Hitler from the world."

"You can never erase what he represented. The rotten maggots of hate squirm out of sight, waiting for another Hitler to release them."

David hid behind Alex when Jacob returned. "You're a coward. You can't face me," Jacob shouted.

"Count to ten. Tadek, apologize to Geniek for what you did," ordered Alex.

"I'm sorry I messed up your stamp," David whispered.

No one made a sound. Jacob took a stamp from his pocket and held it up. "Surprise! I found another one."

"All is not lost," said Alex. "Do you accept Tadek's apology?"

"I didn't think you would get so angry," said David.

"You and your brother agreed to share the album. Sharing means taking action together, not alone. I despise what the stamp represents. Think of it as an object indicating the end of a monster in human form." He turned to Jacob. "You understand why he destroyed the stamp? No more arguments. I have a meeting with Major Grishen. Tell Mama I'll return before supper."

"Can I go with you?" David begged.

"Not this time. Do your homework. Go out and play with Shimon when he comes home from school."

Grishen and Alex sat outside a small café, drinking coffee. "Tastes good," said Alex after his first sip. "Like the real thing."

"It is real. I asked them to keep it for me when I entertain good friends."

Alex raised his cup. "My family appreciates your goodwill."

"It's difficult having us occupy Poland. The war has not been won and we have to remain on alert."

"Hitler's dead. Berlin's fallen. When will Germany surrender?" asked Alex.

"They were told we would slaughter the entire city in revenge for Stalingrad."

"I worry they have one last piece of ammunition in their arsenal."

"Rumors run wild German scientists have a bomb so devastating, so dangerous, it could wipe out Europe. The Norwegians built a plant producing something called heavy water, used for making such a weapon. The Allies blew up the factory in 1943. Intelligence decoded a message from Hitler to his commanders a few days before his death ordering them to expect *Götterdammerung*, the destruction of the world," reported Grishen.

"He got his wish. His world destroyed."

"There's hope we'll emerge from the tragedy of battle. Before Roosevelt died, he, Churchill, and Stalin agreed to allow free elections in Poland."

"As you say in Russia, *Vashe zdorov'ye*."

"If there's anything I can do for you, just ask. I have a bit of influence and would like to help."

Alex shook the major's hand. "We won't take advantage."

Everyone had an opinion based on someone who "knew the truth." Hitler was alive waiting to counterattack. Americans, Russians, or British stole his body. They planned to place it on display in a museum or string it up in public. Other rumors had Germany leading Russians into a trap. A few people claimed they had first-hand knowledge V2 rockets, stored away to bomb London, would soar into the sky wreaking havoc on Britain, Russia, and the United States.

"No one knows what they're talking about. The major expects it to be over soon. Once the dust settles we have to make plans," said Alex.

"You'll open a shop in Łódź and settle down," smiled Mela, looking ahead to a new life.

"We don't belong in Poland. Our so-called friends and neighbors turned on us."

"Jurek is buried in Warsaw. I will not leave him alone, forgotten in an unmarked grave."

"I promise we'll return and bury him next to my grandfather."

"We'll never find him." She sat on a bench and wept.

Alex smoothed out a ragged piece of paper. "I drew a map showing his burial place in the old Warsaw Jewish cemetery. I'm giving a copy to Isaac Feldsheim."

"Jurek is not a Jew. He won't help," snapped Mela.

"He will help. We never asked anything for rescuing Tadek and Geniek."

Mela kissed his hand. "I always trusted you to do right. If you want to leave Poland, we'll go. Do you have a plan?"

"We'll go to the British zone and tell them we want to take Tadek and Geniek to their father in Palestine. Ella wrote a letter to him about how smart the boys are and how we treat them as if they were our children."

"They are our sons. We lived with them through terrifying times. We tended to them when they were sick. We carried them when they couldn't walk."

"I want to see Palestine. I want to see what Jews pray for every day," said Alex. "And, my little believer, you'll walk on the same land Jesus walked. The rocks and the walls of Jerusalem still stand after two thousand years. "

Chapter Ten

Nightmare's End

Sun rose over Łódź on Friday, May 4, 1945, waking birds nesting in charred broken lindens. Bees hovered over pale-yellow flowers blossoming miraculously along scorched branches. Shopkeepers swept sidewalks in front of their stores, hoping the end of Hitler would bring the city back to life.

Ella shared with Alex and Mela a letter she wrote to Nahum Gutgeld in Tel Aviv:

> "As your children's tutor, I feel obliged to tell you what I know about them. I have been tutoring Tadek and Geniek (David and Jacob) since April. I have never met children with so much talent, almost genius. The people who care for them are exceptionally good to the boys. They are not in need of anything, except they miss their true parents and a Jewish atmosphere. In particular, their guardians give them the maximum of what someone who substitutes for parents can give. Tadek adores them."

The letter stunned the Roslans with its insight and tenderness. Ella caught their deep feeling of love for the boys. Overcome with emotion, Mela wept, weight of years guarding Geniek and Tadek from the fate of uncounted dead, lifted from Alex's shoulders. He coughed uneasily. "I wish I could see their father when he reads your letter." He picked up a sheaf of paper. "I have to fill these orders." Before leaving, he smiled.

"I expect you to be a tyrant, not a poet, preparing them for their entrance exams."

He spent the early morning at Ludmila's warehouse, packing goods in official military boxes Major Grishen's subordinates gave him for shipment across the border to Russia. Afterwards, he wheeled his cart to the square setting up his new kiosk. Baranski arrived, hauling his sewing machine. Excited women showed up, arguing, discussing with the tailor designs they saw in time-worn prewar fashion magazines. "Where are your partners, Geniek and Tadek?" one of them inquired.

"Maybe this weekend," replied Alex.

An elderly woman, hobbling on a cane, took an inordinate amount of time sifting through fabric, trying to make a decision.

"Over here," shouted someone from the street.

"What's going on?" the woman asked a man who ran past.

"News. It's big."

Alex folded a piece of cloth and handed it to her. "Keep it. No charge."

A crowd ran from every corner of the square to a shop with a loudspeaker broadcasting music. Every few seconds a voice alerted listeners the BBC was about to air a special announcement. The gathering crowded near the loudspeaker intently waiting. Then:

> "This is London. About six hours ago in a weather-stained tent not far from Hamburg, Field Marshall Bernard Montgomery accepted the surrender of more than a million German troops. All of the enemy forces in northwest Germany, Holland, and Denmark have surrendered unconditionally. The ceasefire becomes effective one minute before eight o'clock tomorrow, Saturday, May 5, seven hours from now."

Faces registered disbelief or confusion, until a woman threw her hat in the air and screamed: "It's over!"

The crowd erupted in cheers. Strangers hugged. An elderly man grabbed Alex, kissing him on both cheeks. Throngs converged on boulevards and avenues. Trolleys halted on rails. Conductors rang bells in one continuous metallic clang.

Alex, Mela, Ella, David, Jacob, and Marisia waited with Dov, Ida, and Shimon outside the apartment house. "Our teacher sent us all home," shouted Marisia. "No more war!"

"Don't celebrate too fast. The Germans swore an oath to die rather than surrender. They will keep killing until eight o'clock tomorrow morning. Who knows how many murderers will escape? Who knows who will protect them? Celebrate when the last German general is arrested," warned Alex.

Two days later, the BBC, on May 7, broadcast the announcement everyone hoped and prayed for:

> "Germany has signed an unconditional surrender, bringing to an end six years of war in Europe, according to reports from France. The BBC's Thomas Cadett watched the official signing at a schoolhouse in Reims, northeastern France, which serves as the advance headquarters of the supreme commander in Europe, General Dwight D. Eisenhower. He said the signing, which took place in the early hours of this morning, was carried out 'on a cold and businesslike basis.'"

British prime minister Winston Churchill, who led his country in battle, broadcast a statement to the world:

> "My dear friends, this is your hour. This is not victory of a party or of any class. It's a victory of the great

British nation as a whole. We were the first, in this ancient island, to draw the sword against tyranny. After a while we were left all alone against the most tremendous military power that has been seen. We were all alone for a whole year. There we stood, alone. Did anyone want to give in? Were we downhearted? The lights went out and the bombs came down. But every man, woman, and child in the country had no thought of quitting the struggle. London can take it. So, we came back after long months from the jaws of death, out of the mouth of hell, while all the world wondered. When shall the reputation and faith of this generation of English men and women fail? I say that in the long years to come not only will the people of this island but of the world, wherever the bird of freedom chirps in human hearts, look back to what we've done, and they will say 'do not despair, do not yield to violence and tyranny, march straight forward and die if need be—unconquered.' Now we have emerged from one deadly struggle—a terrible foe has been cast on the ground and awaits our judgment and our mercy."

"We're heading to Źródliska Park to celebrate," said Dov. "Let's have a picnic and talk about the future."

Mela grasped Alex's hand. Their future did not lie in Poland. They would leave for Palestine with Tadek and Geniek. She had difficulty imagining life in a country she only knew from her Bible.

"No school! No school!" yelled Shimon, kicking his soccer ball against a wall. He tossed it to David. "Come on. We'll get up a game in the park."

"Start without me!" shouted David. "I want to look around."

Burying her feelings, Mela gave him several groschen. "Enjoy. Buy something as sweet as you."

Grass almost disappeared under a mass of happy, excited men, women, and children crying, hollering, shouting with joy. Fireworks exploded over an ancient stone grotto covered with ivy. Sparklers spun rainbows atop an ornate nineteenth-century wooden gazebo. Sausages, cheese, and bread passed from one family to another. Old brass-and-copper charcoal-burning samovars boiled water for hot black tea.

A woman wearing a headscarf and patched housedress sat on a box. She patted David on the head. "Such a nice little boy," she said through missing teeth. "The war is over; we'll finally get some peace."

A mustachioed man drank beer and wiped the foam on his sleeve. "Rzeszów found Jews hiding in a basement. They beat the hell out of them."

"Good work. Poland's for Polish people, not goddamned foreigners who steal our money," grunted a grizzled old man.

"How many dirty Jews did Hitler leave alive? The bastard promised to exterminate them," grumbled the same woman who wore the shabby housedress.

Savage whispers from men and women who witnessed catastrophe at the hands of Nazi oppressors shook David.

At the other end of the park, Marisia introduced Jacob to her school friends as her cousin Geniek. Before long, conversations among the fifth graders drifted toward the difficulties they had when Germans occupied the city.

A boy chewed on a sausage. "My mother and father said the war and all our troubles came from Jews. They controlled the banks. Right here in Łódź, most of them owned factories. They took advantage of us."

Jacob yanked the boy to his feet. "Nazis murdered Jews, and your mother and father probably did nothing. Before the war, Jews helped Marisia's father."

The boy cowered at Jacob's sudden outburst: "I didn't mean anything. Just repeating what they told me."

"They're ignorant and don't know what they're talking about. This is their country as much as ours." He walked away. The day of liberation had turned sullen and dark, violence boiling under the surface. "I can't wait to get away from those people," Jacob said to Marisia. "It will be different when we get to Palestine." David sat atop the algae-covered grotto, his knees drawn up to his chest, a determined, enraged expression on his face. "I thought you were playing with Shimon," said Jacob.

David clawed at the moss, his fingers stained sickly green. "They're always here. Always waiting to drag us into their den of wolves."

"Let them keep talking. I started writing down all the hateful things people say. If I know their names, I put them in a column marked 'Enemies.' When we arrive in Palestine, I'm showing it to our father and grandfather. They'll put it in one of the newspapers."

"I don't want to go to some faraway place surrounded by people I don't know."

"Mama and Papa Roslan are going with us. Can you imagine what kind of welcome we'll have? They call it 'the land of milk and honey.' Not bad. We'll go to school and make new friends—Jewish friends. We won't have to hide any longer."

Ella knelt next to the boys. "What's going on?"

"He doesn't want to go to Palestine to meet our father," Jacob said.

"Papa Alex is my father," David insisted.

"I came to help you and Geniek. It wasn't a sacrifice to leave my family, it was an obligation. Someday I'll return. We can see each other when we're all in Tel Aviv. Theodore Herzl, a very great man, imagined a homeland for us in the Land of Israel," said Ella. She turned to Jacob. "We learned about the Balfour Declaration. What does it say?"

"It says one day Palestine will be home for the Jewish people."

"Not just a home; a national home. After two thousand years in exile, we will return, a nation among nations, living in peace." Ella's enthusiasm lifted David's spirits, but not for long. Alex and Mela would become distant relatives who might visit occasionally. He wanted them to remain as close as they were on that warm spring day in May.

On May 8, the liberated people of Europe heard the voice of the new president of the United States for the first time. "From the Radio Room of the White House, President Harry S. Truman." After the eloquence of Winston Churchill and Franklin Roosevelt, the simple Missouri nasal twang of Truman issuing a message of strength and hope sounded anticlimactic:

> "I only wish that Franklin D. Roosevelt had lived to witness this day. General Eisenhower informs me that the forces of Germany have surrendered to the United Nations. The flags of freedom fly over all Europe. . . . We must work to finish the war. Our victory is but half-won. The West is free, but the East is still in bondage to the treacherous tyranny of the Japanese. When the last Japanese division has surrendered unconditionally, then only will our fighting be done. . . . And now, I want to read to you my formal proclamation of this occasion: 'A proclamation—The Allied armies, through sacrifice and devotion and with

God's help have wrung from Germany a final and un-conditional surrender. The Western world has been freed of the evil forces which for five years and longer have imprisoned the bodies and broken the lives of millions upon millions of free-born men. They have violated their churches, destroyed their homes, cor-rupted their children, and murdered their loved ones. Our Armies of Liberation have restored freedom to these suffering peoples, whose spirit and will the oppressors could never enslave. Much remains to be done. The victory won in the West must now be won in the East. The whole world must be cleansed of the evil from which half the world has been freed. United, the peace-loving nations have demonstrated in the West that their arms are stronger by far than the might of the dictators or the tyranny of mili-tary cliques that once called us soft and weak. The power of our peoples to defend themselves against all enemies will be proved in the Pacific war as it has been proved in Europe. . . . In Witness Whereof, I have hereunto set my hand and caused the seal of the United States of America to be affixed.'"

The world veered in ominous directions. Germany did not use the formidable weapon Major Grishen foresaw. August 6, 1945, President Truman ordered the United States Army Air Force to drop an atom bomb on Japan. It wiped out the entire city of Hiroshima, killing eighty thousand. Three days later, another bomb devastated Nagasaki, a city on the northwest coast of the island of Kyushu, decimating forty thousand in-dividuals. President Truman followed the bombing raid with his report:

"Sixteen hours ago an American airplane dropped one bomb on Hiroshima, an important Japanese Army base. That bomb had more power than twenty thousand tons of TNT. We are now prepared to obliterate more rapidly and completely every productive enterprise the Japanese have above ground in any city. We shall destroy their docks, their factories, and their communications. Let there be no mistake; we shall completely destroy Japan's power to make war. I shall recommend that the Congress of the United States consider promptly the establishment of an appropriate commission to control the production and use of atomic power within the United States. I shall give further consideration and make further recommendations to the Congress as to how atomic power can become a powerful and forceful influence towards the maintenance of world peace."

Sudden and unexpected destruction forced Japan to surrender unconditionally on August 15. News of the bomb's ferocious power rocketed around the globe. The war in Asia came to a fiery end.

Major Grishen confided in Alex his confidence the Soviet Union would come to its senses and grant independence to Poland. Alex avoided discussing news with the children. It was more important for them to concentrate on their education. Unaware the science producing weapons of mass destruction and the use of medical nuclear isotopes would become his life's work, Jacob took his seventh grade exams. David tested for third grade a month later.

Proud of their achievements, Ella wrote to Nahum Gutgeld:

"Geniek passed his entrance exams for the first year in Junior High School with no restrictions. Tadek digested material for two school years in 5 months. Both of their talents are above average. A lesson with them turns into a big thinking celebration. Geniek appears very talented in every aspect. I lack the words to adequately describe his thinking and intellect. I talk to him after our lesson as I would with an adult, although he is only 12. Tadek reads fluently. He is well above the level of his class in writing and arithmetic. In addition, he is handsome as a dream."

Ella was the big sister or beautiful aunt showering David with compliments. She no longer tutored the boys but continued visiting several times a week. Her genuine admiration for the boys expressed with hugs, gifts of pens, pencils, and writing tablets.

They flourished with newfound confidence. Public school in Łódź would be the same as their experience with her, except they could share it with boys and girls their own age.

She spent evenings discussing her future with Alex and Mela. Ella's aunts, uncles, and cousins in Poland had not survived. She was anxious to continue her college education and contacted relatives in England in the hope they would sponsor her.

On the first day of class, reality hit the brothers hard. School books, tests, essays, fell far below their intellectual level, holding little interest for David. Jacob ran through math and science texts with ease. Given the opportunity, the boys preferred challenges.

A major upheaval came a few weeks into the term. The Provisional Government of the Republic of Poland under control of the Soviet Union removed Polish books from libraries, stores, and schools, replacing them with Russian texts. Teachers who objected vanished and Soviet-approved Polish instructors appeared demanding students read and memorize passages emphasizing Soviet principles.

Science followed Soviet rules, insisting Party doctrine and scientific truth buttress one another. Teachers constantly hammered away, with no explanation and no context, how Marxism and Leninism defeated worker slavery. Students in lower classes were ordered to repeat pages and pages they did not understand. Students in upper classes obeyed. A few, including Jacob, slinked off, objecting to a Soviet system with no room for scientific ideas conflicting with Marxism. The Gutgeld brothers commiserated with each other promising not to complain to Alex, who despised Communism as much as he loathed Fascism.

Autumn turned to winter. The first snow fell the end of November. Alex kept busy at his stall all week. Mela pleaded with him to accompany her to church the following Sunday. "If you don't go to church, the children won't believe in God," she insisted.

"Leave Tadek and Geniek alone. Take Marisia. We promised their aunt Hanka the boys would never forget who they are. A priest will want to baptize them."

"I would never allow it," Mela said.

"What will you tell your emissary of God? 'I forgot the boys are Jewish. This has all been pretend.' A bomb will go off in our faces."

"You told Isaac Feldsheim. Ella knows the truth."

"I trust them. Go to church, my love. Make peace with your God."

The door banged open. David stomped in, shaking snow from his shoes. "I hate school," he yelled. "It's boring. No one's allowed to ask questions. I wish Ella was my teacher again." He yanked a red kerchief off his neck and threw it on the table.

Alex recognized the symbol of the Soviet Young Pioneers. "Who gave that to you?"

"School makes everyone wear them. They think calling me Pioneer First Class will make me a better student. It doesn't. Soon we'll all have to wear uniforms. All I hear in class is how the wonderful Soviet Union beat the Germans at Stalingrad and saved the world from Hitler. Not one mention of the Americans or British. We even have to learn to read Russian," complained David. "I already know how to speak Russian."

"Marisia, Geniek, in here!" Alex shouted.

"We're doing homework," called Marisia from behind a closed door.

"Right now."

Marisia ran in, followed by Jacob, wondering what troubled Alex. He snatched the red kerchief from his daughter's neck.

"Geniek?" He threw the balled-up kerchief on a chair.

"I told you," said David.

"No one—not teachers, not school—will force my children to wear these symbols of oppression. You want new clothes? My tailor will make them for you. Major Grishen hoped his country would come to its senses. We didn't fight a war so Communists could indoctrinate you." Alex stormed out the door.

"Where is Miss Ulinski?" Alex asked, towering over the school receptionist. The frightened woman squeaked an answer he could not hear. "Speak up. Miss Ulinski, the school registrar."

No one knows where she is," she cried.

"The school must have records."

"They're all gone. Taken away." The receptionist opened an empty file drawer. New posters had taken the place of the Nazi posters. There was a picture of women working on girders. Underneath, the caption read: "Create Happiness." Another poster showed a Young Pioneer, wearing a red kerchief and uniform standing at a blackboard: "Pioneer Students, Work Hard and Learn." Alex composed himself, trying to look as if nothing was wrong.

He returned to the apartment and took the children aside. "Wear the kerchiefs. Be clever; do what they say and don't stand out. It won't last long. On Saturday night, the major and his wife are coming for dinner. Mama and I expect your best behavior."

"I like his uniform," said David. "I wish I had one just like it."

"War isn't a game," snapped Mela.

"You think I don't know? Dead bodies, people hurt, so many children who'll never grow up." For a few moments David looked much older than seven.

"The children who survived will show the world haters did not succeed," said Alex. "I can't predict what road you'll take. I hope it leads to a life of goodness."

"I don't know anything about the future, except maybe the major will bring cake from the army baker," wished David.

"Good prediction," said Alex.

On a snowy Saturday afternoon, Alex presented Mela with a duck wrapped in newspaper. "From a farmer outside the city. I traded yards of fabric for the bird." He warmed his hands in front of the wood-burning stove. Snow clinging to his jacket melted away.

Jacob and David carried frost-covered logs into the apartment and dropped them in an old copper bucket. "I hope the wood burns," said Jacob.

Silhouetted against the dull, gray horizon, David could see the ghetto's shadow and hear the muffled cries of the girl who wrote the letter in the tin box.

"What's wrong? You look so far away," Marisia said.

David straightened up. "Snow hides all the ugliness."

Jacob slapped his brother on the back. "My brother, the seven-year-old philosopher."

"Mother Nature knows what she's doing. Snow takes away sharp edges. Rain brings flowers. Sun gives life to the world," said Mela, basting the duck.

The major and Kristina arrived with a gift for the children. Kristina handed a box of pastries to David. "This should satisfy your sweet tooth." Golden-brown buns stuffed with cottage cheese and crushed fruit filled the box.

Mela took them away before the children snatched them. "First dinner, then dessert," she said.

"What are they called?" David asked.

"*Vatrushka*," said Kristina. "The major and I have eaten them since we were little children. The recipe comes from ancient tribes living on the steppes of Russia reaching all the way to Mongolia. When you eat *vatrushka*, you eat history."

David's imagination raced across the vast lands. People lived in tents and children ate pastries on open grasslands stretching to the horizon. He waited, his eyes on the *vatrushka*, while Mela chatted with Mrs. Grishen and the major talked with Alex.

After dinner, Mela gave the children pastries and glasses of milk.

"Major Grishen and I are going outside," said Alex, shrugging on his parka. The major wore a heavy overcoat and pulled a fur hat over his head.

Outside, Alex said, "You asked if I needed a favor. Now is the time."

Grishen lit a cigarette. The smoke swirled in the frigid air. "If it's in my power."

"Berlin's divided into American, British, French, and Soviet zones. I want to go to the British zone."

The major ground his cigarette out with the heel of his boot. "Easier said than done, Roslan. We have orders Polish citizens are not allowed to leave."

"There must be a way," said Alex.

"It would be easier if you were Jewish," said Grishen. "Moscow inaugurated the 'Green Border Policy' for Jews who want to leave. The Soviet Union supports Zionist settlement in Palestine. Unfortunately, your family is not Jewish."

Alex thought: If Grishen knew the truth, he'd never trust me again. "Is there any way you can help?" he asked.

Grishen pulled up his collar to keep out the chill. "It costs. No one wants to put his career on the line without compensation. Tomorrow's Sunday. After church, let's meet at the café on Piotrkowska Street."

"I leave religion to Mela."

"You would make a good comrade."

Sunday morning, Mela and Marisia attended the imposing St. Stanislaus Kostka Cathedral, with its soaring steeple and basilica clad in aging, fluorescent-green copper.

Alex, David, and Jacob walked along snow-covered sidewalks to a small, cozy bistro warmed by a brick oven. Alex ordered the specialty of the house—homemade sausage over scrambled eggs, with thick slices of sourdough rye and jam.

"Delicious," smiled Jacob.

"Not as good as Mama's cooking," said David.

"Second best," Jacob countered.

"Mama's cooking has one ingredient never found in cafés. Love. Eat up and enjoy. You may not see sausage and eggs for a while. We're leaving Łódź," Alex revealed.

The news alarmed David. "I don't want to go."

"Why do we have to leave? I'm getting good grades and have friends," argued Jacob.

The boys' sudden reluctance to leave Łódź took Alex by surprise. "After all your complaining about school, teachers, uniforms, and the wonderful Red Pioneers? We're under the Soviet boot. You can make friends anywhere. Truth and knowledge lie deeper than the garbage they teach you. I will not have my kids' minds twisted by Communists. We suffered under Hitler. You will not suffer under Stalin."

"Where are we going?" asked Jacob.

"It's our secret. Berlin. The British zone. No one must know. As long as we stay in Poland and the Russians believe you're my sons, they won't let us out and it will be a long time before you see your family."

"I want to stay with you!" cried David.

"Mama and I will never leave you on your own."

"You have a good business," remarked Jacob.

"Until some commissar decides to collect a little on the side," said Alex.

"When are we leaving?" asked Jacob.

"I'll let you know. I already told Mama. Do not let anyone suspect our plan."

Their new life in the city had seemed as if it would last forever. All of a sudden, Jacob and David had to keep their mouths closed.

"Don't look so glum. Think of it as an adventure," said Alex.

"Some of us don't like adventures," stammered David.

"Says the boy who jumps on trams, taking off for God knows where," Alex replied.

The major met Alex at the café later in the day. "I made arrangements to get you out of Łódź. Every two or three days, our vans and trucks head to Berlin for supplies. Fortunately, the cold weather is our friend. We're anticipating heavy snow tomorrow night, patrols will be few and far between, making it safer for a trip west. Dress as if you're in Siberia. Take as little as necessary. Wait on the corner near your apartment at midnight tomorrow. I'll drive your family in my official car close to the German border. A truck will take you across. The driver is loyal to me. I spoke on his behalf when he was accused of drunk driving. He's taking a risk smuggling you out of Poland and expects payment upfront. The guards at the border crossing are familiar with the back-and-forth trip. They'll only give the truck a quick look."

"Are you sure you want to do this?"

"You're a good man, Roslan. You have your reasons."

"How much will it cost?"

"The truck driver wants two hundred thousand zlotys. He would prefer twenty-five American."

"He'll get his payment. I have another favor to ask. Not for me, for a friend."

"If it's in my power."

"Ludmila Sobanski manufactures the textiles I sold. She needs to start up again. I would appreciate it if you help her."

Grishen clenched his jaw. "Poland's under our sphere of influence. The government will control most businesses."

"I'm asking assistance for someone who helped me."

"No guarantees, but I'll do what I can."

Ludmila brought Alex to the crowded second floor office that served as her living quarters. "Who would imagine after enduring the misery of the past years you would return? I can't thank you enough for unloading my merchandise. And the Russians—what a windfall. So, how many yards do you need tomorrow?"

"There's no tomorrow for Roslan and Sons. We're leaving Łódź."

The news hit hard. "But your business! You built it out of nothing; and now you're abandoning it? A lot of women will not be happy."

"It's important to me, Ludmila. As my partner, I didn't want to just disappear." He placed a pile of bills on the table. "My last transaction. By the way, I know Tadek slipped a few extra zloty into your earnings."

"I thought it was your idea."

"The clever little boy wanted to make sure you got what you deserved."

"Tadek has your brain for numbers. He'll go a long way in this world." She took his hand. "You're the best damned sales-man I ever had. Your little stall on the square gave me enough money to begin manufacturing in a small way again. Here's hoping the Russians let me keep the factory."

"Sobanski, the tailor, will do what he can to trade your textiles. Use his shop as cover. Unless the Soviets find out, it ought to work. The officer who arranged my Soviet link will do what he can for you. He's an honorable man. We'll be gone this time tomorrow."

Ludmila rummaged through her bolts of cloth. She cut a long piece of orange-and-white wool, sat at a foot-operated sewing machine and hemmed it. She wrapped it around Alex's neck. "To keep you warm, and a reminder of our partnership."

Chapter Eleven

Trail to Freedom

Wrapped in wool jackets, parkas, fur caps, and heavy boots caked with snow, the Roslans, Jacob and David braved a white blizzard whistling around them. Marisia draped the long orange-and-white muffler made by Ludmila tightly around her neck. Frost cloaked duffle bags and sacks of food.

Mela stamped her feet. "What if the major doesn't come?"

"He made a commitment. I trust him."

"You're the one who always checks twice before believing," Mela said, clutching him for warmth.

"The major will keep his word."

"My father used to say, 'The Lord's grace rides on a sick horse.'" A green-and-black camouflaged car rolled to the curb. Alex smiled with satisfaction. "Looks as if the horse had a good doctor."

Major Grishen leaned out the window. "Get in. We have a three-hour ride." Mela and the children squeezed into the back seat. Alex handed Grishen twenty American dollars. "You made the truck driver's day."

Gearshift crunched. The car plowed through driving snow, past the town square, and along a frozen stream forming the boundary of Poniatowski Park, explored by David his first day in the city. Łódź rapidly receded behind a curtain of snow. Roots planted in the city by David were cut out from under him. He trusted Alex to do the right thing, but moving from one place to another over and over filled him with dread. He squeezed his eyes closed, trying to shut down his feelings.

With Marisia between them, Jacob slouched against the car door, eyes staring into the icy gloom. He innately understood the Roslan's need to leave a Poland where freedom had become shackled by another occupier. He also felt his brother's apprehension – an apprehension he buried for David's sake.

David's birth in 1938, followed by their mother's untimely death, leaving a father who abandoned both of them. Five years older than David, not yet a teen, feeling as if he were an old man carrying a heavy responsibility that would have crushed him except for the Roslan's courageous example.

Car wipers flicked back and forth with little impact on brittle rime caking the windshield. Grishen halted in a snowbank, leaving the car running, and scraped it off.

"I travel this road at least once a month to confer with our British and American allies. Markers by the side of the road guide us for nighttime driving."

"We trust you to get us across safely, Major Grishen," Alex said.

"It's time you called me Nikolai."

"Nikolai, the last Russian emperor. Any relation?"

"Not even close. My uncle's name. His wife was Jewish. They perished in Belzec, along with my father's entire family. They survived Stalin's Jewish purges, only to be caught by the Nazi blood libel."

"You are Jewish?" asked an astonished Alex.

"Quite frankly, I have no idea what I am. God never protected the millions. We lost an entire future—peacemakers, scientists, artists, scholars. Taking you and your children out of Poland may be the best thing I have ever done."

"Fate brought Kristina to my kiosk in the square. You lit a spark that will never be extinguished," said Alex. He fixed his eyes on the road, imagining a new life in Palestine.

"The truck is ten kilometers from the crossing. I do not dare get any closer," said Grishen. "The driver has shipping blankets to keep you warm and crates in which to hide in the event guards search the vehicle. It's very cold. I don't expect it to happen."

"My family and I are grateful for your help. Someday I'll repay you."

"You repaid me by making Kristina happy."

A camouflaged canvas-covered truck, parked by the side of the road, loomed through snow flurries. The major blinked his headlights. Lights blinked back. "We're here," said Grishen. The children stumbled out, dragging duffle bags, and looked around at a snow-covered countryside broken by scattered remains of burned-out tanks and armored cars. Marisia, Jacob, and David clambered into the back of the truck.

Grishen and Alex shook hands. The major said: "My aunt's mother always said a prayer for travelers. All I recall are a few words. 'Lead me to peace, my steps to peace, support me toward peace . . .' Good luck to you all," he said.

Alex helped Mela into the back and hoisted himself behind her. The driver secured the tarpaulin covering the back of the truck. "Listen to me," he said. "When we approach the gate into Germany, I'll bang on the wall of the truck, get inside the crates and keep quiet." I'm already late and need to make up time to keep on schedule or the guards will want to know why, so hold on tight. The road's full of potholes."

The children rolled themselves up in threadbare quilts. Alex and Mela sat against the walls of the truck. After a few kilometers careening and bouncing over icy depressions, they approached the border. British soldiers bundled in heavy greatcoats, carrying rifles slung over their backs, came out of a guardhouse. A sergeant asked for identification and signaled to his men. They raised the red-and-white-striped barrier.

True to Major Grishen's prediction, they drove into Germany without incident. Alex peered through the tarp. Cars and trucks with British and American insignia rolled along the highway, releasing an immense burden he carried from the first day he rescued the boys. Twisted steel and broken stone materialized through the haze. A broad rubble-lined avenue sliced through Berlin, leading to British headquarters. The truck braked; the driver yanked back the tarp. The children shielded their eyes from morning sunlight glaring off sleet-coated streets.

"I can't stay. Ask for asylum," the driver said, his wheels spinning on the wet road.

"Another bunch of Polacks getting away from the Russkies," a guard muttered in English; he pushed open the gate motioning the Roslans to follow him into an office.

A young lieutenant wearily looked up. The nameplate on his desk identified him as Lt. Smyth-Martin. "No need to tell me how you managed to get here," he said in Polish. "Names, relationships, and where you're from."

"Alex and Amelia Roslan. Our daughter is Marisia. Originally from Warsaw. We came from Łódź."

Smyth-Martin dutifully recorded their names in a ledger. "And your sons?"

Alex revealed the secret only Isaac Feldsheim and Ella Rosenberg knew. "Not our sons. We rescued them from the

Warsaw Ghetto. The older one is Jacob. The little one David. Last name Gutgeld."

"Are you aware they could cross the border legally?"

"Russia's 'Green Border Policy' meant abandoning them to the dubious pleasure of creeping across Europe. They hid behind Polish names, Geniek and Tadek, for over three years. We heard news, rumors about Jews murdered, thrown out of towns and villages. The day Germany surrendered, people cheered reports of those coming out of hiding, accosted and beaten, driven from homes they lived in for generations. Life in Palestine will be best for them. My wife and daughter agree we must deliver them personally to their family."

"You have evidence their family survived?"

Alex fished out the letter given to him by Isaac Feldsheim. "The Jewish Agency in Łódź found this letter from their father, Nahum Gutgeld, living in Tel Aviv. He's been searching for his sons. Since then, their tutor and Jacob have communicated with him."

"Documentation goes a long way toward receiving permission to emigrate. As far as going with them, impossible."

"The boys are our responsibility. We insist on caring for them until they reach their father."

"I'm only the intake officer," Smyth-Martin said with a look of disbelief. "I'll make a request. You'll be asked to present your case to my superiors. In the meantime, we'll find accommodations for you and your wife."

Alex rose to his full height. "We stay together."

"Mr. Roslan, you are under British authority. Regulations require children below the age of eighteen must be housed where they will receive proper nutrition and periodic medical examinations to insure their health and safety. We will provide arrangements for you and your wife to reside with a German family."

Alex shook his head. "We've had our fill of Germans."

"The Allies embarked on a massive de-Nazification program to rid the country of Fascists and Fascism."

"Let's hope they achieve their noble dream."

Smyth-Martin conducted the Roslans to his captain, shuffling papers on his desk.

"Lieutenant, please translate for me." He turned to the Roslans. "A Polish national requesting immigration to Palestine is quite unusual. Jacob and David are another matter, although it will take time to authorize transportation. The Home Office will make the final decision regarding Nahum Gutgeld's request for his children to enter Palestine. They will contact the Jewish Agency in order for direct communication with Mr. Gutgeld. The Palestine High Commission will review your request. We cannot guarantee approval."

"I promised Tadek and Geniek I would personally deliver them to their father," said Alex.

"Who in the world are Tadek and Geniek?" the captain asked Smyth-Martin.

"Names we gave to the children to shield their identities."

The captain looked into Alex's piercing blue eyes. "No one suspected?"

"Suspected, never caught. We don't know what happened to their family in Warsaw."

"I'll pass the information up the ladder of command."

A nurse handed Alex a paper to sign. The lieutenant whispered to the nurse. "There's been an error," she said to Alex.

"Mr. Roslan, you, your wife, and daughter need to request asylum," said Smyth-Martin. "Jacob and David have special status?"

"You may remain with the children for a few days until transfer to temporary housing," said the nurse.

"How far from here?" asked Mela.

"Approximately thirty minutes by rail."

The Roslans and children boarded a truck with the admitting nurse and drove to a gated area. A sign at the entrance read: "United Nations Relief and Rehabilitation—Displaced Persons Camp."

A train rumbled on elevated tracks near the children's dormitories, shaking simple bunk beds lining walls. Boys ranging from five to sixteen stood around a small coal-burning stove working on arts and crafts, playing board games.

"The boys' dormitory. Girls live on another floor," the nurse explained.

David ran to Alex and Mela. "I don't want to live here. I want to stay with you."   "We'll see you as often as possible. I'm sure you can visit." Mela turned to the nurse. "No rules against it?"

"None at all. We encourage families to see one another. It will be comparatively easy once you become familiar with the rail schedule."

"I don't want you to go!" cried David.

"You'll make friends and have a wonderful time," said Mela.

"Everything's going to be all right," reassured Jacob.

"Palestine's a terrible place!" yelled David.

"You don't know what you're talking about."

"Pal-a-stine. Like a monster in a fairy tale," said David, stomping his foot on the floor.

The nurse knelt down and spoke in a calm, reassuring voice. "Perhaps no one told you we serve ice cream once a day."

"Ice cream! How bad can it be?" asked Marisia.

"In 'Hansel and Gretl,' the old witch had a gingerbread house, but she really wanted to eat the boy and girl," David whispered.

"No one's going to hurt you," said the nurse. "This is only until you have permission to join your father."

David grasped Alex's hand. "This is my father. I'm staying with him."

"I'm getting tired of your whining and crying," snapped Jacob.

Marisia pushed Jacob aside, "Leave him alone. If it makes you feel better, David, I'll read you one of your favorite fairy tales."

"I can read myself; I'm not a baby!" yelled David.

"Let's calm down," said the nurse. "First things first." The nurse attached numbered tags to the children's jackets. "Everyone's registered with UNRRA." Bunk beds had the same numbers stenciled on their posts. "Place all belongings in foot lockers with the same number as your bunk. Lock it and keep your key with you at all times. Tomorrow, the medical staff will examine you. We want to keep everyone in our charge healthy. Before long, you'll make friends and think of this as your home."

Mela kissed David. "Until Papa and I have a place to stay, we'll be right here."

"Come here, all of you," said Alex gathering the children in his arms. "There's nothing to be afraid of anymore. The war's over. We're out from under Russian domination . . . in other words, we're free. Free to have supper with you this evening and breakfast tomorrow."

"Come along. I'll take Marisia to the girl's dormitory. We have temporary billets for adults," said the nurse, leading them out of the boys' barracks.

Jacob pulled on his coat. "I'm exploring outside. Want to come?"

"Leave me alone," David said, dropping on his bunk.

"It's up to you." Jacob ran outside.

The scarred, wooden building with row upon row of beds was not home. It stored children like textiles in Ludmila's warehouse. Boys around the stove ignored frigid winter wind racing between barracks, sifting between cracks in walls, drifting with chill fingers through the building.

David expected to see despair and loneliness on the boys' faces. Instead, they laughed and drank hot cocoa as if they were on vacation, sitting around a campfire in the middle of a forest. One of the boys broke away and spoke German to David, who flinched at the sound of the language.

"I don't understand."

The boy pointed at his chest. "Gershon."

"Tadek," David said quietly.

"Polnisch," said Gershon, rattling off questions in German until he realized David had no idea what he said. He motioned him to join the other boys.

They greeted David in a mixture of German, Russian, Hungarian, Latvian, and Yiddish. Sketches and drawings they made of nightmare scenes, hands clutching barbed wire, wide, bleeding eyes peering through slats of cattle cars, black slashes across a scarlet field, contrasted with their outward behavior. David had enough grim experiences in his young life. He chose to craft a symbol of beauty and hope, an illustration of Rebekah Landau's tin box adorned with pink flowers.

He stepped into the frosty air where boys and girls played in the snow and jumped rope. Older boys skidded and sloshed across a muddy soccer field. Perhaps Rebekah Landau passed through the British camp, traveling out of the same dark, fearful world David encountered. Every minute of every day in Warsaw he expected police or Gestapo.

"Time for dinner, dreamer," said Jacob coming up behind his brother. "The nurse said Mama and Papa can eat with us until they find a place."

David, Jacob, Gershon, and the other boys from the dormitory trotted to the cafeteria. They picked up tin trays and walked along steaming containers of potatoes, turnips, and chicken. White-uniformed servers dished out the hot food, speaking languages from every corner of Europe.

The Roslans joined the children. A banner hanging on a wall proclaimed Jewish organizations subsidized the UNRRA camp. "Jews help all refugees. It doesn't matter what country they come from or what religion they practice—or don't practice. It's one reason we want to go to Palestine," said Alex.

David choked on a piece of potato. He could not understand why someone who didn't know him, who abandoned him and his brothers, demanded he break all ties to those who raised, nurtured, loved, and sacrificed for them. The old slave in Uncle Tom's Cabin surrendered his life to save others escaping to freedom. Uncle Tom did not run from his slave master. He stood his ground, and in the end the slave master was defeated. David's father and grandfather should have been brave and escaped with their entire family.

Alex and Mela gathered the children together. "Mama and I made a request to leave for the American zone. From there we can go by train and find passage to Palestine. It may take a few weeks. We're waiting for papers from the British. In the morning they're taking us to a private home not far away."

For two days, doctors and nurses examined the children. An official stamped their Displaced Person Registration Record. Camp rules did not require them to attend school, since most children left within a few days or weeks.

To Jacob and Marisia's joy, the British screened old movies in a small theater. They rushed to be first in line. It didn't matter if they knew the language. Images on the screen portrayed brave England battling the Nazi horde and winning. One afternoon they watched a movie based on Shakespeare's play *Henry V.* Heroic English king Henry faced a great army. His stirring speech drove a small band of warriors to overcome a formidable enemy.

Rain and snow fell almost every day, blanketing the ruined, broken city in a cloak of gray. It did not stop David from wandering between the piles of rubble that led to the east bank of the River Spree. Bomb-blasted Berlin Cathedral rose on the other side of a footbridge. He entered its smoke-and-soot-blackened interior. An Allied bombing raid destroyed the dome, leaving a massive hole open to the sky. Melting snow dripped into a crater in the floor.

David climbed down a broken marble staircase. Ornate stone coffins held remains of Germany's imperial rulers. Men saluted the dead. Women making the sign of the Cross and counting beads on their rosaries, knelt on cracked tile. Defeated, demoralized people dressed in rags yearned for regal leaders to return. David wondered what they hoped for in a church where Nazis, praying with guns slung across backs, prepared to kill innocent people.

A blue-and-white banner painted with Hebrew letters and an eight-branched candelabra covering the wall greeted the children entering the dining room for breakfast. Alex and Mela joined them.

A girl jumped up, shouting: "Hanukkah's coming!"

"What's she yelling about?" David asked Jacob.

"Some kind of Jewish holiday."

"Not some kind of Jewish holiday. One we should all celebrate," said Alex. "Mela, remember in Bialystock, the candles our Jewish friends lit for eight days? They recalled a time when a small group called the Maccabees, the first partisan army, defeated an army of thousands. That's history, not a Bible story."

"I remember," said Jacob. "Once a year about this time, our grandmother would set a large brass menorah near the window. It had tiny birds and places for candles. They used a big one to light the others. Afterwards, our grandfather would hand me and Shalom a small sack of candy. You were a baby, David, but they held you up to see the lights."

Candles, holidays, were mere sketches for David, stories told by his brother, holding no meaning. David's mother— a vague memory, kept alive by a black-and-white photograph taken in more halcyon days; his father in a business suit, sitting primly on a picnic blanket, looking away from the camera.

A British lieutenant stood on a chair at the far end and called out in Polish, "Who can tell the story of Hanukkah?" Hands went up. He pointed at Gershon. "Let's hear it."

The boy turned red with embarrassment. The other children began clapping, shouting, "Tell the story!"

"A long time ago a bad king made everyone bow down to his statue. One man with seven sons, who called themselves Maccabees, refused." He kept his voice low afraid he would make a mistake.

"The brave man was Mattathias. What happened next?" the officer asked.

"The king's soldiers tried to kill him and his sons. They escaped into the mountains, beat the king's army, and rescued the Holy Temple in Jerusalem. That's why we celebrate Hanukkah." Gershon sat down, exhausted.

"I learned the story when I went to Hebrew school in England," said the lieutenant. "'Hanukkah' means dedication. When the Maccabees liberated the Temple in Jerusalem, they cleaned it up and had a huge celebration."

A girl raised her hand. "Are we going to have a Christmas tree?" she asked in a timid voice.

"Of course we are," a nurse promised. "The Jewish holiday comes in November. We celebrate Christmas in a few weeks."

The officer held up a slab of polished wood with nine empty shell casings. One in the middle stood slightly taller than the others. "I made this special candleholder; we use it during the darkest time of the year." He inserted small orange candles in the casings and turned the lights off. The lieutenant flicked on his brass cylindrical cigarette lighter igniting the middle one. "This one's the servant." He took it out of its casing and slowly lit the other eight. "On the first day, we light one candle, and every day we light another. By the end of the holiday all eight candles, plus the servant, burn bright, reminding us we have light all around us and in our hearts."

A hush fell over the room as flames danced. Someone yelled: "It's beautiful!" The children clapped spontaneously.

Lights clicked back on. The kitchen staff marched out with platters of potato pancakes, jars of applesauce, and milk containers. The children dived in, eating with gusto. "We should celebrate Hanukkah every year," said a girl wearing a gold cross.

A nurse pointed out the Roslans to the camp administrator. "Mr. and Mrs. Roslan," he said, speaking Polish. "Good news. We found a couple, the Stampfs, with a lovely home in Spandau, willing to take you in. Be prepared to leave with your belongings within the hour."

David's heart sank. "Is there any way they can stay?"

"I have to follow orders, young man. However, once they're settled, we'll make arrangements for you to visit,"

"Numbers 405, 406, and 407, please report to the office immediately after breakfast," another nurse announced.

"Looks as if it's your turn," Alex said to the children.

In the office, the head nurse opened a file and glanced at Marisia's, Jacob's, and David's tags. "We have instructions to make sure Jewish children have an opportunity to participate in religious life. Since this is Saturday, the Jewish Sabbath, you may attend services in the camp synagogue."

"Can I attend?" asked Marisia excitedly.

Flipping through their intake papers, the nurse looked up. "You're listed as Catholic. We require your parents' permission to attend."

David folded his arms. "I don't want to go."

"I'd rather play with the other boys," Jacob insisted.

"No one's forcing you. I'm presenting you with a choice. Tomorrow's Sunday. Marisia's parents, your guardians, will be in Spandau. Regulations permit one of you to visit for a day with Mr. and Mrs. Roslan. You must decide who goes first, second, and third."

Jacob raised his hand. "Marisia should go first. She's Mama's and Papa's real daughter."

Are you alright with that, Tadek?" asked Marisia.

David tried not to look disappointed. "Have a good time."

The nurse held two slips of paper between her fingers. "Very well. I suggest the boys draw for turns. Whoever picks the short one will visit next Sunday and set your routine while in camp. Close your eyes and make your choice."

David drew the short slip of paper. He would see Alex and Mela in one week. He stuffed the lucky paper in his pocket.

"How will we know where to get off?" asked Jacob.

"The first time, one of our sergeants will accompany all of you. Mr. and Mrs. Roslan will meet you at Spandau train stop. You and David will return with your guard."

David woke early the next morning and ran to the closed dining hall. He banged on the door until a cook let him in. "Our food's so good you can't wait?" The kitchen staff lit stoves and soon the room smelled of pancakes, eggs, and fried potatoes. One of the cooks gave David a job carrying jugs of milk outside and placing them on beds of snow. When he finished, she kissed him on both cheeks. "Ring the dinner bell, Mr. 406."

A tall, blonde baker with a short beard handed David a metal rod. "Go on." A steel triangle hung near the door. He rang it with all his might, rousing everyone for a hearty breakfast.

"I helped!" David said to Jacob and Marisia when they entered the dining hall.

"Just because you're little everyone lets you do what you want," groused Jacob.

"I came early and had nothing to do."

"Cook's pet."

"What's wrong with you two? One minute, happy brothers, the next at each other's throats. Today's special. I won't let you ruin it," complained Marisia.

They ate breakfast without saying another word. The nurse gave them woolen coats and heavy rubber boots. A British sergeant dressed in winter uniform escorted them up rusted iron stairs to an elevated railroad platform. The soldier saw David looking at the pistol strapped to his belt. He pulled it out of his holster. "Howdy, pardner," the sergeant said with a broad smile. He twirled the gun around.

"Cowboy!" shouted Jacob.

"Cowboy," smiled the soldier as the train rattled to a stop.

High above the city, Berlin looked like a toy town smashed beneath boots. Buildings were leveled, trees uprooted. Bomb craters dotted the landscape. People dug with hands in ruins of demolished homes, searching for remnants of their lives. The train squealed to a stop. A bullet-riddled sign read: "Spandau."

The children ran into the waiting arms of Alex and Mela. "We told you nothing can keep us apart," said Mela.

David hugged her. "I want to stay."

"You have to take your turn."

"I'll be here next Sunday."

The sergeant pointed to his watch. "Time for the boys to return."

"When you come back, tell us all about your visit," Jacob said to Marisia.

Back at camp Jacob ran behind the kitchen to build snowmen with boys and girls. David wandered away from laughing and giggling to the quiet library, searching for books about trolls, gallant princes and princesses, magic and mystery. He fantasized mystical powers gave him the ability to make wishes come true in a big world rolling forward without stopping. In a children's astronomy book he read about light years and the distance of the moon from the Earth. His fingers traced diagrams of Ursa Major, the Greater Bear, and Ursa Minor, the Lesser Bear with the North Star at the end of its tail. The book explained: "Keep the North Star or Polaris in sight. It helps you know the direction in which you're moving: north, east, south, or west." He wanted to go in any direction his Papa Alex and Mama Mela took him.

"The British pay the old couple for taking in refugees," Marisia told the boys when she returned. "Mrs. Stampf is a nice lady who made us lunch. Mama and Papa took me for a walk along a frozen river. Papa told me he's sure the British will give permission for all of us to immigrate."

"He's a great salesman," said Jacob.

"I'm not going to Palestine. I want to go to America," demanded David.

"All your crying and complaining won't make the British send you anywhere, except to Palestine. Get used to it. Our father's making arrangements for us to travel and when we get the right papers we're going. There's nothing we can do about it," Jacob said sadly.

"We could run away, and if anyone asks who we are we'll tell them we're Tadek and Geniek Roslan going to America."

"Or maybe we run away, and they find us. We could end up in Poland with the Communists."

Boxed in, David longed for a life far away from the ugliness surrounding him in the camp. The next seven days dragged by. Clocks ran slower. Weather changed from sun to rain, to sleet and snow. Icy winds pummeled the camp. His life constantly altered, at night he searched for never-changing stars, planets, and constellations. How many days, weeks, years had he traveled since escaping from the Warsaw Ghetto?

Early on Sunday morning, David dressed in his warmest clothes. He shoveled down his breakfast and presented himself to a British sister.

"Anxious, are we?" she asked, bundling him into a parka. The nurse escorted him to the train platform and handed him a travel pass. "It permits you to travel on public transportation throughout Berlin. Show it to the train conductor. Do you remember your stop?"

"Spandau."

"Correct. On your return, look for a train with the name Charlottenburg on the front. Don't be late. Someone will be waiting."

David climbed squeaking iron steps and boarded a car. Army trucks plowed through heavy snow on the street below. Winter haze softened the broken spire of Kaiser Wilhelm Church. The train squealed to a stop at Spandau station. David hurried into Alex and Mela's embrace.

"So healthy and strong," admired Alex.

A short hall in the Stampf apartment led to a large living room with an ornate Persian rug. Heidi Stampf, gray hair tied in a bun, sat on a threadbare couch. Her husband, stout, white-haired Wilhelm, occupied a large, worn, leather-upholstered chair. He stood, brushed bits of *Streuseltaler* crumb cake from his shirt, wiped hands on his dark canvas pants held up by broad suspenders, and ran a finger along his bristly moustache.

"Tadek, meet Mr. and Mrs. Stampf. They kindly opened their home to us," said Alex.

"Pleased to meet you, young man," said Wilhelm, struggling with the Polish language.

Heidi kissed David on his cheek. "Would you like tea and cake?"

David nodded, then froze. Adolf Hitler's portrait hung on the wall. The same face pasted in Jacob's album. Germany lost the war, and a picture of the dead dictator held a place of honor. He quickly sat with his back to the picture, feeling cold, dark eyes boring into him.

Heidi Stampf set tea and cake on the table. The cake stuck in his throat. Had Marisia been so happy to visit her mother and father she didn't notice the picture? She suffered during the war as much as David and Jacob. Marisia witnessed executions and atrocities. The portrait proved to him Germans continued loyalty to the biggest wolf, the beast who made the destruction of every Jew in the world his life's work.

Fright and anxiety on David's face were too much for Mela. "We're going for a walk along the river."

Alex thrust his hands in pockets of his heavy wool coat, trudging through drifts and low-lying fog. "It's only for a short time," he said, as if reading David's mind. "The British made many arrangements with people like the Stampfs. They need them. We need them, and they can't do us any harm." He stood overlooking frozen Havel River. "Germany's like the river. When it melts, hurt and hate will flow to the sea."

"Will things change?" David wondered.

"As much as I believed the war would end and Nazis defeated. Takes time. Challenges make life interesting. Overcoming challenges makes life worthwhile."

"You've done so much for me and Geniek. I want to do something for you."

"A little child and his brother survived and flourished when others gave up. A skinny, handsome, wise young boy gave us love when it was in short supply. What more can you do?"

"Remember how you enjoyed hearing Ella Rosenberg read fairy tales? You liked the ones where the younger brother made believe he killed seven giants, married the princess, and lived happily ever after in a castle," laughed Mela.

Fog slowly evaporated, revealing a red-brick fortress with two turrets on the opposite bank. "It's a castle like in the stories!" David shouted. "Can we go in?"

"Only if you break the law," said Alex. "It's an old prison."

"Are bad people inside?" David asked, thinking about robbers and gangsters in movies at the Łódź movie theater.

"Behind bars, Tadek, where they can't hurt anyone."

"What's going to happen to them?"

"Remember what Major Grishen told us? The Allies will place Germany's leaders on trial for . . . what did he call it? Crimes against humanity."

"Will they send Mr. and Mrs. Stampf to prison?"

"They didn't do anything to anyone," answered Mela.

David took her hand. "They didn't help like you and Papa Alex." Mela dusted snow from a bench, wiped away her tears, and sat down.

"Promise we'll go somewhere else next time. I don't want to see that ugly picture again," begged David.

"There's a café on the riverbank. Good food will put you in a better mood," said Alex.

British flags flew outside a *hofbräu*. British soldiers drank beer and played cards. Alex, Mela, and David looked over the German-language menus. A portly waiter, with a black moustache curled at the ends, bowed slightly. He rattled off the day's specials. It didn't surprise David when Alex responded in German.

The Gestapo and Polish policemen barged into the Roslans' small apartment in Warsaw, searching for hidden Jews. Alex broke into German, cleverly disarming them with vodka. The intruders left, stumbling drunkenly to the street. "I hope the prisoners stay in a dungeon for the rest of their lives. I hope they grow old and die without seeing sun or flowers or snow in winter," David said solemnly. "Why did we live when so many died?"

"No one can answer. Someday, you and Geniek will give gifts to the world and make us proud," Mela said.

David warned Jacob about the portrait. "It's almost the same picture on your stupid stamp."

"Ever touch the replacement, I'll get even."

"All you can think about is how much your stamp is worth. The Stampfs are Nazis."

"The Geniek and Tadek Junior Military Police will handcuff the Stampfs and march them to prison," Jacob said sarcastically.

"Suppose they find out we're Jewish."

"Mama and Papa Roslan won't say anything. We'll be out of here in no time."

"Wait until you see the picture," grumbled David.

He stomped out of the dormitory. Broken people wandered through rubble of an apartment building, searching for anything of value to trade for food. David had an eerie feeling they still pledged allegiance to the defeated leader who plunged them into a senseless war and committed suicide rather than face justice.

He trudged through snow to camp. Alex and Mela surprised him outside the dormitory. "We should have warned you about the picture. Grown-ups don't realize how things affect children," said Alex.

Mela kissed David. "You don't have to go there again."

David nodded. "It hurt, Mama."

"No more hurt," said Mela. "We're having a picnic. Find Marisia and Jacob."

Black bread sandwiches with jam, a flask of hot tea, fresh-baked *vatrushka* covered the table. Sunshine broke through for the first time in weeks.

"It's impossible to know how long until it snows or rains again," said Alex.

"We're celebrating. Papa and I filled out forms asking permission to go with you to Palestine."

"Mama is very excited. She wants to see the land of Jesus," said Alex.

"You don't believe in Jesus," David reminded him.

"Someone who comes back from the dead? No. If God exists, He wants us to fix the world and make it better. Religious hocus-pocus doesn't impress me."

"That's what I think," said Jacob. "What kind of god let our aunts and grandmother suffer?"

"Out of the mouths of babes. The children have seen too much misery to believe in God waving a magic wand, making miracles," Alex stated.

"They follow your lead, Mr. Roslan. One day, who knows?" said Mela, "They'll agree with me."

"We've been having this same argument from the first day we met—when we were children. It doesn't make a difference.

I love Mama and I hope Mama loves me, or it's been a long disagreement without purpose."

They gave the children boxes of pastries and kissed them goodbye. "We'll see you in two weeks," Mela said to David.

"We'll go to a café for breakfast. Maybe have pancakes with strawberry jam," promised Alex.

"What about me?" asked Marisia.

"Next Sunday; special lunch. Rouladen, spaetzle, red cabbage. And for Geniek? Ice fishing on the Spree with David. He showed what a good fisherman he was in Łódź."

Chapter Twelve

The Little Colonel

Frost etched fanciful images on dormitory windows veiling another numbing day looming ahead in Berlin. Beds creaked; grunts and murmurs from sleepy boys bounced off walls and ceiling. David dressed in his warmest clothes, trying not to make noise. Picking up rubber overshoes, he slipped outside and pulled them on without buckling the flaps.

David slogged through swirling snow to the dining hall. Boots slapped his legs, metal snaps ringing out a merry sound. Aroma of bread baking in wood-burning ovens mingled with the scent of a tall fir tree in a corner.

"In a few days everyone's taking turns decorating our Christmas tree," one of the cooks said in Polish.

"I don't celebrate Christmas," said David.

"You don't have to. Everyone took turns lighting candles for your holiday. Decorate the tree so other boys and girls can enjoy it."

It was true. Marisia lit Hanukkah candles. Boys and girls took turns over the eight-day holiday, lighting a candle every day. During the darkest days in Warsaw, Mela insisted on going to church with her at Easter, returning with toy sheep woven from straw for David and Jacob.

"Remember when the British officer said your candles light the darkness? It's the same when we light candles on the tree. We have different ways of celebrating. It all comes down to people doing the right thing," the cook said.

David finished breakfast by the time Marisia and Jacob joined him. He shrugged into his coat, pulled on a woolen hat, and snapped closed the buckles on his boots.

"Ready to brave *Das Hundewetter*?" asked Jacob pompously.

"All of a sudden you're talking German."

"They have good words for some things. Take a look outside. *Das Hundewetter* means horrible, howling-like-a-dog weather."

"Ignore your brother. He's showing off." Marisia took off her bright orange-and-white wool scarf and gave it to David. "To keep you warm." She shoved a small paper bag into his pocket. "I saved cookies."

Jacob wagged a finger in his face. "There won't be any left by the time you get off the train."

A sister bundled in a knee-length macintosh swept through doors at the far end of the dormitory. "Time to go!" She walked David to stairs leading up to the platform. "Remember, get off at Spandau station." She checked her watch. "Get along. You don't want to be late."

Gaunt, vacant-eyed passengers, huddled in ragged coats and jackets, scarves pulled over their heads, sat silently in the car. Frightened, David snuggled into his coat, tightened Marisia's scarf around his neck, and closed his eyes to protect himself from the world outside hoping he wouldn't have to feel Hitler's piercing eyes in the Stampf's framed picture boring into him.

Alex and Mela warmed their hands at a metal barrel filled with charcoal embers where chestnuts roasted beneath Spandau's rail stop. Rivulets of melted snow spread under the hot container, freezing into delicate six-armed icy starfish clinging to cement.

"Buy chestnuts for David," said Mela. The vendor wore a soiled gray Wehrmacht winter jacket. Alex hesitated. "Don't ask for his history. Just buy them," ordered Mela.

The train clattered to a stop. Passengers trooped down to ice-covered streets, scattering in the face of glacial winds.

"He's not here. Maybe he missed his train. Maybe he's sick and couldn't come," Mela called out.

"The camp would have contacted us. The next train's due in thirty minutes. We'll wait." Half an hour passed. Another train screeched to a halt. "This isn't like him," Alex said anxiously.

"Remember Łódź when he went off by himself?" Mela reminded Alex. "Who knows what can happen in a big city. Everything and everyone can be bought and sold. I'm contacting the camp."

Twenty minutes later, the train carrying David ground to a shuddering stop, jolting him awake. He rubbed sleep from his eyes. Passengers scurried out of the car. Dense snow hid the ironwork rail station and city beyond.

A conductor tapped him on the shoulder. "Hoch. Hoch. Ende der Zeile." He pushed David through the door.

Gray skies obscured the sun. The eight-year-old lowered his head, plunging through freezing wet snow clinging to his clothes, seeping through gloves, and under his scarf. Dodging under a rail trestle to escape heavy snowfall, he emerged next to a newspaper kiosk. A short, stout old man, with a white beard, wearing a heavy coat and wool cap, purchased tobacco, tamping it into his pipe. In the matchlight, he looked like pictures of avuncular St. Nicholas tacked on camp walls.

David followed him onto a train, hoping it traveled back to Spandau station. He wanted to ask the stranger for help, but the old man fell asleep, snoring into his beard. David waited for the next stop. The train skidded to a halt on ice-coated rails.

A heavy-set scowling Russian officer, wearing a tall, gray wool hat, long dark coat with gold braid on its shoulders, high black boots, and a pistol in his holster, stomped into the car, barring David's exit. Doors slammed shut and the train lurched forward.

A boisterous pack of Soviet soldiers, with rifles slung over their shoulders, staggered aboard at the next stop, passing bottles of vodka to each other. A young soldier stood on a bench, threw his hat in the air, singing with drunken enthusiasm. His comrades stamped and cheered him on.

The officer marched in front of them, feet apart, thumbs in belt. "Attention!" he bellowed in Russian. The troops leaped to their feet, shouldering their rifles. Their faces paled under the glare of the angry, unyielding captain. "You disgrace your uniform and the Red Army. We did not conquer Hitler and Nazi Germany by playing the fool. You will comport yourselves as warriors, not *p'yanitsy.*"

David spoke enough Russian to know he called them drunkards. The captain's blazing eyes terrified David as much as they did the soldiers. He squeezed into a seat at the other end of the carriage. Hail clattered overhead, bouncing off tracks, striking against the misty windows.

The train groaned to a stop between train stations. Darkness crept over the city. Silhouettes of a railway crew scraped ice off tracks. The train rolled forward slowly through a blinding snowstorm. Obscure ice-coated signs alongside tracks gave David no idea where he was or where the train headed. He waited uncomfortably until it groaned to a halt at the end of the line. Vodka-besotted soldiers scrambled off the train disappearing in the blizzard.

The formidable officer paused in the carriage doorway, muttering angrily to himself. He pulled his lambswool collar tight and stepped into the storm. David followed, hoping against hope he could find a way back to the camp. The captain lit a cigarette and strode into the night, leaving a trail of cigarette smoke mingling with his frosty breath.

An ornate iron fence surrounded a gray, granite three-story house with a steep roof surmounted by a red flag with a hammer and sickle under a star. The captain thumped hard on the door. "Proklyatiye, yest' kto-nibud' zdes'?" he spit out in Russian. Some of the first Russian words David learned were blasphemous oaths, and the captain did not hesitate to use them. "Goddamn. Is anyone here?"

David ran, slipping on dark, frost-covered sidewalks. Biting wind howled down empty streets. His hands froze and feet cramped. His eyelashes grew heavy with frozen tears. He pulled Marisia's scarf over his nose and mouth, feeling frigid fingers tightening around him.

Music floated faintly out of the dark shadows. A shaft of light spilled through leaded windows of a small beer hall. Two young men, one playing an accordion, the other a harmonica, sat before a crackling fireplace. David pushed through the door, clutching a chair against a wall. Warmth from the blazing fire brought life back to his hands and feet. The tall, thin accordion player ran fingers up and down the keyboard and sang a German drinking song. His friend joined him on the harmonica. The bartender thumped beer steins down. People, living ordinary lives, unmoored David. He cried uncontrollably.

"My singing's so bad it made the kid cry," the accordion player said. "Hey, little man, what's the trouble?" he called in German across the room.

His face, the image of captured Wehrmacht herded past the barn on the way to Łódź, panicked David. He slipped off the chair, looking for a place to hide. The musicians pulled him to the fireplace.

"Where the hell did you come from?" asked the harmonica player.

"Hitler promised to exterminate the Jews," said the old lady in the park, venom in her voice.

David had to think fast. "I don't understand," he answered in Russian.

"A Bolshevik kid. Anyone here speak the language?" the accordionist asked.

"A little. Helps when they come in for beer," said the bartender. He knelt next to David. "Who are you, little fellow?"

The only Russian name he remembered was the soldier in Kaminsk. "Vasily," David murmured.

"How did you get here? You have a family?"

David searched for an answer. "My mother died a long time ago. My father went away." It was the truth. He hoped they believed him.

The harmonica player threw his overcoat around David's shoulders. "You can't wander around in this blizzard."

"What the hell do you want us to do?" asked the accordionist.

"Take him to the Soviet garrison."

They walked David to a brightly lit fenced area. A Russian sentry stepped out of the guardhouse. "State your business," he demanded.

The accordionist pushed David forward. "We found this Russian boy; calls himself Vasily. Too damned cold to leave him on the streets. Take care of him until his family's found— if he has family."

"This isn't an orphanage. Get the brat out of here," ordered the sentry.

"He's Russian. You're Russian. He doesn't speak German."

"What's going on?" boomed a voice out of the dark. A sergeant appeared and stopped at the sorry sight of David's cheeks burned red from numbing cold and frost clinging to eyelashes. "Holy Mother and the saints. You had a rough time."

The sergeant pulled a blanket from the guardhouse and wrapped it around David's shoulders. He brought him to a brick barracks. Troopers gathered around a black stove drank tea from a large brass samovar.

"Who's your prisoner?" yelled a soldier.

"None of your fucking business."

"You can't bring a kid in here without an explanation."

"A couple of Germans found him freezing in the snow. Says his mother and father are dead. Reporting to Colonel Kozlovsky. No more questions."

The sergeant poured a cup of tea, dropped in a lump of sugar, placed a jar of jam and loaf of bread on a table. "Don't pay attention to my men. To them, you're a curiosity. Matter of fact, to me you're not what I expected in my barracks. Eat as much as you like, Vasily. My commanding officer will figure out what to do with you in the morning." He pointed to an empty cot. "Sleep here."

Hot tea warmed David's frozen fingers. Heat from the stove made him drowsy. He took one more sip, clutched a blanket to his chest, and fell asleep.

"Little Vasily; time for mess."

David bolted up. Vasily, the soldier who gave him the book. The name he adopted. A tall, broad-shouldered officer wearing a cap with gold braid and a heavy gray overcoat stood over him.

"I'll take charge of the boy. Tell my steward to prepare a healthy breakfast for me and the lad," he ordered the sergeant.

The tall, imposing officer led David to a large office with windows overlooking a garrison blanketed with snow. A long table held a feast the boy had never seen: eggs, sliced white fish and salmon, fresh-baked bread, a pitcher of hot chocolate.

"My name is Maxim Kozlovsky, colonel and commander of Rifle and Mechanized Unit. You know all about me. What about you? They tell me you have no family."

The colonel's gold-braided uniform, polished black boots, forest of medals stretching across his chest overawed David. His fear of discovery as a Jewish boy, not the Russian orphan Vasily, made him stutter.

"No family."

"Two words. Eating a good breakfast will grease your vocal cords." The colonel poured hot chocolate and shoved a plate of eggs across the table. "Eat up, boy. You're as thin as a pole. Good food, yes? No charge, courtesy of the Red Army. This war hurt so many people. Especially children. You're my guest, Vasily." Kozlovsky called his aide. "Tell the sergeant I'm driving back to my apartment with the boy."

They traveled along bomb-shattered boulevards to a gray, granite building. "We're here," said the colonel

"I thought all soldiers stayed in camp."

"He has a voice and is quite curious! Officers have certain privileges."

The colonel's housekeeper, Frau Helga, a stern, determined woman, opened the door with a curt nod. David peeped out from behind her employer.

"Who is this child, Herr Colonel?"

"Wandering streets. An orphan."

"Believe *ist nicht hier oder dort*. Report him to civilian authorities. They know how to handle such cases."

"Frau Helga, do your job, I'll do mine. Vasily needs a place to stay, good food, and from the way he looks, decent clothes. He'll use the other bedroom."

"Colonel is always right," she said imperiously.

Elegant furnishings filled the high-ceilinged apartment. Sparkling crystal chandeliers cast rainbow prisms along walls. A photograph of a woman on the mantelpiece of a marble fireplace sat between tall porcelain candlesticks holding candles decorated with entwined purple, white, and yellow flowers.

"My wife, Valentina. She lives at home in Moscow. You know Moscow?"

"I've seen maps. I can read."

Kozlovsky smiled. "Smart boy. The photograph was taken at our dacha, a cottage in the south. I haven't seen her in a long time."

David reached out to touch a flower on one of the candlesticks. The colonel carefully pushed his hand away. "They're very old. The apartment belonged to the Rozenzweigs, a Jewish family sent to a concentration camp. A Nazi Generalmajor occupied it. When we liberated Berlin we found it just as it was left.

A chill ran through David. Family fates played out over and over wherever he turned. Gutgeld, Landau, Rosenzweig. "Did they have children?"

"Two daughters. We found records listing the family transported to Treblinka."

"How many children do you have?"

"No children. You have no mother or father. Let's not talk about sad things." He turned David around. "You need a hot bath and decent clothes."

Alex barged into the camp administration building, followed by a distraught Mela, and visibly upset Jacob. A guard pulled out a pistol.

Lt. Smyth-Martin stepped out of his office. "Put away the weapon, corporal." He switched to Polish. "Stand down, Mr. Roslan."

"My husband doesn't mean harm. He's upset. We're all concerned," explained Mela.

Alex collapsed on a chair. "I apologize. Please help us."

"What's this all about?" asked the lieutenant.

"Tadek left camp yesterday to visit us in Spandau. He never showed up."

"You need to notify us through regular channels."

"We've been taking care of the boy for a long time. We can't lose him now."

The lieutenant sifted through a file. "Tadek. I have it here. His birth name David Gutgeld, eight years old. I was the admitting officer." He thumbed through papers. "We received information the boy's father lives in the Palestine Mandate. Several rather important individuals support your request for immigration."

"If we can't find the boy, it won't do us any good. Heavy snow fell last night. He could have had a serious accident."

"Tadek—David—is like one of our children," said Mela desperately.

The officer glanced at a pile of papers and files on his desk. "We can't stop everything to find one little boy. With all you people trotting into Berlin every day, we barely have enough time to get our work done. You must wait your turn."

Alex's face flushed red. "All you people? Jews? Survivors? Those of us not English, American? We're talking about an eight-year-old under our care for almost four years."

The lieutenant pounded a rubber stamp on forms. "We'll make a note of it and see what we can do."

"A note does nothing for 'us people,'" glared Alex.

"We do not take missing children lightly." He glanced at the file once more. "We have your location and will be in touch as soon as possible."

"My brother is lost in Berlin. You need to help right away!" Jacob shouted.

"These cases usually end when the boy or girl finishes exploring and returns."

"Not if he freezes to death," insisted Jacob.

"I will not wait for camp authorities. We need to work together to find Tadek," said Alex when they returned to the dormitory.

"A café had a notice in its window from someone looking for a missing woman," said Marisia.

"Make posters offering a reward. We'll place them in every damned British, Russian, and American shop," said Alex.

"I know where we can find cardboard for posters," announced Jacob.

They cut out pieces from boxes they dragged into the dormitory from a garbage heap. "What should we write?" asked Marisia.

"Lost Boy, David Gutgeld, eight-years-old, light-brown hair, brown eyes. Scar over right eye," replied Alex.

"He wore a wool cap and my orange-and-white scarf," said Marisia.

"Add the description to the poster, along with a reward and camp phone number." Alex turned to Mela. "How much do we have in the money box?"

"About ten thousand German marks."

"Five thousand marks will get attention." He picked up a container of crayons used in the dormitory. "Use red-and-blue crayons. The brighter the better."

Alex wrote the first one with the reward in large numbers. "Make at least fifty posters."

"We need to write them in English, German, and Russian," suggested Jacob.

"I know who can help!" shouted Marisia. She ran out of the dormitory, returning with three nurses.

"We heard David went missing. He's a clever boy. I wouldn't be surprised if he shows up soon," said one of them.

"We don't have time for 'maybe' or 'could be,'" said Alex.

"My parents emigrated from Poland when they were quite young. Polish was my first language," said a nurse. "Edwina speaks Russian. Sylvia's the German specialist."

Tears flowed down Alex's cheeks. He turned away, embarrassed by his sudden show of emotion. "Get to work. Tomorrow we drop off as many as we can." He snapped his fingers. "Every day, the Stampfs buy a newspaper. It has a section with notices from people searching for missing relatives. What's the most popular paper in Berlin?"

"*Berliner Zeitung*, the Berlin Daily News," Sylvia said.

"How do we place a notice?" asked Alex.

"All you have to do is call. It's a free service."

"Call for me. Your German's much better than mine. Use the information we wrote on the cardboard."

Sylvia called and everyone pitched in. Mela hugged the nurses after they finished. "We'll never forget you."

From sunup to sundown they plodded through snow, along wet streets, down dank alleys, tacking reward notices on streetlamps and fences. Store-owners placed the signs in their shop windows.

"All we can do is wait," said Alex.

"And pray," Mela reminded him.

Kozlovsky towed David into the camp's dusty tailor shop and accosted a sergeant bending over a humming sewing machine.

"Sergeant Nesterov," the colonel called.

He turned off the machine and saluted. "What can I do for the colonel?" he asked, curious why his commanding officer had a boy with him.

"Make little Vasily a uniform."

Alex rejected his school uniform. He hated the red kerchief. David believed his rescuer wanted to make him a Pioneer.

"What style?" asked the tailor.

"Like mine. Every button, every seam—all the same."

"What about medals?" asked the tailor with a smirk.

David had a hard time believing the colonel's request. The officer winked at the boy. "Leave them off until he earns them. Make sure he gets a nice pair of leather boots."

"We don't have them in children's sizes."

"Get the bootmaker busy," snapped Kozlovsky. "I want everything by the end of day."

The tailor shrugged his shoulders. "By the end of the day," he repeated with a sigh. "Who reimburses my department?"

"It's official business. Vasily's a Russian orphan. We have an obligation."

"But a uniform?" snorted Nesterov.

"There's no regulation it can't be a uniform. If necessary, I'll pay from my account. Get to work. That's an order. His field uniform can wait a few days."

Nesterov grumbled under his breath about a custom-made uniform and boots for delivery by the end of day.

"Let's find one of those famous German toymakers. One or two must still be around," the colonel said.

An old man wearing a leather apron matching his weathered and wrinkled face led Kozlovsky and David down wooden steps into a basement filled with a jumble of small wooden cars, electric trains and tracks, dolls, toy guns of all kinds, and an assortment of large and small balls crowding dusty shelves.

"Very nice collection," noted the colonel.

"I thought I would go back in business after the war," said the toymaker.

"Lucky for little Vasily." Kozlovsky turned to David. "Pick out whatever you want."

The old man smiled. "You're lucky to have a father like the colonel."

The idea Kozlovsky was his father made David uneasy. Having a uniform and receiving gifts didn't seem important. The Roslans expected him to show up. Marisia and his brother would panic if he didn't return to camp.

"When will I get paid?" asked the toymaker as Kozlovsky lugged a box of toys up the stairs.

The colonel handed him a voucher. "This is as good as money in the Russian sector."

The toymaker turned the document over. "Won't buy bread."

Early in the evening the tailor arrived at the colonel's apartment with a miniature version of his uniform, right down to belt and boots. David's dream of wearing military regalia came true.

Kozlovsky held them up to the light. "You like it? Of course you do." He placed the uniform in a closet. "First, clean up. Then we'll try it on."

"Off with your clothes," ordered Frau Helga.

David jumped back. "I don't need any help. I can wash myself."

"A real man, Frau Helga. Make sure the tub has hot water."

Frau Helga peered at the scar on his forehead. "Where did you get that?"

David shrugged his shoulders. "In a fight."

Vasily Grossman's advice to make the scar a romantic and danger-filled story, would appeal to girls. One look at Frau Helga, David knew she didn't have one spark of kindness in her.

Life with the Roslans had been spent in bombed-out apartments. Water came from wells. The British dormitory had cold showers. The colonel's apartment had cold and hot water and electricity. A hot bath seemed an unreachable luxury. Steaming water relaxed David. He lathered his arms and legs with rose-scented soap drying himself with a large, luxurious soft towel embroidered with "Hotel Adlon—Berlin."

David poked his head out of the bathroom door. "I need my clothes."

Frau Helga handed him underwear, socks, and newly tailored uniform trousers. The colonel waited with a white shirt, blue tie, and officer's jacket.

David held up the bath towel. "Are we in a hotel?"

"The Adlon was almost destroyed in the last weeks of the war. We found those towels in the basement and decided victors deserve a bit of luxury."

The colonel helped David with his boots and shoulder belt, tucked in his shirt, knotted his tie, and planted him in front of a full-length mirror. "Now you look like a loyal soldier of the Soviet Union."

A gold-braided cap completed the miniature officer's outfit. David looked different on the outside. Inside, he yearned for his family.

The colonel snapped a salute. "Little colonel, my first command: eat dinner."

Frau Helga served roast duck with mashed potatoes and gravy, freshly baked bread, and a small crock of rarely seen butter. Russia treated its officers like kings, thought David, while bands of people roamed streets and alleys searching for scraps of food.

After dinner the colonel sipped a glass of vodka. David waited to see how he reacted. The colonel smacked his lips, enjoying the drink. David tightened his stomach, remembering the incredibly hot, harsh taste.

"My wife will like you." Kozlovsky waved his arms around at the apartment. "You could have anything you desire."

David had no idea what the colonel meant. He spent his short life running, hiding, and surviving with unconditional love from Alex and Mela. They gave him a home and protection. His Polish name concealed his identity. Vasily tore him away from everyone he loved. The colonel had no idea the boy he believed was a Russian orphan who endured insufferable hardship in the Warsaw Ghetto.

Frau Helga cleared her throat. "Colonel, may I speak with you?"

The officer looked menacingly at her. "I'm trying to explain things to Vasily, Frau Helga."

"A moment, Herr Colonel," she insisted. They stepped into the kitchen. "You don't know this boy. You can't take him with you," she whispered.

"It's none of your business. Vasily needs a home. Besides, he's intelligent."

"Too intelligent," she smirked. "How did he get to Berlin?"

"It's good you speak Russian, or I would fire you."

For the first time in three years David had new clothes and abundant food. They could not take the Roslans' place, or Jacob's and Marisia's companionship. The deep emotional impact of separation hit hard. He broke into heaving sobs.

The colonel glared at Frau Helga. "Enough. You frightened the boy." He put an arm around David's shoulder. "Go to bed; get a good night's rest. You have nothing to worry about."

Lt. Smyth-Martin held a poster offering a reward for information about David. "Your plan worked, Mr. Roslan. We received calls from across the city and outlying areas."

"He's been found?"

"Unfortunately, people thought they saw him or heard about someone who found him. None of the sightings were true."

"It's been almost two weeks!" cried Jacob.

"Berlin's in ruins and so many are missing," lamented Mela.

"He could have been kidnapped, or worse," insisted Jacob.

"For all we know, the person who found him is looking for us," said Alex.

"I should have treated my brother better. It's my fault he's missing," cried Jacob.

"Don't blame yourself. We'll find out what happened once he returns," said Mela.

"What if he never comes back? What will I tell my father when we reach Palestine? I'm supposed to look after him. All I did was make fun of Tadek or ignore him."

"Maybe someone found him and took him home. Once they see the posters or newspaper notice, they'll call," said Marisia.

"An alert sent to all British units in Berlin requested they be on the lookout," said Lt. Smyth-Martin.

Alex buried his face in his hands. "How could this happen after all we've been through?"

In the Russian garrison, Kozlovsky paused in front of a mirror. He smoothed David's military jacket and adjusted his shoulder belt. "Stand up straight. Look in command. This morning we review my troops," said the colonel. "Now, let me see the salute I taught you." David turned to the colonel and saluted smartly. "Excellent. One day you'll make a great officer."

Men stood at attention next to Harley Davidson chain-driven cycles, low-slung Indian motorbikes, and British Slopers given to the Soviet military when Germany invaded. The colonel and David, wearing matching heavy gray over-coats, marched onto the parade ground to inspect his mo-tor rifle unit. The colonel's troops stood steadfast as bitter wind swirled across the river. After inspection, they saluted David.

"I have a surprise," said the colonel.

Troops hunkered behind sandbags. Shots rang out; machine guns chattered. David covered his ears. Smell of gunpowder and the sound of gunshots brought back horrific memories of Nazi soldiers firing indiscriminately at anyone resisting the occupation.

"It's frightening, but you'll get used to it soon enough," said the colonel.

"I don't want to get used to it," David whispered, wanting to run from guns and fighting.

In the evening, the colonel opened a cabinet taking out a rifle. "This weapon helped free the world of Nazis. I call her my Simonova." He ran a hand over the polished wooden stock and grip. With a flick of a finger a chamber opened over the barrel. "Ten bullets go in here." He closed the chamber, lifted the rifle to his shoulder, and aimed. "Don't worry. It's not loaded. I wouldn't want to put holes in the wall." The colonel handed the rifle to David.

"You killed people?"

"Before they had a chance to kill me. Now it's up to politicians to keep the peace. I only hope they know what they're doing." Kozlovsky locked up the rifle. He pulled out a chessboard. "No one gets hurt in this game of war." Kozlovsky held up the tallest piece. "The goal is to checkmate the king. He's never captured, only threatened with capture. It's a tactic we use in the army. The threatened enemy always tells you what you want to know."

David made mental calculations, determining how many moves he needed to checkmate the colonel's king. After a few games David understood the basics. Chess became a nightly activity after dinner.

During the week, the officer and young boy lunched in the officers' mess at the commissary. Women behind the counter gave David extra fruit and cake. They whispered to the colonel, "He's adorable, but so serious."

On weekends, Koslovsky's fellow officers joined him in the Unter den Linden apartment to drink and listen to phonograph recordings of Russian songs. When they discovered the boy could do complicated mathematics, they congratulated Kozlovsky on his decision to adopt him. David panicked. It was the first time he heard the word "adoption." Did they hear something he hadn't known about?

"He'll make you proud one day," one of the officers commented.

The attention, good food, and warm bed meant nothing when David heard the news. The colonel had no right to take him away. The Roslans couldn't give him the things Kozlovsky offered, they gave him something more precious. He owed his life to them, and they gave him their devotion.

With the colonel busy in the garrison, Frau Helga treated David as if he were a prisoner. He feared telling Kozlovsky the truth would send him and his family back to Poland. His eight-year-old imagination conjured Alex's description of prison, work camps, and Siberia. By keeping silent about the truth, he faced a dilemma. The colonel planned to scoop him up and present him as gift to his wife.

During his third week with the colonel, Frau Helga walked quickly along an icy street toward the apartment. She pulled her thin cloth coat around her shoulders to keep out the chill. She was confident Kozlovsky had grand plans for a sly little boy who, she was convinced, planned to steal the silver.

The smell of fresh coffee drifting out the door of a small café pushed these suspicions to the back of her mind. She purchased the *Berliner Zeitung* and a cup of coffee with a big dollop of cream. Sitting alone with no obligations for few minutes made bearable the next eight hours catering to the colonel and the strange orphan who was too smart for comfort.

Reports of tensions between the Russians and Allies over control of Berlin and East Germany dominated the news. Gossip held more interest for Frau Helga. A notice in the missing persons section caught her attention. A reward of five thousand marks for an eight-year-old. She could use the money to return to her family farm in Hoppenradde, far from the Russians.

The housekeeper folded the paper and read the notice about a boy named David with a scar on his forehead, last seen wearing an orange-and-white scarf. Frau Helga found her secret treasure. She looked at her watch. The hands had not moved since she left her miserable flat. According to the clock on the café wall, she was almost thirty minutes late.

Frau Helga hurried out of the café. The colonel stood on the corner, next to his official limousine. David peeked out a car window. "Inspection was over half an hour ago," the colonel barked at her.

"I'm sorry, Herr Colonel. The train was delayed because of snow."

"Another few minutes and I would have taken Vasily to my staff meeting," he growled, putting on his overcoat.

"When will you return?" the housekeeper asked.

"Three, four hours." He opened the car door. "Frau Helga will take care of you, Vasily."

She slammed the apartment door closed and whispered, "I know who you are—David."

He looked at her with wide, frightened eyes. "How did you find out?"

"I'm not *dummkopf*. You know what that means?" David shook his head. "Stupid. Just because I keep house for a colonel who wants to adopt a boy called Vasily who isn't an orphan and isn't Vasily doesn't mean I'm stupid. Am I correct, little David?"

He grabbed her skirt. "Don't tell the colonel. Please."

"I'll get you back where you belong," she said abruptly. "Be a good boy and you won't have to worry about a thing. I'm going to help you."

"I want to go home!" pleaded David. "I don't want this uniform. I want my own clothes, my own family."

Frau Helga dialed the phone. "I saw a notice about a lost boy named David. He's with me. Pick him up before it's too late."

"Too late for what?" asked Lt. Smyth-Martin.

"Before he's taken to Russia."

"We need corroboration you're telling the truth."

"Speak to the child." She handed the phone to David.

"Hello," he said, his voice quaking.

"Is this David?" asked the lieutenant.

"Yes."

"Your last name?"

"Roslan . . . Gutgeld. Please come and take me back to Mama and Papa Roslan," he implored.

"I need an address."

"Frau Helga knows." He gave the phone back to the housekeeper.

"I am employed by Colonel Maxim Koslovsky, commandant of a Soviet garrison in Berlin. The boy lives in his apartment at the corner of Unter den Linden and Friedrichstrasse in the Soviet zone. The colonel plans to adopt the boy. He believes he's a Russian orphan."

Lt. Smyth-Martin called Alex and Mela with the news. "We're sending a car for you." He ordered an aide to immediately take an official car, drive to Spandau, pick up the Roslans, and return posthaste to camp. Alex and Mela stormed into the administration building on their arrival.

"Where is Tadek?" Alex demanded.

"He's been taken by a Soviet officer, Colonel Maxim Kozlovsky." Smyth-Martin paused for a moment. "His housekeeper reports the colonel wants to adopt him."

"This is unbelievable. We have to get him before it's too late!" cried Mela.

"You must go with us, lieutenant," Alex insisted.

"I need permission from my commanding officer."

Alex pulled himself up to his full height. "We waited a hell of a long time for you to act. Take charge, dammit."

Smyth-Martin backed against a wall. "Paperwork takes time"

"A Soviet officer wants to adopt Tadek and take him to Russia. He doesn't belong there. He belongs with us. He's not Russian. What happens when the colonel discovers he's Jewish?"

The lieutenant sat down at his desk. "If my superiors discover what I did there'll be hell to pay."

"And if we don't go, Tadek ends up in Moscow."

Frau Helga checked the clock. "It won't be long." David broke into tears. "What are you crying about, *Kleiner Jude*? Your mother and father will be here soon."

"Suppose they don't come on time. You have to help me."

She poked his chest. "I let you go, I'll have my own troubles. The colonel will fire me. I won't have a job. He doesn't always pay on time, but there's always food I take home to my family. And what about the reward? I don't suppose you have money for it."

Time crept by. Each second a minute. Each minute an hour. David had visions of the Roslans celebrating his bravery. After all, he refused to divulge his relationship with Mama Mela and Papa Alex out of fear Russians would put them all in prison.

After what seemed like an eternity the Roslans and a British officer appeared at the door. David rushed into Mela's arms. She looked bewildered at the sight of his uniform. "What are you wearing?"

"The colonel made it for me."

"Well, Mister Colonel Tadek, what do you have to say in your defense?" Alex asked.

David experienced intense guilt for making everyone upset. This was not the hero's welcome he expected. "I was afraid if I told the truth we would all be sent back to Poland."

"You almost ended up in Moscow," said Alex.

"I didn't know how to get back to you. I was scared." David wiped tears from his eyes.

"We'll discuss it when we have more time." He looked over Frau Helga's shoulder. "Where is this Colonel Kozlovsky who wants to take my boy to Russia?"

"He's not here. Leave before he returns," urged Frau Helga.

"His clothes," Mela demanded.

The housekeeper returned with David's belongings. The door banged open. Maxim Kozlovsky confronted a British lieutenant and very angry man and woman. Frau Helga retreated into a corner. "What is the meaning of this?" the colonel roared.

"What is the meaning of even considering taking our boy to Russia?" Alex said, a knife edge in his voice.

Kozlovsky glared at Frau Helga. "Your boy? Vasily told me he's an orphan."

Although a head shorter than the colonel, Mela glared at him menacingly. "We won't let you or anyone else separate us."

Kozlovsky pushed past her. "Vasily, tell them who you are."

Color left David's face. He tried to talk. His voice cracked.

"Don't be afraid. Tell him your real name," coaxed Alex.

"David Gutgeld."

The colonel blanched. "I don't understand."

"He and his brother lived with us for almost four years after escaping the Warsaw Ghetto. They are like our own children," explained Mela.

"Jewish?" asked an astonished Kozlovsky.

Alex placed a protective arm around David. "Is Gutgeld Jewish enough for you? We're taking him home."

"Wait a moment," interrupted Frau Helga. "My reward."

"Reward?" Kozlovsky's interest was piqued.

Alex shoved bills into the housekeeper's hand. The colonel looked at the wad of money.

"This reward you offered for Vasily—David's return was meant for the person who found him?"

"Correct. Frau Helga called us . . ."

"Not to put too fine a point on it, I rescued him from freezing to death on the street. I gave him a warm bed, fed and clothed him at great expense. I should share the reward," Kozlovsky said, pacing the room.

David looked up at the colonel. "I thought you liked me."

The colonel shrugged his shoulders. "I do like you. You're a very clever, good-looking boy. Business is business. The uniform cost a fortune. I fed you for three weeks. Bought you toys."

"Whatever it cost, it's worth having Tadek back with us," said Mela.

"This is between you and your housekeeper," said Alex. "I suggest you split the reward with her." The housekeeper peeled off half the bills, handing them to the colonel who glared at her. Frau Helga quickly gave him all the money.

The colonel smiled at David. "We had good times. Remember me next time it snows."

David walked into the night with Alex and Mela. A beautiful blanket of snow draped ruins of the war-torn city.

Jacob and Marisia bombarded David with questions. He swore escape was on his mind every minute. He told them the colonel or his housekeeper never let him out of their sight. "I made up a story about being Russian because I didn't know what those German boys might do. Once I was in the Russian camp, suppose they caught me lying?"

Jacob pointed a finger at his brother. "Put you against a wall and shoot you."

Marisia poked Jacob in the chest. "Don't pay Geniek any attention. He's glad you're back."

"He wanted to go to Russia with his uniform and play soldier," said Jacob.

"Not true!" yelled David.

"How did the colonel treat you?" asked Marisia.

"He liked Vasily. The minute he found out I was David he changed."

"You had nice clothes and plenty of food to eat. What did you do for three weeks?" asked Jacob.

"Helped the colonel review his men."

Jacob laughed. "A real little colonel. Bet they saluted, making you feel important. You're back with us and no more saluting."

"I learned to play chess," announced David.

"A game you never played."

"The colonel taught me. I beat him once."

"I bet he lost on purpose."

"No he didn't. When I called 'checkmate' he looked surprised, then told his officers. They challenged me to games every time they came to the colonel's apartment."

"You're going to tell me you always beat them as well?" said an unconvinced Jacob.

"Sometimes. When I won, they gave me extra dessert."

Nurse Penny joined them. "Mr. and Mrs. Roslan will be here soon."

"This is going to be the best day of my life," smiled David.

"It won't be when Papa gets through with you."

"You're not funny. What if the colonel took me to Moscow? How would you feel?"

"Don't believe a word about the way he felt. Geniek was so angry, he yelled at the British officers. He took charge of making posters. It was his idea we print them in English, Polish, and Russian. We worked together putting them up on walls and in store windows," said Marisia.

"You're my brother. What was I supposed to do?" murmured Jacob, self-consciously.

Alex pushed through the door, followed by Mela. "There's news! Tadek and Geniek were granted permission for Palestine."

"Did you get your papers?" asked Jacob.

"We're still waiting for certificates from the British. It takes time. The commander of the camp gave me a copy of a letter your grandfather wrote in 1942. The high commissioner of Palestine requested entrance permits for your grandmother and your aunts, along with both of you and Shalom, in March 1943; but it was too late," said Alex. "We also have another letter from your father to the American State Department. In the event we can't travel with you, he requested the United States give us immigration status for America."

"You have to go with us!" cried David.

"Don't jump to conclusions. Everything's a possibility. In the meantime, I made arrangements to travel into the American zone. Get your bags packed."

David dragged his duffle to a corner of the dormitory and sat on it, staring out the window. The future he dreamed of when the Roslans brought him to his father might never happen. "I'm tired of running from one place to another."

"You could have gone to Moscow with the colonel, 'Vasily'," Jacob uttered sarcastically.

"It's back to arguments. We all want to finish our journey. It's a long time but eventually we'll find peace and quiet," Mela said.

A packed British lorry took them to Potsdamer Bahnhof where they boarded the westbound train. It rolled past icy rivers and streams, through ravaged villages and towns. After two hours it stopped near a British depot. A convoy of American trucks rolled in to refuel.

Alex hefted Mela's duffel over one shoulder and his own duffel over the other. "Stay here," he said when they reached street level. He crossed the road to the convoy's commanding officer.

"Great. Another one who can't speak English." The captain blew a whistle. "Malkowski, front and center."

A tall, broad-shouldered soldier jogged to the captain and saluted. "What can I do for you, sir?"

"You're a Polack. Translate for me."

"What do you need?" Malkowski asked Alex in Polish.

Alex grasped the soldier's hand. "Where does your family come from?"

"Chicago."

"I heard of Chicago. America. Where in Poland did your family live?"

"I don't know. My grandfather never talked about it."

"What's he saying?" asked the captain.

"Asking about my family," Malkowski answered in English.

"We don't have time for social chit-chat. Find out what he wants."

"I think he's Jewish. Something about immigration," the soldier reported.

"We're driving to Hanover. He can catch a train to Frankfurt. A large DP camp's in operation."

Alex waved for Mela and the children to join him. Soldiers searched through their backpacks and gave candy and chocolate bars to the children, who grabbed as much as they could carry. Instead of gray Russian uniforms, American soldiers wore olive-colored winter jackets and khaki or fatigues with camouflage patterns. A Black driver wearing the same uniform as other soldiers hopped out of his truck.

"We're taking these folks to Hanover, Jenkins," said the captain.

David stared intently at the driver. "What's your problem, kid?" Jenkins asked in English.

David whispered to him in Polish.

"Malkowski, I need help with the kid's lingo!" Jenkins shouted.

"He wants to know if you're a slave," laughed Malkowski.

"Yeah. A slave to good old Uncle Sam."

"It's above my pay grade," said Malkowski.

Jenkins sat on the back of the truck. "How did a little Polish boy learn about slaves?"

David explained to Malkowski he read *Uncle Tom's Cabin*, given to him by a teacher in Łódź.

"Ain't no Uncle Tom. I'm a soldier in the United States army," said Jenkins. He looked David squarely in the face as Malkowski translated. "When you grow up, tell your friends you met a Black man who drove you to safety. Black folks were once slaves like the Israelites who came out of Egypt, just like your family when Nazis occupied Poland. You tell them what I said. Might make all the difference in the world."

David had no idea what he meant by Israelites and Egypt, except that it had to do with Jews enslaved by Germans.

Jenkins opened a canvas flap in back of his truck and pulled down a ramp. The Roslans and children clambered into the cargo space. Jenkins tossed their duffel bags inside, slipping David an extra chocolate bar. Jacob and Marisia attacked their chocolate with relish, remembering from birthdays or after dinner with friends before war shattered lives. David enjoyed treats brought by Major Grishen and his wife, ice cream served in the dormitory, cakes and pastries in the Russian camp. Jenkins's kind gift fell into a separate category, a link between enslavement and freedom.

"You think the children can overcome everything they faced?" Mela wondered.

"No one will forget," replied Alex.

The truck braked to a halt near Hanover Hauptbahnhof, the city's central station. A bronze equestrian statue of Ernst August, king of Hanover, stood undamaged among the terminal's ruins.

An anxious, impatient crowd wearing frayed jackets and coats scarred by stitches from yellow six-pointed stars they ripped off, stepped over broken glass and bent metal beams in their harried rush to board the southbound train.

"Don't let the look of the place fool you," said Malkowski. "Brits and Americans have the trains running. You'll have delays on account of ruptured tracks. Frankfurt's a four- or five-hour ride."

"Don't forget me," Jenkins whispered to David.

David spoke the two English words he knew. "Thank you."

People dashed from one group to another, yelling, "*Amcha, amcha!*" "What are they shouting?" Alex asked an elderly man wearing a shabby jacket.

"*Amcha*, 'your people' in Hebrew. If someone recognizes it, he's a Jew who might find relatives." The old man shook his head. "Always reaching for hope."

"Is the next train going to Frankfurt?" asked Alex.

"So I've been told. See the clerk inside for a ticket. Germans are good at organizing, whether its running trains on time or killing us."

A short, portly, ticket master wearing an ill-fitting blue uniform with dull brass buttons stood behind a counter near the platform. "Courtesy of the American army," he murmured, handing tickets to Alex.

A train whistle set off a frenzied surge toward the tracks. Doors hissed open. Passengers pushed and shoved to get inside. Alex forged ahead, securing a place in the crowded car. Younger men and women carrying suitcases and bundles precariously perched atop carriage roofs. They rolled south, past forests of frost-covered fir trees, muddy fields scarred by tank treads. Ancient towns dating to the Fifth Century CE, shattered, their broken stone bridges crossing rivers clogged with ice floes. Everyone seemed brighter and more alert as they moved farther and farther south. Late in the afternoon the train pulled into the vast, undamaged Frankfurt terminal.

Passengers rushed to counters staffed by United Nations Relief and Rehabilitation representatives in gray-and-blue uniforms, who patiently took names and handed out numbered tags indicating their assigned camps in the American zone.

"Roslan, Alex Roslan, Poland," Alex informed an administrator.

"Family?" she asked.

"My wife, Amelia. Daughter, Marisia. Two Jewish boys, Jacob and David Gutgeld."

"Where did you pick up the children?" the administrator asked.

"They lived with us since 1943. First Warsaw, then Łódź and Berlin."

She made notes on a form. "Sounds like something out of a movie."

"We did what was necessary."

"Your bus leaves in thirty minutes for Zeilsheim camp where you have been assigned." The administrator gave Alex a numbered tag. "Show this to the bus driver."

Chapter Thirteen

Torch of Liberty

An eight-story building spared by Allied bombers rose out of Frankfurt's desolate ruins. Surrounded by over fourteen acres of parkland, it was one of the foremost architectural triumphs of Germany's Weimar Republic. Its impressive rotunda and exterior emulated an ancient temple. A green flag emblazoned with the emblem of the Supreme Headquarters, Allied European Forces (SHAEF) fluttered over the dome. It bore the Latin motto: "Viglia Pretium Libertatis." Protect the Price of Liberty.

Passengers aboard the army bus cheered, buoyed by the sign on the front of the building with the SHAEF insignia: a rainbow above a flaming sword. Unknown to survivors passing the facility, it had been headquarters of IG Farben, the chemical company that manufactured deadly Zyklon B poison used in Nazi extermination camps. The bus traveled west to the eighth-century village of Zeilsheim. Its cobblestone streets and steep-roofed, whitewashed, half-timbered houses had escaped the war's devastation. Church steeples rose at one end of the town. Beyond the church, an American flag and a banner with a Star of David between blue stripes flapped in the winter wind. Over a guard gate, a sign read: "UNRRA TEAM 503, Zeilsheim." Refugees hesitantly disembarked from the bus staring in disbelief at a Jewish pennant flying over German soil.

An American sergeant checked tags. Speaking Polish, he ordered everyone to line up at the administration building.

The Roslans inched forward slowly reaching a woman in uniform who wrote their names in a ledger.

"Considering you have been guardians of David and Jacob for quite a while, we consider you a family unit," she informed Alex, placing a form on her desk. "This lists everyone in your party." She handed Alex five cards with their names written out. The cards stated they were part of UNRRA Team 503. "These cards will allow you to receive food and other supplies. Photos will be taken in the billeting office to my left for permanent cards. Within a few days, interviews will be conducted in order to determine status."

Mela slipped sweaters she purchased before they left Łódź on David and Jacob. "I want you to look as if you're on vacation."

"This doesn't look like the Łódź carnival," said Jacob.

"There's an old saying: 'don't judge a book by its cover.' Look at the flag. It's almost like being in America," said Alex.

After the photographer took identification pictures, another UNRRA representative escorted the Roslans and the boys to a military truck. "As the non-Jewish guardians of Jacob and David, we assigned a home for you outside the camp. It's a short walk to Team 503. You'll find bedding, towels, plenty of soap, and best of all, hot water. We also provided food for several days. A brochure on the kitchen table has our weekly schedule. The objective is to have you become an integral part of the Zeilsheim family for as long as necessary."

Icicles hung from eaves of a two-story wooden house surrounded by snow. It had a working kitchen, a living room with a sofa and chairs on the first floor; two bedrooms and bathroom with tub on the second.

"I suggest your family join us in the camp dining room this evening. Tomorrow you'll have an opportunity to get your bearings. Anytime you need assistance, look for someone wearing an UNRRA uniform."

After dropping their duffels on the floor, the Roslans inspected the rooms, marveling at their cleanliness; they turned water on and off, adjusting a heater.

"I'm hungry," complained Jacob.

"Let's find the dining room. I could eat a horse . . . except Princess Roza," Alex said with a grin.

He and Mela led the children to the camp gate. Guards gave directions to the dining hall packed with refugees. Murals of farmers and fairy tale characters covered two walls. A colorful painting on another wall illustrated a traditional European Passover Seder.

Servers behind hot food counters doled out roasted meat, steamed turnips and potatoes, chicken soup, and fresh-baked bread.

"I don't see milk for the children," Mela whispered to Alex.

A woman leaned over. "Not tonight. We keep kosher. Tonight, the *mashgiach* comes in, scrubs down everything with lye to *Kasher* the counter. Tomorrow, they serve dairy and vegetables."

"Thank you," said Mela, who had no idea what the woman talked about, except that it seemed hard on kitchen help.

"Roslan!" Dov Lazik stood at the other end of the table.

"I thought we left you in Łódź," said Alex.

"A cousin in America sponsored me. I have a teaching job waiting for me at university in America—Pennsylvania," explained Dov.

"Never thought we'd see you again. What are you doing in a Jewish camp?" Ida Lazik asked Mela.

"We kept Tadek and Geniek's identity secret. With Jews hunted down after the war, we couldn't take chances. We applied for permission to take them to their father in Palestine."

"The French have a saying: 'Plus ça change, plus c'est le même chose.' The more things change, the more they stay the same. Anti-Jewish riots erupted in Polish cities and towns. Survivors killed in Kielce, Łosice, and Klementów. A meeting of the Polish Peasant Party cheered a resolution thanking Hitler for murdering Jews. We have no future in Europe. Your boys have no future here," said Ida.

"A war was fought to free us, and once it's over, bitter, hostile, poison-filled snakes crawl out. Thank God we won't have to witness it much longer," Mela said, steel in her voice.

"When things got bad my mother used to say, 'Sher tzu zein a yid,' it's hard to be a Jew. At least no one's coming after us in Zeilsheim."

At the other end of the table David sat with Shimon picking at his food. "What's the matter? This looks like a great place."

"I'm going to America with my grandparents," said Shimon.

"I want to go to America."

"What about your father?"

"He's a ghost, a phantom who left us to the Germans."

"All the time we went to school and played in Łódź my parents fought with Jewish partisans." He broke down and cried. "They were killed fighting in a Polish forest two weeks before Germany surrendered. I don't know where they're buried." Shimon pushed away the plate of food. "Someday I'll come back and find them."

Every person David met traveled his or her own road. Shimon and his grandparents would find a new life in America. Jacob dreamed of the father who abandoned him. At every turn, David's wish to remain with the Roslans seemed hopeless.

Men and women worked full time in the bustling camp, patching, sewing, making new clothes out of old cloth for refugees to wear on their journeys across continents and oceans. Customers lined up outside a Rumanian bakery. A Hungarian hairdresser opened for business on a corner. On another corner, cobblers mended broken boots and shoes. The coffee shop bustled as a lively center where *Unterwegs*, the newspaper written and published in the camp, was scoured daily for gossip; news on how to make travel arrangements, 'bintel briefs,' artitcles and letters about families in Palestine, the United States, and Great Britain.

Next door, Jewish GIs had rebuilt a barn to house a synagogue and schoolhouse flying the American flag.

"Do we have to go to school?" David asked Mela.

"It depends on how long we have to stay. Would you like to go?"

"Is it going to be like Łódź?"

"A school for Jewish children? Not likely. If you want to attend, Papa and I will see what we can do."

An UNRRA representative, holding a large folder, waited at the cottage. He gave the Roslans and children their permanent identification cards with photos, Displaced Person identification card numbers, with the camp's name. "Sign your ID cards. Do not hesitate to ask for information from any United Nations personnel or representatives of the Jewish Agency."

David's registration number was 896190.1645. His Displaced Person identification number 11.02100351. Impersonal, demeaning numbers almost the same as those tattooed on thousands who walked out of concentration camps.

He turned over the card and saw his name, not a number: "David Gutgeld." He picked up a pen to sign but could not move. Writing "David" instead of "Tadek" felt as a betrayal of the Roslans.

"What are you waiting for? Sign the card," urged Jacob. The look in his brother's eyes was frightening. He leaned close, whispering, "You'll always be Tadek inside. Geniek is also part of me. We have to take one step at a time, learning we're part of Papa Alex and Mama Mela, as well as the Gutgeld brothers.

In tears, David signed, one letter at a time. Each stroke peeled off pieces of the shell guarding him against tragedies of bigotry, death at the hands of those seeking to destroy the surviving remnant. Shadows of wary years facing imminent death slowly dissipated as the aroma of roasted vegetables, white borscht, cabbage, fried onions, and *karpatka* baking wafted from the cottage oven.

"Mama's cooking up something special to celebrate the Laziks' trip to America. You'll have a chance to say goodbye to your buddy, Shimon," said Alex.

They gathered around the table, toasting Dov's good fortune. "Nothing like this in Pennsylvania!" he exclaimed.

"Keep it as memory of our time together," said Mela.

"We walked a very long, hard road," Ida reminisced. "In the end, we survived. Shimon and Tadek became friends."

"Your grandson taught Tadek how to steal rides on the tram," laughed Alex.

"Shimon took me to Poniatowski Park, where Papa caught a hen."

"The one you wouldn't eat," Alex recalled.

"I saw it alive. Then it was roasted."

"Chickens lay eggs. Chickens get roasted. It's Mother Nature doing her best to keep us healthy."

"If I ever eat chicken again, I'll remember that poor hen," said David.

"In America you can eat chicken, fish, strawberries, peaches all day long," Dov said to Shimon. "School is open to everyone, rich and poor, Jew and Gentile. As my grandson, you can go to university without paying tuition. Who knows how far you'll go?"

"I want to go to America one day," said David.

"America may be the golden country, but nothing compares with Mela's baking," Dov said, eating his third piece of *karpatka*.

He wrote down his address in Pennsylvania. They hugged, kissed, and cried. Shimon shook David's hand. "Wish I had known you were Jewish."

"Would it have made a difference?"

Embarrassed, Shimon looked away. "I said things about you that weren't true."

"Papa Alex warned me and my brother never to do anything to make people suspicious."

"You did a good job. Glad it's over?"

"Not over for me. We live in a neighborhood with German families. Who knows how they feel?"

"My grandfather said you'll be leaving soon. Maybe we'll meet again."

After the Laziks left, David sat on the front steps of the house, listening to tree sparrows chip, chip, chipping in snow-blanketed trees. A blonde, blue-eyed boy approached David. "Ziehen Sie einfach hierher?" he asked.

David searched for words and phrases similar to Yiddish he picked up in Berlin. *"Ich verstehe nicht,"* he said haltingly.

The boy patted himself on the chest. "Manfred." Then he pointed at David.

The old fear reared its head. "Tadek."

Manfred ran into his house. What would his parents or other children do if they found out their neighbors were Jews? Manfred's parents might have a picture of Hitler in their home. Perhaps they secretly hoped every Jew in Germany would leave.

Chanting echoed over the camp. David joined a somber crowd marching to a stone monument surrounded by dark green branches. A bearded man wearing a purple-and-white prayer shawl and black satin head covering read an engraved plaque on the monument: "'In Memory of Our Loved Ones, Six Million Murdered during the Nazi Regime'. Together we say Kaddish. The Mourner's Prayer is written in Aramaic, the common language of the ancient people of Israel. Not about death. An affirmation of faith in the future."

David ran home. "Why did they put up a stone to six million people who died? Who were they?"

Jacob took his brother aside. "Remember the radio news about Buchenwald? Germans tried to murder every Jew in Europe. If it wasn't for Mama and Papa Roslan, we'd be part of the six million."

"There's time for Tadek to learn what happened. He's had enough for one day," interrupted Alex.

It wasn't enough. David wanted to write Rebekah Landau's name on the monument so others would know about the short life of an innocent girl.

Hiding behind Polish identities, Jacob and David picked up German. Adults gathered around makeshift fires, roasting chestnuts, drinking beer, conversations veering into antisemitic rants. Boys and girls repeated tropes learned from parents about secret Jewish cabals. They repeated assassinated Gestapo chief Reinhard Heydrich's nonsensical mantra "Jews are nothing but Bolsheviks hiding in tuxedoes."

"They are puppets. Parents pull strings, and children say what they're told. One day, the truth will come out. Don't fall into the trap of trying to convince them with facts. Right now, they believe," warned Alex.

To neighborhood boys and girls, Geniek and Tadek were Polish refugees who had remarkable talents for numbers. Before long Jacob tutored older children. Younger students flocked around David. Zeilsheim's camp school took a back seat. They had everything they needed from Manfred and his friends' books, notes, and tests.

A fierce, blinding November snowstorm hit Zeilsheim, shaking dormitories in the camp and homes in the village. In the morning sun broke through morning clouds, revealing crystal snow, tree branches sparkling with ice, winter birds clacking pinecones.

Schools closed for road clearance, freeing students to race through the woods. They collected winter heather, spiky winter thyme thrusting long stems through snow, and fir branches to decorate window frames.

Manfred packed snow in a circle. "I claim Zeilsheim in the name of Kaiser Manfred. Who wants to be captain of the other army?"

"Our fort will never be taken!" Jacob shouted, helping Marisia build walls out of snow blocks.

Snowballs rained from both sides. Boys and girls dodged around snowdrifts, huddling together making strategic decisions about where and who to pelt with their ammunition.

Alex surprised David when he joined his team. He lined up a dozen snowballs. "Here's how you beat them. Believe it or not, I once built snow forts and had snowball fights. Start throwing and don't stop."

A wet ball of snow smacked Alex in the chest. He fell down, jumped to his feet, pelting Manfred and Jacob, who objected it wasn't fair for a grown-up to help. Marisia shoved a handful of snow down the back of his jacket. He dumped a bucket of frozen ice over her. She shrieked at the top of her lungs, shoving him down, proclaiming, "I am St. George and you are the dragon."

"St. George was a man!" yelled Jacob.

"Then I'm St. Georgette."

Roads cleared and their brief vacation ended. Manfred and neighborhood children returned to school. David and Jacob were invited to join a nascent junior soccer league in camp. Refugees gave them envelopes from America, Palestine, South America, and Europe. They steamed off stamps with images of Abraham Lincoln and Einstein, a fourteen-cent stamp with a Native American in full regalia, a three-cent stamp honoring General George S. Patton who led the Third Army to victory over the Nazi horde.

On days when temperatures dropped below freezing, David plied Jacob with questions about math and science as they played chess in front of the cottage's roaring fireplace.

Winter gave way to blue skies of spring. Grass sprouted between patches of melting snow. Flocks of birds returned, filling the forest with song. The camp organized an adult Zeilsheim workers' soccer team, Hapoel Zeilsheim, with former sports stars who survived concentration camps. The Jewish Agency and Joint Distribution Committee provided uniforms as an added incentive to engender loyalty from refugees for the team.

For a few hours, cheering crowds forgot they were in a sea awash with uncertainty. American GIs helped establish a new league in Frankfurt, Eintracht Frankfurt. The Roslans traveled with the children over twelve miles in camp buses to root for their local team. Adults drank steins of beer and munched salty pretzels. Youngsters filled up on Kosher sausages and cola drinks, courtesy of the Allies.

Track-and-field competitions sprang up during spring and summer. The boys eagerly devoured *SportSchau* (Sport Look Magazine), memorizing statistics, information about teams, players, and track stars. Determined to become a famous soccer player and compete on track teams, David ran on village streets and paths through the forest every day.

After a sprint, he returned home to find a young man, Baruch, representative of Team 503 council in Zeilsheim, holding a meeting with Mela, Alex, and Jacob.

"You and Geniek have been invited to attend a special dinner tomorrow evening in the camp to celebrate Passover," said Alex. "When I first came to Warsaw a friend invited me to a Passover meal. I'll never forget chicken soup with dumplings . . ."

"Matzah balls," explained Baruch. "Always made for the holiday."

"A special dish with carrots, sweet potatoes and a little touch of honey," Alex remembered.

"Tell David the part about wine," insisted Jacob with a sly smile.

David glared at his brother. Jacob never missed a chance to remind him of the vodka episode in Kaminsk.

"For this one night you're allowed to drink. It's supposed to be four glasses of wine… or grape juice," Baruch suggested.

Round tables covered with white cloths replaced long communal benches in the camp dining room. Large plates in the center held symbolic objects—roasted shank bones, roasted eggs, parsley, horseradish, haroset, made with nuts, apples, red wine. Almost the entire population of UNRRA Team 503 crowded into the dining room.

Baruch handed Jacob and David small satin caps: "To wear for reading the Haggadah, the story of our freedom from slavery." Every seat had booklets in Hebrew, Yiddish, and Polish. Baruch held up a large, hard round cracker. "This is matzah; special unleavened bread made just for Passover. We're forbidden to eat regular bread for eight days. You'll hear why in a few minutes."

A woman at the head table with a colorful kerchief around her head, wearing a long skirt down to her ankles stood and lit two candles. "Bless candles with me." Other women and girls stood, their faces beaming with joy, and covered their eyes, chanting in Hebrew.

"I remember our grandmother lighting candles on Friday nights," Jacob whispered to David.

"What are they saying?" asked David.

"I wish I knew."

A short man, barely five feet tall, also stood at the head table. "For those who do not know me, I am Rabbi Jacob Kret," he announced in a strong voice belying his height. "In 1940 I fled from the Nazis to Lithuania, where I believed I would find haven. Russians had other ideas. They shipped me to a Siberian labor camp."

David sat up. What would have happened if he had gone to Moscow with Colonel Koslovsky? He might have been sent to Siberia, the place Alex called 'a prison with no walls.'"

"Good came out of evil." The rabbi held the hand of the woman who blessed the candles. She smiled, her gray-tinged brunette hair peeking from under her kerchief. "Chana and I labored together on the frozen steppes of Siberia where we married. With her encouragement and strength, I survived. Thank all of you for making this Passover, our first since liberation, a unique moment.

"We begin with the traditional Haggadah. However, when we tell the story of our slavery in Egypt, we will use Musaph l'Haggadah Shel Pesach arranged and illustrated by concentration camp survivors author and poet Yosef Dov Sheinson and artist Miklos Adler, as a reminder to every generation pharaohs, kings, and dictators attempt to erase us from history. We thank the United States Third Army Corps for printing the supplement. Our escape from Egyptian bondage in the distant past is intertwined with our escape from Hitler's slavery. We, the surviving remnant of Jewish life in Europe, need to tell our story and the story of ancestors who overcame oppression."

Third Army Corps' capital *A*, encircled by red against a blue background, decorated the supplement's cover, along with a woodcut of a door labeled "Brause Bad"—shower-bath. Sketches of concentration camp victims, fire, smoking chimneys surrounded the door. Baruch translated a sentence in Yiddish printed in the center: "We were slaves to Hitler in Germany."

The rabbi and congregation chanted rituals, blessings, journey to Egypt, enslavement by Pharoah. Neither David nor Jacob understood the occasion's solemnity. Baruch handed a sheet of paper to David. "Traditionally, this part is always read by the youngest person at each table. We wrote the Hebrew in Polish so you could read it aloud."

David expected dinner, not a chore with words making no sense to him. "I can't do it."

"Of course you can. You're a smart young man."

Jacob smiled at his brother's frustration and unease. "What would Mama and Papa Roslan think if you turned down this fantastic opportunity to be a star."

"Shut up," whispered David, gulping down a glass of water. After struggling through the exercise, he dropped into his chair, exhausted and humiliated.

A woman leaned over and kissed him. "Beautiful."

"What did I read?" David asked Baruch.

"The first question you asked was, 'Why is this night different from all other nights?'"

"What's the answer?"

"Every generation responds in its own way."

"Turn to the new supplement," announced Rabbi Kret. "It expresses our torment under Nazi tyranny and humiliation." His voice rose with fervent intensity:

> "When the righteous among the nations of the world saw that Hitler decided to exterminate Israel, their great assembly came together and out of their great sorrow decided to keep silent. And the righteous among them said: 'How can we in our weakness save Israel from the hands of the evil man? Perhaps this is the hand of God and who are we to interfere in

the conduct of this world?' And the people saw how Israel swam in their blood and they passed by. And the children of Israel groaned and cried out but were not heard. And they cried out to the Lord, the God of their fathers, who saw their suffering and oppression, and their cry went up. And that man of evil, Hitler, made instruments of destruction which he sent across the sea, killing many."

The Black army truck driver, Jenkins, told David his own people were slaves who found freedom. Jews were slaves to Hitler just as Blacks were slaves in America. He hung on to the rabbi's words:

"Finally, the enemies of that man of evil grew indignant, and they girded themselves and unleashed against that man of evil and his people great wrath, rage and fury, disaster, and a band of avenging angels, afflicting them with two hundred and fifty plagues. And God hardened Hitler's heart. And instruments of destruction, and eagles of iron and copper showered fire and brimstone upon his garrison cities, killing man and beasts alike. And a multitude of chariots, as plentiful as the sands of the sea, swept across the land of the evil man, and destroyed him, and the Holocaust survivors were rescued and redeemed. When peace came down on earth, the people of Israel were gathering. The surviving remnants came out of caves, out of forests, out of death camps, and returned to the land of their exile. The people of those lands greeted them and said: 'We thought you were no longer alive, and here you are, so many of you.' And they sent the survivors all sorts of messages, telling them to leave the land, even killing them. And the people of Israel ran for their lives; they sneaked across borders only to be robbed of everything they had. And they

> abandoned their homes, and they saved their lives,
> and they went up to our Holy Land, Eretz Yisrael."

The Haggadah burrowed into the deepest part of David's heart. He and his brother, the "surviving remnant," escaped, crossing borders to safety in a camp where everyone dreamed of new lands, where they could live free from fear.

Rabbi Kret held a large round matzah above his head and intoned the blessing over bread. They ate their meal of freedom and wandered back to the cottage.

"Had a good time?" asked Mela.

"It was terrible. They forced me to read words I didn't understand," David complained.

"It wasn't so terrible. Dinner was delicious," said Jacob.

"You sat in your chair waiting to eat."

"He loves to complain and moan. When he finished, people cried as if they found something lost."

"Memories. Of another time, when they told stories, celebrated without worrying about a knock on the door. They drank wine after years of deprivation remembering what they lost for five, long, terrorizing years," said Alex.

"Doesn't make me feel better," said David.

"After a good night's sleep you'll feel different," said Mela.

Before they slept David turned to his brother. "You didn't make it any better by laughing at me."

"I couldn't help it. You looked as if you were going to faint."

"I hope you have a terrible night." David pulled the blanket over his head. He fell asleep with the rabbi's reading swirling through his head: ". . . And they sent the survivors all sorts of messages, telling them to leave the land, even killing them."

Chapter Fourteen

A New Year

Atrocities, bitterness, hatred in the harsh, angry language of the Passover service, written and illustrated by survivors of Dachau and Theresienstadt, paralleled demonstrations by Zeilsheim's refugees. They marched, holding banners, signs, flags, comparing the oppressive Egyptian pharaoh thousands of years ago with inhumane treatment of Jews under brutal Nazi occupation and British quotas limiting immigration to Palestine.

Refugees' newfound freedom released sources of strength within the displaced and dispossessed marching, condemning Great Britain's callous refusal to recognize torment and agony of those who witnessed systematic efforts to destroy an entire people. Chants rang through the air. Hopes and dreams ended with the cry, "Am Yisrael chai"—the people of Israel live.

Zeilsheim village boys and girls, oblivious to protests, played on narrow lanes and ran over meadows, their lives far removed from the angry turmoil behind camp gates.

Manfred trotted over to David. "We're playing hide-and-seek."

"Who's 'it?'" asked David.

"Last one in. You. Count to twenty, then find as many of us as you can."

Everyone scattered into trees, gardens, behind houses. In twenty seconds David calculated how many players hid within fifty feet. After ten minutes he located almost all of them.

"You're a great player. If you were in the army, Jews wouldn't have a chance to hide and escape," laughed Manfred.

The unconscious, insensitive comment, shook David. Manfred asked Tadek for help with his math. Changing names flipped a switch, making him blind to boys hiding behind Polish masks.

Jacob and Marisia emerged from the forest, carrying pinecones to decorate. The idyllic moment countered David's shock at latent antisemitism infecting youngest Germans growing up under Hitler's domination.

"Where's Papa Alex?" David asked.

Jacob dropped pinecones on the kitchen table. "The camp called them to pick up immigration papers."

"It's wonderful! We'll go with you!" cried Marisia, spontaneously hugging David and Jacob.

Order restored until Mela and Alex returned from the camp. Their usual enthusiastic nature vanished. "The news is not good for Mama and me. The British denied our request to accompany you to Palestine," said Alex.

"We're all going to America!" shouted a relieved David. His enthusiastic expectation pained Alex. Overwhelming political forces exerted intense pressure, crushing dreams of a new, exciting world.

"The British have strict rules about who can immigrate to Palestine. They turned down our request. It's beyond my power. Your father made arrangements for you to join him in Palestine," Alex said, his voice trembling with emotion.

This disappointing news jolted David. "I won't go. Take me to America. I promise to be good. I won't give you trouble."

"Your father and grandfather want what's best for you," Mela said.

"You're what's best for me. I don't know the person you call my father."

"Why do we have to go to Palestine?" asked Jacob unexpectedly.

"You always wanted to go," Marisia said. "What changed your mind?"

"We're supposed to go together," insisted Jacob.

Marisia clenched her jaw. Unexpectedly, a volcano of rage erupted. "Mama and Papa are not your family. For years I watched how they took care of you. When you were sick they gave you the best food. I ate leftovers."

"We're best friends. What's happened?" asked Jacob.

"You and your brother always come first. It isn't fair."

Mela clasped arms around her daughter. "You have to understand what your brothers experienced."

"I went through the same thing!" she cried. "When neighbors reported us to the Germans, I thought they would kill us. When the police and Gestapo raided our home, I thought it was the end of my life. When Jurek was murdered, part of me died." Marisia's outburst surprised David. She was his older sister. Was it all an act?

Dismayed by his daughter's outburst, Alex tried to calm her down. "You're not angry with Geniek and Tadek. You're angry about being torn away from your brothers. New countries, bright futures. You told me you wanted to marry Geniek when you grew up, remember?"

Jacob looked as if cold water splashed over him. "No she didn't," he insisted.

"It was a long time ago. I was young and stupid," said Marisia.

"You're still young, and no one in this house is stupid. We have to get on with our lives," said Mela.

"It's because I'm a girl. But I'm your daughter. You are my mother and father."

"You have a big heart like Mama. We don't favor one over the other. But Tadek and Geniek carry a very heavy burden. They also lost a brother and if we hadn't taken them in, they would have become part of the six million. When we first brought Geniek into our lives you were ex- cited because he was your age."

Marisia sniffled and pressed against her father's chest. "Cry, cry, it's all right," said Mela. "They will never take Jurek's place, but the three of you are like sister and brothers, friends who walked out of fire stronger and braver."

Marisia turned to David and Jacob. "I didn't mean what I said."

"Did you really want to marry Geniek?" asked David.

"He is good-looking and very clever." Marisia smiled.

Jacob's face reddened. "I wish everyone would keep quiet."

"Feel better?" Alex asked his daughter. She nodded and sat between the boys. "We're not leaving Geniek and Tadek in Zeilsheim. Mama and I stay until the boys receive their travel arrangements. Another few weeks or months won't make a dif- ference. For the time being, let's make the best of things."

Fearing Alex and Mela's steadfast support would vanish once they separated, drove David into a dark tunnel of anxiety. He ran blindly into the forest. Branches slapped his face and arms. Thorn bushes gouged his legs. He tripped over a fallen log, crashing into a brook. Sopping wet, shivering in night air, he leaned against a moss-covered tree and cried.

Nightingales and warblers sang. Owls hooted across the valley. Stars, constant as David's life was unsteady, peeked through trees. He trudged out of the woods wanting only to sleep in the safety of his bed. Mela took one look at his wet clothes, bloody legs and arms, and quickly cleaned him. "Punishing yourself won't help, young man."

"I didn't feel anything," he said. "I wanted to smell the trees and listen to sounds of the forest, from the loudest raven to scared rabbits."

Mela made him a cup of hot chocolate. "We all have memories. Some good, some, well, not so happy. Don't let bad times blind you."

"Why did you save me and Geniek?" he suddenly asked.

Taken aback, Mela sought an answer. "Papa Alex did something very brave. A Jewish ghetto fighter took him behind the walls where he saw children starving, dying. He said we need to do something, anything. A friend knew your family and knew the Gutgeld brothers needed help. As simple as that. If anyone asks the same question, we have an answer. When it looked impossible, we saved a life," Mela said matter-of-factly. "Wherever you go, you will always be in our hearts. In the morning we'll talk about what's waiting ahead."

Months crawled by while mountains of paperwork made their circuitous way through British bureaucracy to approve entry into the Mandate. With all the strength he could muster, David hoped they would deny the request. Alex and Mela would have no choice but take him to America, an almost mythical country.

Talk of separation never arose again. The family traveled to Frankfurt for the regional soccer championship. David joined the junior league Hasmoni team, named after the dynasty established by the Maccabees and organized by men who played in Poland, Russia, Hungary, and Czechoslovakia. Daily workouts, weekly games, and camaraderie with team members overcame David's apprehension.

Summer slowly turned to fall. Organized games ended. David brought home a trophy after his team won the junior league championship. The Roslans beamed with pride when the camp held a celebration for the team. Jacob toasted his brother with a glass of grape juice. "To my brother, the champion goalie." Hasmoni continued practice twice a week.

At the end of September 1946, a flurry of activity surrounded the synagogue. Crowds of men and women crammed inside the small building. Chanting and singing echoed along lanes. Zeilsheim celebrated Rosh Hashanah, the Jewish New Year.

At soccer practice a week later, on October 5, the ball rolled to the edge of the playing field. A man wearing a prayer shawl and head covering stopped it with his foot. The children yelled for him to kick it back. "Not today," he responded. "It's Yom Kippur, the most solemn day in the Jewish calendar. In here," he ordered, pointing to the door.

The boys dutifully entered the building. A velvet purple curtain with a large Star of David hung in front of a cabinet against the far wall. Two tall candles in silver holders flickered on a table draped with a white satin cloth. Rabbi Kret, who led Passover services, wore a tall white hat and loose white robe and chanted a sad, tearful dirge.

David felt as awkward in the midst of the solemnity as he did at the Passover service. Papa Alex equated religion with unrealistic outcomes. He had more confidence in science rather than a god ruling the universe, a tenet proved over and over under Nazi occupation.

Herschel, one of David's teammates, nudged him. "Let's get out of here." The soccer players inched their way off chairs and, one by one, tiptoed into sunlight and fresh air.

"Herschel, I've been looking for you," called a woman.

"It's my mother. I hope she doesn't make me go back," he said.

She handed him an apple and bread. "You don't have to fast on Yom Kippur until you're thirteen."

"How come your mother didn't show up?" Herschel asked David.

"I told her I would come home for lunch," he prevaricated, feeling guilty.

They picked up their game. David played as if he fought for another championship. He raced toward a line drawn in the earth representing the net, kicked the ball, and scored. His team whooped and hollered. Flushed with excitement, he raised his arms and yelled, "We won!"

"Such a noise on the holiest of days!" exclaimed Rabbi Kret, standing in the doorway. "Come—come all of you. It's time to close the gates of heaven."

David expected to see real gates creaking. Except for candles melted halfway down, everything looked the same. Rabbi Kret opened a book. "We are counted one by one and asked if we have been good and kind and respectful of others. Have we given charity even when our own pockets have holes? Have we fed others by dividing our daily food in half? The gates of heaven close, a new year begins. Our journey begins in this camp. We choose our road. As it is written: 'See, I have placed before you good and evil, and you must choose good.'" The rabbi looked up. "One of you boys, tell me when you see three stars in the sky."

David ran outside waiting until three stars flickered on the eastern horizon, minute flames in the dark-blue sky. He stood in wonder as the majesty between dusk and night with its blanket of stars emerged engulfing the lonely trio. Coming out of his momentary trance, he remembered his mission and waved to the rabbi.

"The gates close for another year. New beginnings. Let us make this coming year one of peace and forgiveness."

Kret lifted a large ram's horn over his head. "We are not permitted to blow the Shofar, the ram's horn, when Yom Kippur, the Day of Atonement, falls on Shabbat, as it did this year. At sunset, Shabbat ends. Listen with your heart to its pure call ushering in a New Year of harmony."

A trembling blast rose into the air, resounding off walls, wafting into the heavens. The primeval sound stirred a profound feeling in David, one he would recognize years later as an uplifting call to repair the world. The last note reverberated, rose steadily, thinned out, and faded away. A hush fell over the room. No one moved until the rabbi stepped off the platform and made his way to the door. The North Star blazed in the sky, centering David in a changing world.

Alex met David head-on the moment he returned from camp. Without warning, he slapped his face. It was the first time Alex physically punished him. "Berlin all over again. You never learn. We looked all over the camp. We asked children in the neighborhood if they saw you."

Mela's eyes bored into Alex. "Never, ever, strike one of the children again or you will have me to reckon with." She knelt next to David. "We thought someone kidnapped you."

Alex sobbed uncontrollably. "I'm sorry. I'm sorry. You frightened us. After enduring, hoping, living moment to moment, we thought something dreadful happened."

"It wasn't my fault. The rabbi ordered our team to stop playing and go into the synagogue. We had to wait until night when they blew some kind of trumpet made from the horn of a sheep. It made a sound I never heard."

"I know this holiday. Like Catholic confession. Say prayers, listen to the sound of a horn, all will be forgiven," said Alex with a note of disbelief.

Mela pulled him back. "He did what he was told. What if it is something you don't like? When Tadek and Geniek grow up, they'll decide how to lead their lives."

"The only way to get forgiveness is do the right thing. The earlier children learn that the world is not black or white, Christian or Jewish, the better off they'll be."

"Enough sermons. Have milk, a piece of cake, and go to bed," Mela said to David.

"I'll join you with milk and Mama's cake," said Alex. He ate slowly, then took David's hand. "You are my bright boy who helped in Łódź. Please forgive your old papa." They hugged, rocking back and forth. "Promise never worry me again," whispered Alex.

"I promise," David said softly, before slipping into bed.

"One thing you're good at is getting in trouble," Jacob said. "Maybe you should ask to be forgiven."

Leaves turned yellow, brown, and purple. Red squirrels scampered up oak trees, gathering acorns for the long winter. The Earth continued spinning, hurtling David toward disconnected foreign lands with exotic languages and a family of gray, out-of-focus images. He and Jacob endured monthly physical exams. Doctors and nurses weighed and measured, took their blood pressure, thumped their chests and backs, examined their ears and eyes. In the end pronouncing the boys healthy.

The first snow of winter brought unsettling news for David. The Jewish Agency sent a telegram to Team 503. British authorities approved the request for him and Jacob to emigrate to the Mandate.

"I won't go unless you and Mama go with us," complained David.

"We tried hard as possible to get permission. The power of Britain is against us. We'll be with you until you leave," Alex assured him.

"Your father lived for years not knowing if you were alive or dead. He wants you to come home," said Mela.

"My home is with you!" cried David.

Jacob tried to calm him. "Think of it this way, we have Mama and Papa Roslan, and we have our own father. Can you believe we have two fathers, a mother, and Marisia, our sister?"

"I'm not going to Palestine," protested David.

"The United Nations wants to keep families together. The war ripped children away from their homes. Many of them have no place to go. You're lucky," Alex said.

"Don't leave me," David implored.

"We'll be together," said Jacob.

"I wish . . . I wish," Alex stammered, not knowing how to respond to David's fervent plea. "Mama and I did everything to make the British understand our commitment to Aunt Hanka and Devorah. It's no longer in our hands. This was not our plan, not what we wanted. We will always love our Geniek and Tadek." He sobbed uncontrollably. "Mama, show them the letter."

Mela smoothed a sheet of paper on the table and cleared her throat. "The Joint Distribution Committee sent us an express letter from the JOINT-Jerusalem from your grandfather, Wolf Gutgeld in Tel Aviv. Jacob read it aloud.

> "Dear Sir, a letter from our office in Paris related to your grandchildren arrived in our office today. Here is the letter verbatim: 'We regret the delay that occurred in the final arrangements with Mr. Roslan regarding the children. We are in contact with our Frankfurt office and hope to be informed concerning the conclusion of negotiations about the case in a few days. In the meantime, our representative in Paris is making the necessary preparations for the arrival of the children in France in order to continue their trip to Eretz Yisroel at the earliest.' A worker in our Frankfurt office has seen the children and reported they feel well and are in good health. We shall notify you when we receive additional information. Sincerely, Joint, Jerusalem Office."

Invisible bonds wrapped around David, dragging him from the refuge created by the Roslans on the long, tortuous trek to freedom.

Alex opened an envelope. "Your travel documents are in here with instructions. You board a train in Frankfurt for travel to Paris. Those in charge will make sure you have a place to stay. The Joint Distribution Committee paid for all your needs. As soon as possible, you'll go to Marseille in the south of France. After final emigration papers arrive, you board a ship to Palestine."

Words spiraled inside David's head. So matter of fact. So absolute. So final. He said nothing, remembering how his adopted mother and father lived up to their promise. They survived.

"When do you leave for America?" asked Jacob.

"A few days after we see you off in Frankfurt. We start our new life with money saved and funds from the Jewish Agency," said Mela.

"What about Marisia?" Jacob asked.

"I'm going to be American. I'll go to school and learn English. If you're lucky, maybe you'll come to America someday and we can see each other."

"Even when we're far apart we'll still be family," said Mela. "Now, off to bed with all of you."

Nightmares about helmeted, gray-clad German soldiers overwhelmed David. Jurek ran joyously into the street, shot to death. David ran through muddy fields, but his legs wouldn't obey. Dark, frightening, slavering wolves crept toward him. David opened his mouth to scream. The scream turned to a whimper.

He woke at daybreak, stumbling into the kitchen. Mela served an old-fashioned Polish breakfast. He wanted to engrave the picture in his mind of Marisia bouncing up and down waiting to taste dumplings. Broad-shouldered, self-confident Alex battling a cruel, indifferent world.

With a swipe of his napkin over his chin, Alex stood up. "Off to the tailor for suits you'll wear when you meet your father and grandfather. I don't want to hear we sent you looking like vagabonds."

Piles of fabric lay on tailor shop tables and floor. An old man with a gray beard, a cap on his head, long fringes hanging under his soiled vest, pressed a pair of trousers with a heavy iron. Other tailors pedaled foot-powered sewing machines, stitching jackets, pants, and shirts.

Alex flipped through swatches of cloth. Mela either said "no" or shrugged her shoulders. The fitter tapped his fingers impatiently on a counter covered with trousers and jackets in various stages of alteration. David and Jacob waited restlessly on hard, wooden chairs for a decision. At last, Alex held up dark-blue serge. Mela nodded her approval. "This is it," he announced.

The fitter ordered the boys to stand on platforms in front of full-length mirrors. He turned them right and left, writing down their measurements and shouting in Yiddish across the shop. "You will look elegant upon your arrival in Eretz Yisrael," winked the tailor.

David played soccer and raced the village boys through the forest. Intense, serious, exhilarating challenges pushed aside the inevitable. He had no desire to enter the camp with flags, demonstrations, and confusion. Zionism held little meaning until he was older, living in a country that didn't exist in 1946.

Exhausted and tired, he threw himself on his bed. The door banged open, and Jacob, with a benign smile, lugged an armful of books to a table.

"Find another Hitler stamp?" David asked mockingly.

"I'm learning. Rabbi Kret introduced me to a professor of mathematics. Instead of playing with Nazi kids, he's going to teach me math and physics."

Alex pushed open the bedroom door. "All done." He held up their new suits. "Get dressed. Mama and Marisia want to see how handsome you are."

Jacob shook out the pants and grunted with utter embarrassment. "They buckle at my knees. I'll never wear them," he said, tossing them on his bed. "I'm old enough to wear long pants."

"I didn't wear long pants until I was fifteen. Get dressed," ordered Alex.

Jacob yanked on his suit, looked down at his bare legs, and muttered, "I look like a clown."

"If I didn't know better I would think you're going to a dance," Mela smiled when they stepped into the living room.

"Girls in Palestine will go crazy over you, Geniek," said Marisia.

"Not in knee pants."

"I want to remember you just the way you are," said Mela.

David did not want to be remembered. His entire life with Alex and Mela unraveled stitch by stitch. No one asked his opinion. Decisions made by faceless organizations controlled his life. Alex shook him by the shoulder. "Daydreaming again?"

"Geniek's right. We want long pants."

"No arguments. Mama and I made an appointment to have your picture taken."

"Looking like this?" Jacob complained.

"Like young gentlemen. Be proud," said Mela, marching them to the billeting photographer. The brothers smiled awkwardly for the camera.

Day after day during the month of December temperatures fell below freezing. Trucks delivered blankets, sweaters, heavy coats, and boots to the camp. The boys joined children in the neighborhood, scouring the forest floor for pinecones, sprinkling them with tinsel and twining holly branches to make wreaths. Christmas trees perfumed the air with the scent of pine. The aroma of Christmas bread stuffed with dried fruit and nuts floated through the village. Streams froze. Ice clogged rivers. Night and day, branches snapped under the weight of snow. The boys and girls ignored frigid weather, jumping into snowbanks with joy.

David, Jacob, and Marisia, noses and cheeks red from bitter cold, returned home to hot chocolate and a surprise announcement. The Jewish Agency sent travel orders for the boys. They were to leave for Frankfurt in two days, take the train to Paris on their first leg south to Marseille, where a ship waited to transport them to the Mandate. It was all becoming frightening real for David. He ran outside, siting on the frost-covered steps, clutching his knees to his chest.

Alex wanted desperately for his Tadek to understand life takes strange turns. "One day you'll thank us for sending you to your father. When you grow up, you'll visit your old Mama and Papa Roslan. Only we won't be Mama and Papa any longer. We'll be Uncle Alex and Aunt Mela."

David buried his face against Alex's chest. "You'll always be my papa."

"Always, but I'll feel even better when you go to school and become educated. You and Jacob are so good with numbers. It's as if they were your first language. I never went to university, but I knew how to add, multiply, and divide. I could do fractions and figure out the best way to make a profit. You and your brother understand so much more. I'm amazed at the books you read. Science, astronomy, books about insects, how machines work. Even the story Ella Rosenberg gave you about slaves in America made you want to learn more."

"You're smarter than me," sniffled David.

"By the time you're my age you'll be a professor or doctor. I could only dream. Make your dreams come true."

"I don't want you to go away," said David.

"Sailing on a ship across the sea is an adventure. Who knows? One day you'll come to America. We'll sit and talk about old times."

Displaced persons, the "surviving remnant" dragged meager belongings to an army bus parked on a snow-banked street outside UNRRA Team 503 gate. Mela, Alex, and Marisia accompanied the boys. The driver wrote their names on tags, tying them to the boys' bags, looping them around their necks on a ribbon—leashes pulling them into a dark cave filled with unseen monsters.

Steady clank of snow chains accompanied them on the drive to Frankfurt over slick, frost-covered roads. The rail terminal looked the same, except for fewer refugees and less confusion. Emissaries from Jewish organizations stamped their documents. Baruch, the young man who asked David to read at the Passover service, waited on the platform. "The train leaves in twenty minutes."

Mela handed the boys a small burlap sack. "In case you get hungry," she said, holding back tears.

Marisia kissed Jacob and David. It was the first time in years they would not be part of the Roslan family.

"Geniek, take care of your brother," said Alex. "Tadek, you're the best salesman I ever met." A whistle shrieked. "We'll write once we're in America. Write back. Let us know how you are."

"Whenever we look at Happy Bear's crooked smile, we'll remember you," said Mela.

Chapter Fifteen

La Ville de Lumière

The train jettisoned steam, drifting a cloud over Alex, Mela, and Marisia standing on the platform waving forlorn good-byes. David already missed the small house on Zeilsheim's rutted streets where Alex piled up snowballs to pelt Jacob and Manfred; where Marisia made snow angels; where trees filled the countryside with the scent of pine.

They rolled past villages, through forests echoing with the sound of axes wielded by gangs of men chopping down trees for firewood. Gray clouds unleashed rain and sleet, battering train carriages and rattling windows. In the distance, explosions boomed, followed by geysers of smoke and snow.

Baruch peered through binoculars. "Bomb squads detonating unexploded ordinance. Plenty of bombs still buried in the ground."

"Anyone ever been killed?" asked Jacob.

"They're experienced and remove as many as possible. The Allies worry children and farmers will accidentally set off explosives buried in fields." Another burst, followed by a cloud erupting. "See what I mean? Paris doesn't have that problem. On the other hand it has plenty of shortages. We arrive in a few hours. Maybe we'll see each other near the Eiffel Tower." He saw the blank look on David's face. "You can't miss it. Very tall, in the center of the city near the River Seine. Everyone says, 'Meet me at the tower.'"

David didn't want to think about Paris or towers. The farther he traveled from those he loved, the closer he approached an obscure destiny.

"Don't look so sad," said Jacob. "Someone will meet us when we arrive. We'll just be another couple of kids. They'll stick us in some kind of miserable camp with terrible food. I'm really looking forward to it." He flipped open his sport magazine.

"Reading about soccer when we don't know what's going to happen?!" David shouted.

"We can't stop the train. Shut up and leave me alone."

David stared sullenly out the window. Rain poured down on German refugees carrying packs, guiding old wooden carts pulled by scrawny, straining horses trudging muddy roads next to trail tracks. Weary, miserable, exhausted by years of war, they clamored around American and British trucks carrying food and clothing. The same people once shouted joyfully, saluting Nazi storm troopers, cheering Adolf Hitler. Destroyed German tanks and charred trucks cluttering blasted forests and hedgerows proved the malignant false prophet failed.

Down the line, American troops wearing winter uniforms scanned the earth with metal detectors, pausing to place markers in the ground. "They're searching for buried soldiers," Baruch said to the boys.

"Americans?" asked David.

"Americans, British, even Germans. The war's over. Families need to know what happened to their husbands, fathers, brothers. It's the right thing to do."

"After everything they did to us?" asked a doubtful Jacob.

"Our tradition teaches: 'If two people claim your help, and one is your enemy, help him first.' Converting an enemy into a friend is more important than carrying bitterness for the rest of your life. We can never forget. We can never forgive this generation, but a new generation will come along. We have to make sure no more Hitlers or Nazis threaten the world."

Late in the afternoon the train pulled into Paris's massive Gare de Lyon rail terminal. An enormous clock tower, surmounted by a glistening gold dome, glowed with bright-blue enameled hour and minute hands. Graceful metal beams and girders arched high above, supporting an enormous glass ceiling. Statues and marble figures, flanking entrances, mounted on parapets, symbolized Paris and Marseille. Nineteenth-century stone carvings of bare-breasted nymphs stopped Jacob and David in their tracks.

"The carvings are allegorical, symbolic," said Baruch. The boys didn't move. "They represent engineering, navigation, steam power, and electricity." His explanation didn't work. They couldn't stop staring at the nude figures. Baruch pushed them past passengers lined up at tables divided by the first letters of last names. "Come back after your twenty-first birthday."

People hollered from every direction. "Where's the line for *K*?" "I can't find *C*." "Tell me where to go; my name is Perlmutter."

"Someone's waiting for you behind those barriers," said Baruch.

A man in a heavy black coat held a sign reading: "Jacob/David Gutgeld." The boys dragged their duffels to the fence. "I'm Jacob Gutgeld. This is my brother, David," called Jacob over the din and turmoil.

"The Jewish Agency requested I meet you." He shook hands with Baruch, "Thank you for supervising them."

"Take good care of the boys."

"My duty is to make sure their journey to Eretz Yisrael is uneventful."

He led the brothers to an elegant black 1938 Peugeot four-door sedan parked near the entrance.

"We don't have to show our identity cards?" asked David.

"You're a special case," he said, sliding behind the wheel. "My name's Zvi Salat. I'm a friend of your family in Tel Aviv. My younger brother studied engineering with your uncle Natan at university in Zurich, Switzerland. In 1939, Natan returned to Warsaw for your aunt Hanka's wedding. War broke out. He couldn't return."

Parisians walked leisurely along snow-dusted streets. Cafés, restaurants, shops catered to American, British, and French soldiers, as well as those fortunate enough to have money. They crossed a three-arched iron-and-steel bridge over the River Seine. The Paris coat of arms, depicting a crown above a field of lilies and a sailing ship riding the river, decorated four statues facing north and south.

"It looks as if there had never been a war," said Jacob.

"Germans almost burned Paris. At the last minute they decided to evacuate without destroying it. Maybe they knew the war was lost, or someone in Berlin had a fondness for the city," responded Salat, pulling up to fin de siècle Hotel Mirabeau on Rue Sébastien Mercier, changed little since it was built in the late nineteenth century. Brocade chairs, gilt-trimmed tables and desks, and grand piano looked as they did when the hotel was young. On the fireplace mantelpiece stood a marble bust of the hotel's namesake, eighteenth-century deputy to the French states-general, Honoré Gabriel Riquet, count of Mirabeau.

A shuffling, elderly, wizened porter in a dark uniform with brass buttons led them up a broad staircase laid with deep-red carpet. He paused several times, grabbed his knees, taking deep breaths before leading them down a wide hall to a spacious room. Salat tipped the porter a few francs. He accepted with French aloofness.

"It will take a while to receive final permission to enter the Mandate. It's only a formality. This is your home until you leave for Marseille." Salat opened an inside door. "Your own bathroom with hot water."

A window framed soaring Eiffel Tower. It seemed so close David thought he could almost touch it. He ran back to the living room. A young man in his late twenties sat with Jacob and Salat. "We assigned Benjamin Shapiro as your guardian and guide while in Paris. He speaks excellent Polish, French, and English. Benjamin has a room in the hotel. He'll always be here when you need him," said Salat.

"Friends call me Bennie. We won't do much, since this is your first evening in Paris. We'll have dinner in the hotel and get a good rest. Tomorrow we begin our Parisian adventure."

Salat held up a box. "I have a favor to ask." He lifted out a camera. "When your uncle Natan returned to Warsaw, he left his Zeiss in care of my brother. He requested you return it to him." The black Ikon Ikonta folding camera with chrome trimmings had a lens mounted in a stainless steel adjustable ring attached to a bellows.

Jacob peered at David through the viewfinder. "We'll take good care of it," he promised.

"And Bennie will take good care of you. Now, off to dinner."

Aging waiters in black tuxedoes, frayed white shirts, and bow ties shambled from table to table set with fine porcelain, crystal goblets, and polished silver taking orders from an assemblage of the displaced. For a brief moment, semblance of a bygone era made hardships refugees suffered fade away.

A waiter whispered in French to Bennie. "What did he say?" asked David.

"He regrets the hotel has difficulty getting supplies." Roasted potatoes, leeks, and chicken roasted in herbs did not match the waiter's apology.

Early on their first morning, Bennie led them northwest along narrow confines of Rue Sébastien Mercier, past brick apartment houses with fanciful iron artwork grilles over windows. Paris emerged from the Nazi occupation with a newborn burst of energy.

The street broadened into a garden bordering the River Seine. Bare, thorny rose bush branches laced through trellises arching over walking paths where American and British soldiers walked arm in arm with their new girlfriends. Men, women, and families rushed from local boulangeries with loaves of bread. Parisians lined up at small bistros for cheese-and-ham sandwiches, sliced fish fresh from the Seine, and croissants. "We'll get breakfast after we take a ride on the river," Bennie assured them.

Ice floes glided past an old *bateau-mouche*, a covered wooden barge, moored at a concrete pier jutting into the river. The creaking, slow-moving, sightseeing flat boat chugged along the Seine. Jacob snapped pictures with Uncle Natan's camera of workmen hauling blocks of ice sawed out of frozen banks to horse-drawn sawdust-filled wagons.

They disembarked at a mooring leading up a long esplanade to an impressive building with a steeple atop a gold dome soaring over a great vaulted doorway. "A long time ago, Les Invalides was a hospital for French soldiers. The government made it into an army museum," explained Bennie.

David asked him to buy a postcard from a booth near the entrance. It was the beginning of a collection he maintained for years.

"Why are we going into a hospital museum?" asked Jacob.

"Not just any museum. The tomb of Emperor Napoleon Bonaparte is inside the old hospital chapel."

"I learned about Napoleon in Łódź. I never imagined we'd see Paris or his tomb."

"Napoleon conquered almost all Europe. Claiming he engaged in a scientific expedition, he marched on Egypt and Syria. Overwhelming forces made him withdraw, after which he still claimed victory. He pressed on finally defeating Egypt, a triumph leading him to proclaim himself the new Alexander the Great. Looking east, he believed Russia, under its young czar, had no stomach for battle. Russia's ruthless winter proved Napoleon's downfall. His adventure ended in ice, snow, and frozen lakes. Five hundred thousand French soldiers perished. Hitler should have paid attention to history. Weather was part of the reason Nazis failed to take Stalingrad," said Bennie.

A mosaic of green laurel leaves on the marble floor circled an imposing fifteen-foot-tall red coffin carved from porphyry on a granite base under the dome. Napoleon's statue, emulating a Roman emperor, stood above the sarcophagus. Twelve statues of winged figures, carrying laurel wreaths, swords, trumpets, and palm branches celebrating his victories, surrounded the tomb. Murals, frescoes, mosaics, the tomb of Napoleon's brother Joseph, galleries lined with statues glorified a soldier who rose to be the self-proclaimed emperor of France.

"Napoleon died an exile, confused by the lack of glory to which he felt entitled. It's the story of autocrats, dictators, tyrants through the ages. A lesson ambitious politicians usually ignore," Bennie told the boys.

They crossed Boulevard des Invalides to sculptor August Rodin's villa and studio surrounded by the nineteenth-century artist's monumental masterpieces cloaked with snow. "If you remember one thing about Paris, art lives far longer than conquering heroes," said Bennie.

David and Jacob aimed the camera at immense bronze doors meant for a museum never built. They ventured onto Place de la Concorde, the largest square in Paris, standing at the southeast end of Boulevard Champs-Élysée where a 3,500-year-old yellow granite column given by Egypt to France rose into the air.

Benny read from his guidebook. "'During the French Revolution the statue of Louis the Fourteenth was torn down and the square renamed Place de la Révolution.' The revolutionary government erected a guillotine in the square during what became known as the Reign of Terror. They chopped off heads of those who disagreed with the new government."

"Not much different from what Germans did," said Jacob.

"No one was executed for being Jewish, only for supporting the monarchy. Bad enough."

"Why didn't they just put them in jail?" asked David.

"There's an old saying: 'Power corrupts; absolute power corrupts absolutely.' The French Revolution expected everyone to think alike, and if you didn't . . ." He drew a finger across his neck. "It lasted ten years, two years less than the Third Reich."

"Ten years is still a long time, and people get hurt," said Jacob.

"Today, Paris is free and eager to get back to life. It is La Ville de Lumière—the City of Light," said Bennie.

Marble carvings celebrating French victories ran along the top and down the sides of the grand Arc de Triomphe, a massive structure at the northwest end of Champs-Élysées. From there they climbed to the Eiffel Tower's third level.

"Let's go to the top," insisted Jacob.

"I'll wait here if you want to climb," said Bennie.

"Take the elevator," smiled David.

"It doesn't work. During the German occupation French resistance fighters cut the cables. Nazi soldiers struggled up seventeen hundred stairs to fly the swastika from the top of the tower. Parisians prayed they'd take a misstep and topple 312 meters to Jardin de la Tour Eiffel where they would've ruined the roses."

"Someday, I'm coming back and going all the way up," said David.

Sunny winter days slipped by. They bundled up lunching at small cafés and bistros on sidewalks along the river, watching ice drifting on the water. Bennie pointed the camera at Jacob and David smiling and holding croissants.

He suddenly looked up. "You don't have film in the camera."

"We thought all you had to do was point and click," said David.

"No film, no pictures."

The boys laughed so hard their sides hurt. "Please don't tell Uncle Natan," pleaded Jacob.

Each day brought new experiences. Paris may have been the City of Light, to Jacob and David it was the City of Enlightenment. Around every corner they discovered history in massive flying buttresses, monuments, and ancient buildings. Bennie escorted them to the Grand Synagogue of Paris on Rue de le Victoire. Its classical and Byzantine architecture evoked eternity. Inside, stained-glass windows representing the twelve tribes of Israel glowed along the walls. No one questioned or reviled the boys. They felt safe under the watchful eye of their guardian and agencies paving their way.

Zvi Salat wrote to Nahum Gutgeld in Palestine concerning their progress and state of health. Twice a week, he punctually joined them for lunch. On a cold, bright afternoon he met Bennie and the brothers at a corner bistro. He was not his usual upbeat, ebullient self. After a cup of strong coffee, he leaned forward, holding David's and Jacob's hands. "The Joint compiled lists of those who perished in ghettos and concentration camps. I'm sorry to tell you Hanka, Devorah, and your grandmother died at the hands of the Nazis."

The boys sat in dazed silence. Their grandmother was a rock who faced oppressors, determined not to fall into hopelessness. Hanka and Devorah kept up their spirits even in the darkest of times.

"Authorities believe it happened when Germany knew they lost the war. The Allies found ledgers and records meticulously accounting for every person in work camps and extermination centers. You need to know the truth. It's a lot to absorb."

"What about our uncle Doctor Galler? If it wasn't for him I might have died," cried Jacob.

"He was incredibly brave. From brief records located by the Jewish Agency, it appears someone at the hospital betrayed him. Dr. Abraham Galler is also mentioned in an official announcement of death published in Warsaw on 9 March 1948 (p. 15); according to this source, he was detained and killed at the Krakow railway station."

"Does our father know?" asked Jacob.

"The Joint notified your family in the Mandate."

They abandoned their women and children to murderers. David and his brother survived by chance. David wondered if each step on the path to freedom was an accident or part of some mysterious grand scheme.

Alex had no use for mystical explanations. Chance brought Stasek, their grandfather's chauffeur, to his door and Jacob into his family's life. Mela's obstinate refusal to allow her husband to join Stasek in a reckless adventure saved her husband. David and Shalom, daringly rescued by their uncle hiding under a Polish name. A doctor placing his life on the line to save a boy under eyes of the enemy.

The Gutgeld brothers proved Ella Rosenberg's description written to their father: *"I have never met children with so much talent, almost genius."* Proficient in mathematics, immersed in science at an early age, they intuitively knew each incident could have gone in a different direction. They relied on one another creating a reality, the opportunity to start a new life.

While Jacob seemed reconciled to the notion, it unsettled his younger brother attempting to make sense of a world out of orbit. He clung to Alex and Mela, who took the place of their mother existing as faded photographs, a nonexistent father vanishing before developing physical, emotional, or social bonds. He transferred those feelings to the Roslans. The link between them was destined to break. Mama and Papa Roslan planned to sail thousands of miles away. Łódź, Berlin, Paris milestones marking a road to an obscure fate.

A book of photographs about America from Hotel Mirabeau's library had page after page of images: skyscrapers soaring into the sky, farmland with endless seas of wheat stretching westward to towering mountains, waterfalls and mighty rivers rushing to the sea. A golden land, a fairy tale land was being traded for a sliver of arid territory bordering the Mediterranean.

Bennie hammered on their door early in the morning. "Pack immediately. The train to Marseille leaves in two hours."

"Can't we stay a few more days?" begged David.

"Wish I could help you out. The agency only hired me to keep you safe on your journey."

"It was too good to last," groused Jacob.

"Don't forget Uncle Natan's camera," said David, stuffing his duffel with Vasily Grossman's *In the Town of Berdichev*, along with his collection of Paris postcards he promised to save forever.

"We took great pictures. Too bad we didn't have film," said Jacob.

Refugees given shelter at Mirabeau, other hotels, former military barracks, and abandoned factories packed the truck. A young woman, who could have been Ella Rosenberg's sister, whispered to David: "I'm going to live with my cousin in Eretz Yisrael. What about you?"

"My father's in Palestine," he mumbled.

"How lucky." Her face suddenly turned into a stone mask with haunted eyes. "The Germans murdered my father and mother."

Everyone they met on their long journey carried heart-break and sorrow. David and Jacob felt the weight of Shalom's death. Brave Jurek's senseless killing by a German sniper's bullet. They survived a chaotic world while others, without protectors, perished.

Bennie hustled the Gutgeld brothers through milling crowds anxious to start a new life in a country where they could live without fear. David remembered Rabbi Krets reading words of hope and despair during the Zeilsheim Passover service: ". . . they went up to our holy land Eretz Yisrael." They faced a warning written by survivors of Auschwitz and Dachau: "There is no such thing as 'bad' or 'good' exile. Every exile leads to destruction."

David had no idea if he was leaving or entering exile and took hold of Jacob's hand. "Suppose it's not the place for us. Can we say no?"

"We don't have a choice. Most Poles hate us. You saw what happened when the colonel found out about you. Paris was a holiday we knew wouldn't last forever."

Carriage doors hissed open. Bennie tied name tags on their coats and escorted them aboard the train. Angst-ridden men, women, and children crowded aisles searching for familiar faces.

"You'll do all right once you get used to living in Palestine." Bennie leaped to the platform.

A young woman wearing a dark dress, winter coat, and wool beret clapped her hands for attention. "My name is Laila Dolinsky. My job is to make sure you're comfortable and have everything you need on the trip. It takes approximately eleven hours before our arrival in Marseille. Volunteers at the terminal will take you to hotels and dormitories until you leave for Eretz Yisrael. If your paperwork is ready, you may be able to travel in one or two days. For others, perhaps a week or two. Rest assured: you will receive permission."

The steam engine coughed to life. Iron wheels squealed on tracks leading south out of Gare de Lyon. Passengers, gathered from concentration and death camps, wearing expressions of hope and worry, still carried the fear an SS officer dressed in a neatly pressed uniform would point right toward slave labor, or left to extermination in gas chambers.

David pushed through a sliding door to the platform between cars. Cold rain pelted his face. Tracks paralleled a river through misty, barren hills, past farms nestled in valleys. It looked little different from Poland and Germany's familiar landscapes.

He peered through the downpour, imagining the Palestine Ella described in glowing phrases. Sunshine and warm breezes abounding in a land destined to become home for the dispossessed scattered across the world. Protestors in Zeilsheim clamored for the right to enter their promised land. David had no such illusions. The more he obsessed about his dilemma, the more apprehension increased.

Passengers slept or stared blankly through the storm-splattered windows, their eyes witnesses to unimaginable atrocities. David slumped on the bench next to Jacob.

"Where did you go?" Jacob asked.

"On the platform between the cars. What will happen to us when we reach Palestine?"

"We'll have our own beds. We'll have Grandfather, Father, uncles."

"We'll also need to learn a new language. Remember Passover? I'll never learn to read and write Hebrew," complained David.

"We both speak Polish and a little Russian. In Berlin and Zeilsheim we learned some English and German. We didn't do so bad picking up French. I bet we'll speak, read, and write Hebrew in no time at all."

"You want to bet your collection of *SportSchau* magazines? How about the silver-engraved ashtray you stole from the hotel?"

"It's a souvenir. One of the porters translated the engraving and gave it to me. He said it commemorated Count Mirabeau's death. 'Pleurons la perle de Mirabeau'—Let us cry for the loss of Mirabeau."

French bore no comparison to Hebrew's strange letters and words reading right to left. "Pay me after a week in Tel Aviv," said David.

Laila Dolinsky walked through the car, doling out sandwiches and apples. "All guaranteed kosher."

David stepped out on the platform again, wanting to feel mist wash away the past. To the east and west, gnarled, dry branches stretched in tidy rows over hills where large stone houses stood in meadows and on riverbanks.

"Even in winter it's beautiful," said Laila, joining him outside. "Feel the wind? Mistral brings cold rain in winter from the mountains to the valley. Makes wine special. When spring arrives, those dry branches turn green and blossom. By midsummer they'll be heavy with grapes."

"So many grapes," David said in amazement.

"Stone houses along the River Rhone belong to families who have made wine for hundreds of years."

"How do you know so much about the valley?"

"My father worked for one of the vineyards. When the Germans occupied France this part of the country was turned over to collaborators, French who cooperated with Nazis. They rounded up Jews and shipped them to concentration camps. My mother, father, and I escaped over the Alps to Switzerland and eventually to Palestine."

"You were lucky to get permission."

"Not that lucky. We didn't have papers. The British captured us the moment we landed. They packed us off to Atlit detainment camp south of Haifa on the coast of the Mediterranean. Officers and soldiers divided the men and women and ordered us to take showers. Everyone panicked. Nazi death camps had so-called showers that turned out to be gas chambers. But this time, they were real.

"We spent a year in detention, until they closed the camp in 1942 allowing us to stay in Palestine. When illegal immigrants came after the war they opened Atlit once more. The secret Jewish army, Palmach, raided the camp and freed over two hundred."

Her story seemed incomprehensible. Why throw desperate, homeless people behind barbed wire when all they yearned for was the right to live in peace? Anger, distrust, fear gnawed at David all during the train's steady, unrelenting trip south.

Familiar oak and fir trees gave way to exotic palms and twisted tamarisk until the blue Mediterranean Sea appeared. The sun lowered, casting shadows over Marseille's once elegant Gare de Marseille-Saint-Charles. German and Italian bombing raids reduced the north end of the terminal to a pile of broken stone.

"We need to go over rules before getting off the train," announced Laila. "Line up at tables manned by Jewish organizations. They will provide the number of the bus that will take you to your quarters."

A middle-aged woman checked off David's and Jacob's names. "You're staying in a hotel near the port," she said in Polish. "Line up at bus seven."

They hoisted duffels on their backs and walked down a wide staircase to the street. Old buses, painted blue with white Stars of David and "Jewish Agency" stenciled on doors, lined up in front of the terminal. Refugees milled around carts searching for their luggage. An old man with a scraggly gray beard sat on the steps repeating the same Yiddish phrase over and over again. "Is he all right?" David asked Jacob.

"He's thanking God for his salvation," answered a woman behind them.

The once flourishing gate to the Mediterranean had turned into a ghost city. Empty merchant ships, paint flaking from hulls, waited for cargo that would never arrive. Chains hanging from tall, rusty cranes clanked in the wind. Flocks of starlings flew in dense, black swarms out of bombed ruins.

The bus bounced up a rocky road to a hotel with shuttered windows, neglected gardens, and ivy clinging to fractured stucco walls, where Jewish Agency staff waited. Shmuel, an energetic young man, escorted David and Jacob to their room. Comfortable beds, sturdy chest of drawers, mahogany desk, and separate bathroom had not changed from before the war. Jacob piled his issues of *SportSchau* on a chair.

"We expect you to attend classes in preparation for your arrival in Eretz Yisrael. It may seem like a lot of work, but we don't want to give you too much free time. One: because you must stay in the building. Two: you need to know about our goals for Palestine. Three: language. We'll do as much as we can while you're in our care to teach you Hebrew basics."

"You want us to learn a new language in two weeks?" asked an unconvinced David.

"Basics. When you come home, you'll learn fast enough. Don't be surprised if you learn Arabic at the same time." He looked at his watch. "After dinner get some sleep. Be ready for tomorrow."

"Coming home" meant being with those who loved him, who never failed him. Home was not a foreign land where he would be a stranger. The Haggadah for the first Passover after the end of the war warned those yearning for Erez Yisroel "the unity of Israel is a fable... The remnant answered: all Israel was slaughtered together . . . is not Israel to rebuild together? The emissaries say: The unity of Israel is a fable. The land of Israel is being built by different groups." The "remnant," sitting at tables draped with old linen, in leather chairs cracked from age, did not hear the same alarm bell tolling. They believed "We are all of us, Israel." David would not raise his young voice; he would keep questions to himself. Find his own way.

A French tricolor and Jewish flag stood at one end of the room. An official wearing the insignia of the Jewish Agency in Israel on his lapel raised a hand for silence. "For those who just arrived, shalom, welcome. I am Morris Milstein, administrator for the agency in Marseille. Please join us in singing 'Hatikvah,' which means hope. The pamphlets on your tables have transliterations and translations of Hebrew into Polish, Russian, German, and French."

He sang in a deep baritone. First, one or two joined in. Then more and more, until the room resounded with song. Faces brightened; smiles appeared. Everyone stood straight and proud. David turned over the pamphlet and read the Polish translation of 'Hatikvah':

"As long as the Jewish spirit yearns deep in the heart,
With eyes turned toward the East, looking
                                    toward Zion,
Then our hope—the two-thousand-year-old hope—
                                   will not be lost:
To be a free people in our land,
The land of Zion and Jerusalem."

Marching and clamor of protesters in Zeilsheim began to have meaning. He did not know what Zionism meant, but he understood from the Passover service it was entwined with Jews living in an aspirational Palestine.

"Take your plate to the table up front and pick out what you want," said Shmuel, interrupting David's emerging awareness of what lay ahead.

An unexpected banquet of vegetables, baked fish, bread, grapes, apples, bowls of pickles, turnips, and green olives confronted him. David pointed at the olives. "What are those?" he asked Shmuel.

"Olives; they grow on trees. Palestine's famous for them. People eat them every meal."

David bit into one. He recoiled, spitting it into a napkin. "Not like any fruit I ever tasted."

"Thanks for being my taster," laughed Jacob.

"It's terrible," David said, gulping a glass of water.

"I guess it's what you're used to," said Shmuel, popping an olive in his mouth.

"They're disgusting," said a boy sitting next to David.

"I hope the rest of the food is better."

"We're the Mandelbaums. You and my son, Kazik, have something in common. You don't like olives. What is your name?" asked the boy's mother.

"Tadek. Tadek Roslan. This is my brother."

"It's not his name. We were given Polish names to protect us during the war. He's David. I'm Jacob."

"Did anyone tell you when we're leaving?" asked Kazik.

"We were told on the train some of us might leave in a couple of days or it could take a week or more," said Jacob.

"Maybe we'll be on the same ship," Kazik hoped. "Do you play chess?"

"My brother's better than me, just ask him. Enjoy yourselves. I'm going for a walk outside."

"No one is permitted outside," Shmuel said sternly.

"So we're in another ghetto?" Jacob asked sarcastically.

"Buckle down and pay attention to rules. These walls aren't keeping you in. They're keeping out *Les beaux voyous*, wise guys, gangs looking for *k'nakers*. A kid like you is red meat to them. If they grab you off the street, chances are we'll never see you again unless we pay them off. Don't tempt fate. For your own safety, stay inside."

"Sounds like the Gestapo."

"Except they don't care if you're a Jew, Christian, or Muslim. Your life is only worth what they can collect for your release."

"I get the picture," said a shaken Jacob.

"I hope you do. Boys you'll be going to class with are in the lobby. Most of them wanted to wander around Marseilles. I told them the same thing. I suggest you join them—in the classroom.

"Behave yourself, or Shmuel will cut off your dessert," Jacob whispered to David.

"I heard him. Don't open the hotel door. You won't be rescued by a Russian colonel."

Jacob turned red. "Enjoy your new friend," he glowered, storming out of the room.

"What's going on?" asked Kazik.

"He'll get over it. You want to play chess?"

"They have chessboards in the library. We can play tomorrow after class."

Turmoil of traveling from Paris in the cold north to warmer Marseille, facing head-on the realization his world spun out of control, kept David awake. He threw open the shutters, gazing at silhouettes and shadows of abandoned gantries crisscrossing against a full moon over the port.

Jacob sat up. "Get to bed."

"Those gangs are out there waiting for us to break the rules."

"You're imagination's running away." He peered out the window. "All I see are waves crashing against rocks." Creak of sailboats moored in the harbor, clang of a buoy at the end of a breakwater, rang through still, moist air.

"We stayed safe with Mama and Papa Roslan. Remember how you squeezed under the kitchen cabinets?"

"I handled it, like I'm handling our trip across the ocean. I used a ruler on a map in the library and calculated we're about thirty-six hundred kilometers from Palestine."

David threw himself on the bed. "I still don't want to go." For the first time, he saw tears on Jacob's cheeks. "I wanted Papa and Mama Roslan to go with us. They would have made the whole journey complete. It doesn't seem fair."

From the day they discovered their father survived, Jacob never mentioned his doubts. His insecure despair forged stronger links between the brothers. "You kept it to yourself all this time?" asked David.

"I didn't want to make my kid brother feel bad."

"What are we going to do?"

"Make the best of it. It's not as if our real father and grandfather don't want us. They worked hard to get us this far."

"It doesn't change how I feel," said David.

He fell asleep, dreaming his father and grandfather apologized for leaving them behind. He envisioned sitting at a dinner table, his father praising Alex and Mela for their sacrifices. Reconciliation vanished when he awoke in Marseille, the last stop before crossing the sea to an alien land.

Members of the agency staff dressed in khaki trousers, skirts, and light-blue shirts led daily classes. David's first one focused on Theodore Herzl, a secular Jew, journalist, and author, who lived in Vienna on the cusp of the twentieth century. He witnessed violent antisemitism, wrote about pogroms and the infamous Dreyfus Affair for the Viennese newspaper *Neue Freie Presse*.

His book *Der Judenstaat* presented a conception for establishing a pluralistic society, not limited to Jews, built on socialist principals in biblical Israel, living and working in harmony with the native population.

Ella Rosenberg related how Herzl envisioned Palestine would be a Jewish homeland. At the time he wrote his book everyone thought it was only a dream. His instructor on the *Providence* quoted the writer. "He replied 'If you will it, it is no dream.'" It wasn't a dream for David. It was real enough to worry how life would be in his father's country.

Playing chess with Kazik pushed anxieties in a corner. Neither one of the boys mentioned their pasts until one day David innocently asked about Kazik's father. "Nazis rounded up all the men in the Krakow Ghetto. My father was sent to Plaszow concentration camp. The commandant used Jews for target

practice. He shot my father from the balcony of his office."
Kazik burst into tears.

"Target practice?" stuttered David, shocked by the inhumane image. It brought back bleak, terrible memories of children in Warsaw executed in front of their mothers and fathers.

A cold breeze blew through the room. "Mama was afraid
we'd be next. We escaped to the home of a Polish friend who
had someone make us false identification cards. We traveled
from one place to another, staying away from Germans until
the war ended," said Kazik.

"We did the same in Warsaw. People we thought were
good neighbors reported us to police and Gestapo. We moved
at least five times. Finally, we escaped to a small farming
village."

"Hitler couldn't kill us all," said Kazik. A moment later he
changed the uncomfortable, painful subject. "Are you going to
live with friends, family?"

"With my father and grandfather. They live in a place called
Tel Aviv."

Kazik brightened. "We have family in Tel Aviv! We can
still see each other!" A bell rang twice. "Time to get back to
class."

Shmuel brought his accordion to the room. "Clear a space.
Everyone make a circle. We're going to dance like true sabras.
A sabra is a tough, thorny cactus, but soft and sweet inside. I'm
a sabra, and after a time in Eretz Yisrael you'll become sabras.
So let's dance."

He played a rollicking, happy song. They danced in a circle
with their teachers, who sang in Hebrew. David and Kazik
picked up a few words and bellowed, "Hava nagila, hava nagila,
hava nagila, Ve-nisma-cha."

Shmuel translated: "Gather, come gather 'round me, a joyous sound we'll make today." Music lifted hopes, giving them the promise of life without fear.

After two weeks penned up in the hotel, Morris Milstein called an assembly in the ballroom. "We received papers from the British for many of you to enter the Palestine Mandate. "The ship leaves Marseille tomorrow morning. Be ready to board the bus no later than seven o'clock. Be certain if you do not hear your name, it will not be long before the ship returns to pick you up."

Jacob jumped to his feet and cheered when he heard their names. David sat, unmoving. A gate closed, sealing him off from Alex and Mela.

Chapter Sixteen

Oranges and Home

February 11, 1947. Early morning sea breezes blew across the desolate Port of Marseille. The sleek, white SS *Providence*, with blue-and-white-topped red smokestacks, stood out among empty freighters and oil tankers moored at the battered passenger terminal. The same buses that carried them from Marseille's rail station to their temporary living quarters pulled onto the wharf. Nervous and apprehensive displaced persons, battered, beaten, tattooed, landless, once abandoned, now invigorated with the possibility of having a home after waiting two thousand years, arrived, wondering if, after all the promises, they would be pushed back by strangers claiming, "You are the dead come alive. Return to ashes from which you arose."

Officers wearing crisp, white uniforms checked survivors' names checking off their destinations: Haifa, British Mandate. Disbelief and doubt raced through the throng. They would not believe until they set foot in Eretz Yisrael. The Gutgeld brothers waited patiently in a long line, not for a Promised Land, for their return to the family that abandoned them eight years before.

"Jacob, David," called Zvi Salat, standing next to his Peugeot parked on the wharf. His appearance surprised the boys. He trotted to the purser.

"Mr. Salat, you know these boys?"

"My special friends. It won't be against the rules if I talk with them for a few minutes?"

"We won't leave without them," assured the officer.

"I sent a telegram to your father and grandfather you would arrive at Haifa terminal on February 25. They replied by cable with assurance they will meet you on arrival." He shook their hands. "Get a move on. We don't want to keep the ship waiting. I'm returning to Eretz Yisrael myself."

"Are you coming with us?" asked Jacob.

"I'm traveling east to Turkey on agency business. Then Cyprus, before sailing to the Mandate. You'll get there long before I do."

The purser handed the boys cards marked with the deck and number of their cabin. They clambered down three levels to a cramped stateroom with bunk beds, a small dresser, and bathroom the size of a broom closet.

"After the hotel in Paris, and even the room in Marseille, this is not what I expected. Thank God it's only for two weeks. I don't think I could stand it much longer," complained Jacob.

"We don't have to spend time inside. It's a big ship. Come on. It's going to sail any moment."

They avoided the host of passengers crushed against rails, their faces marveling at the land they dreamed of beyond the horizon. They hoped to find answers to prayers they chanted after every meal. This time, they prayed for their future.

"Have mercy, Lord, our God . . . on Jerusalem, Your city; and on Zion, the resting place of Your glory . . . Rebuild Jerusalem, the city of holiness, speedily in our days. Bring us up into it and gladden us in its rebuilding and let us eat from its fruit and be satisfied with its goodness and bless You upon it in holiness and purity."

Jacob ducked under a chain with a sign in French stretched across the bottom step of a wooden ladder leading to an upper deck. "I don't think they want us up there," warned David.

"No one's throwing us off."

With a sharp blast of its horn, a tugboat nudged the ship out of the bay. Another blast, and under its own power, the *Providence* turned one hundred eighty degrees.

"I found a book of maps in the hotel library," said Jacob. He pointed south. "Over there is Africa. To the west, Spain and the Rock of Gibraltar—the entrance to the Atlantic Ocean. We're going east, past Egypt all the way to Palestine."

"Attention, attention!" the public address system announced. "Welcome aboard SS *Providence*. We will make your voyage as comfortable as possible. Programs for children and adults will be found in your staterooms, along with times for breakfast, lunch, and dinner. Tomorrow morning, classes begin. Study the diagram of the ship provided in order to become familiar with your surroundings."

A recording of "Hatikvah" followed the announcement. Music floated on wind blowing from the west across the Mediterranean. The ship slowly pitched and rolled as it crossed swells. A cool salty mist flowed over the bow.

"We're really on our way," said David.

"In two weeks we'll be with our father and grandfather."

"You're really happy about it?"

"Happy? Our mother died two weeks after you were born. You can't imagine how a five-year-old feels attending his mother's funeral. A year later, Germany invaded. Our father and grandfather picked up and left. They told me to listen to Grandmother, Hanka, and Devorah. Our father asked me to take care of you, a one-and-a-half-year-old baby. I could hardly take care of myself. All of a sudden we were forced to march behind gates with hundreds and thousands of other families. It was all downhill until Papa Alex broke me out. If there's such a thing as a miracle, that was it. Our uncle Avraham brought Shalom to us. You were the last."

"Don't remind me. Over the wall. I thought I was going to die."

"The plan worked. Mama Mela and Papa Alex made us part of their family."

"Aren't you angry our father left us behind?"

"I dreamed he would come back. If he had, the Germans would have killed him." Jacob lifted his hand. "Feel the breeze clearing away all the bad stuff?"

"Nothing will erase what happened to us. And now we're meeting our father. I don't even know what he looks like," David objected.

"I'll know him when I see him."

David had troubling doubts. "Seven years is a long time."

Jacob placed an arm around his brother's shoulder. "Everything will be all right."

The small, knife-shaped sliver of land made of desert, hills, swamps, shown to him by Ella Rosenberg, did not look as if it was anyone's Promised Land. Films they watched in Marseille and on the ship depicted a country shaped, twisted, recreated. Baruch, Laila, and Shmuel pushed the idea of becoming a pioneer in a place ruled by Jews thousands of years ago.

A whistle blasted over the public address system: "Lunch is ready in the restaurant on the observation deck."

"You go first. I'll make sure no one takes our place," said Jacob, sitting at a table.

David stood in line with refugees scooping up eggs, cucumber and onion salad, ever-present olives, grilled fish, pita, and hummus. Baskets of fresh oranges, a fruit David had only seen in photos and illustrations, stood on the counter.

Jewish Agency staff sliced and peeled them, releasing fresh, sweet aromas. David's first taste, sweet mixed with tartness, brought back Mela's *karpatka*—the flaky pastry filled with custard, covered with crushed raspberry, dusted with sugar. Troubled he would never see an orange again, he picked up three and hid them in his stateroom closet.

On the first day at sea, loudspeakers ordered children six to eighteen report to the upper deck. Staff manned long tables piled with wool jackets and sweaters to ward off winter weather at sea. Jacob grabbed a sweater and ran to classes for older children. David bundled in a jacket, walking the wind-blown, sun-drenched deck. He wished Rebekah Landau could see rippling white caps on the Mediterranean, listen to the throb of engines propelling them across an endless ocean. The unknown, mysterious girl, grown into a woman who became a great doctor, artist, or photographer.

Kazik ran down the deck ahead of his mother. "Time for class."

"I'm not interested. Trying to make us learn Hebrew. Stories about draining swamps," said David.

"In Łódź they taught Polish history. It's time we learn our history. Poets, composers, sages, and fools. Survival when subjugated. Overcoming tragedy, embracing life. Thrown out, abandoned, we returned," Mrs. Mandelbaum said fervently.

There had to be more than torment in store for David. Seminars highlighting the modern history of Palestine could not rub out the past. Massacres in towns and villages of

Europe unleashed a slow-moving tide of immigration in the early twentieth century. Jews looked to America, not Palestine, as the New Jerusalem. The Yiddish idiom, Di Goldeneh Medina, the Golden Land, expressed the desire of a people yearning to break chains of oppression. Palestine seemed second best. Why trade Golden Land for deserts and swamp?

After classes, David and Kazik discussed their futures. Newspapers and magazines from the United States portrayed bearded rabbis, students in New York yeshivas studying Hebrew texts, along with images of raucous Lower East Side where the poorest lived in crowded tenements. A picture of Black baseball player Jackie Robinson reminded David of Jenkins, the driver who told the story of his people who once were slaves like the Israelites coming out of Egypt.

The Jewish Agency and Joint Distribution Committee produced films, published magazines, printed newspapers about the "New Jew." Healthy, bronzed young men and women cleared swamps, turning them into farmland, planted forests, picked fruit in lush orchards, played sports, danced, sang. To Kazik, Palestine was paradise. Alex would never settle for crowded tenements of New York. He would have taken David and his brother to the real America of waterfalls, wide rivers, and snow-covered mountains where anything was possible.

Kazik's and David's friendship overrode their differences. After class they explored the ship, daring to sneak into forbidden areas. Burly, soot-covered men in the sweltering engine room on the lowest deck of the *Providence* shoveled coal into nine large furnaces, feeding groaning, growling engines driving the liner across the ocean.

They climbed out of the oppressively hot engine room to the ship's stern. Passengers, mostly elderly, grasped the railing.

The boys ran to find out what was in the water. Sad men and women who never stepped aboard a ship suffered from severe seasickness. Crewmen rushed jugs of water and pills to them. A few passengers fell into deck chairs, faces drawn and gray, clutching their stomachs.

"How are you handling the voyage?" asked a crewman wearing a red six-pointed star armband.

"I'm all right but a lot of passengers look terrible," said Kazik.

"Some have difficulty on the open ocean. After a few days they'll have their sea legs." He helped a woman return to her stateroom. David and Kazik climbed to an upper deck. Sprays and splashing water, followed by clicking sounds filled the air as a pod of dolphins leaped out of the sea.

"That's incredible," yelled David.

"Happens almost every trip," said a ruddy-faced uniformed officer speaking Polish looking over their shoulders. The captain invites you to the bridge—our command center."

Officers in a cabin with ports on three sides bellowed commands into brass tubes.

The captain's blue blazer with gold buttons and four gold sleeve stripes impressed David more than Colonel Koslovsky's uniform. The colors matched sea and sun.

"Do you have medals?" David asked.

The first mate translated for the captain. He answered, "Mes médailles sont des passagers qui ont survécu."

"The captain believes his medals are passengers who survived."

The first mate sat David at the ship's wheel. The compass, housed in a waist-high cylinder, remained level as the ship bobbed through waves. "Keep the arrow pointed to *E*, east."

David moved the wheel slightly right and left. The compass moved with ship's motion. "I did that!" he yelled.

He showed them instruments used to ensure their safe journey from Marseille to Haifa, tracing a line on a large map. "Here's the route we're taking across the Mediterranean." He pointed to Palestine. "Our destination. We arrive in eleven days."

"What do numbers on the map stand for?" asked David.

"Position of our ship. Numbers going north to south indicate latitude. Numbers east and west show longitude."

"Maybe I'll be a sea captain," said Kazik.

"I want to learn all about latitude and longitude. I can be your navigator," said David.

The second mate opened the outside hatch. "You're very lucky lads. The captain doesn't permit passengers up here. Enjoy the rest of your trip."

They climbed to the main deck. Standing at the rail they watched the ship's prow led by leaping dolphins, cutting through the sea. "Can you imagine what it will be like when we reached Eretz Yisrael?" Kazik said.

"Hebrew classes."

"Ought to be easy for someone as smart as you. "

"Jacob believes learning another language will be simple. I don't think so."

"Maybe we'll both be surprised."

David wanted no surprises. Too many times throughout his young life, he had one disappointment after another— promises made, promises broken. Alex and Mela gave their word they would take him to Palestine. He knew it wasn't their fault. At the same time the prospect of not having them as a protective shield provoked profound fear of the unfamiliar.

After classes, David and Jacob stood on the deck watching the sun set. "Ten more days and we're there," said Jacob.

Dark hovered in the east looming over David, concealing an ominous world where great unknowns dwelled. "What do you think it's going to be like living in Palestine with our father?"

"I don't know, except we won't have to move every few months."

"What will I do if I can't make friends?"

Jacob sat up. "Kazik's your friend. In school you'll find more."

"Suppose our father has a new wife," worried David.

"Stop making everything horrible. None of his letters or messages mentioned a wife."

"Wicked stepmothers always try to kill children. Why would anyone tell stories like that if it wasn't true?" asked David.

"Fairy tales are make-believe. Our friends in Berlin and Zeilsheim had fathers who remarried."

"Snow White's stepmother ordered a hunter to cut out her heart."

"If he remarried, and I don't think he did, and she has a long sharp knife, run like hell."

"Stepmothers don't like children," David said defiantly.

Exasperated, Jacob picked up a piece of paper on the deck, folded it, made a boat, and threw it in the water. "Enough with all the doom and gloom. I bet the paper boat gets to Palestine before us."

"Who cares about your stupid boat" David screamed, reminding Jacob of his father's instructions to take care of his brother that fateful day in 1939.

"Tell you what," he said trying to calm David. "If it's true, we'll run where she can't find us."

"We'll write to Papa Roslan in America and tell him. He'll save us. Papa can do anything once he makes up his mind," said David.

Land shimmered on the eastern horizon the morning of February 25, 1947. Kazik and his mother joined David and Jacob on the top deck. Passengers stood three deep, eager for their first view of a land they yearned and prayed for every day of every week. "And to Jerusalem your city may you return. . . . Blessed are you, builder of Jerusalem."

Tel Aviv rose behind broad, white beaches against a background of date palms, acacias, and squat stucco houses with red, tile roofs. Tall minarets dominated the skyline. Prayers of muezzin echoed across the city, 5600 miles west in New York, where unknown to the travelers, debate over partition of Palestine into Jewish and Arab states rattled the United Nations.

The *Providence* steamed north. As they approached theport of Haifa, British naval forces roared across the water, surrounding an old freighter listing to one side. A packed, frightened crowd on the sloping deck of the ship clung to rails and each other. Machine guns rattled through the air.

"Why are they shooting?" shouted David.

"Refugees aboard the ship don't have permission to enter the Mandate. The British are trying to prevent them from jumping in the water and swimming for shore," a teacher told them.

"They were in camps, hiding. They survived. They should be allowed freedom," demanded Jacob.

"The Jewish Resistance rescues of those who make it to shore. Ones caught by the British are sent to internment camps. After the war you would think compassion would be the norm. You're fortunate. You and your brother have authorization to enter legally."

Refugees on the old merchant vessel ducked under British fire. With one hand, the soldiers liberated them from the concentration camps; with the other, they imprisoned them. Inundated by propaganda in Marseille and aboard the ship, contradictions confused Jacob and David, who could do nothing but watch refugees grasping for freedom.

A loud, rasping horn sounded. A tugboat prodded the *Providence* to Haifa's ship terminal, a series of long buildings next to the water. Crowds on shore waited eagerly for friends and relatives to disembark.

"Think our father knows we're here?" David asked Jacob.

"Keep worrying. Maybe your wish for something bad will happen."

David carefully wrapped Vasily Grossman's novel and packed it with the oranges he saved, in his duffel bag. Before exiting the stateroom, he paused in front of a mirror and took a deep breath. He looked the same as Tadek. But Tadek was a mask. The disguise he wore for years slipped away.

"Stop admiring yourself!" shouted Jacob.

"Who do *you* see in the mirror—Geniek or Jacob?"

On the momentous day when the *Providence* entered the harbor, Jacob saw in the mirror Geniek and Tadek Roslan and the Jacob and David they would become. Loudspeakers announced passengers would disembark from the top deck down. Before leaving the stateroom David placed a hand over his mirror image: "My name is David."

The boys joined Kazik and Lisa Mandelbaum on the main deck where fellow passengers searched for familiar faces on docks below.

"Remember to call me," Kazik reminded David.

"Once we're settled, perhaps you and your father will visit," said Mrs. Mandelbaum.

"You were my first friend in Marseille," David said to Kazik, as he and his mother prepared to cross the gangplank to their new life in an old land.

"Feeling better?" Jacob asked David.

"What if our father has a woman with him?"

"I'm not swimming back to France."

"Suppose they miss us?" David asked.

"No one's leaving us behind."

The first mate whistled. "I have orders to escort you off the ship."

"Everything works out for the best," said Jacob.

It may have been best for his brother, nevertheless David had great misgivings about meeting those who deserted him. They followed the mate to an area marked for ship's personnel. A separate gangplank used by the crew stretched to the dock. Four men waited dockside. Bright winter sun made it difficult to see their faces.

The boys took tentative steps forward, when a voice rang out: "Jacob! David!" A slim man wearing a brown hat and dark suit rushed forward. He stopped a few feet away and opened his arms. "Jacob, David, it's your father." He erupted in tears, holding them in his arms. He kissed the boys, looked at their bewildered faces, and kissed them again.

David stood rigid while the man who called himself "father" wept. "You survived. You're alive. Thank God for rescuing you," Nahum Gutgeld cried.

"God had nothing to do with it," interrupted David stoically. "Papa Alex and Mama Mela saved us."

Nahum wiped his eyes. "Of course. We owe them a great deal and won't forget what they did."

"We owe them our lives," insisted Jacob.

Nahum stuttered, failing to comprehend his sons' lack of respect and absence of appreciation for bringing them home. A taller man with gray hair and short beard gently took Nahum's arm and stepped forward.

"Let me see you. So handsome and grown up," he said.

Regaining his composure, Nahum said nervously: "Jacob, remember your grandfather? We worked very hard to bring you here. Now it's done and we're a family once more."

Jacob removed the camera from his duffel bag. "Where is Uncle Natan?"

A handsome man who looked like the singing, dancing, hardworking, suntanned Jewish pioneers in films they viewed in Marseille and on the *Providence* shook their hands. Jacob presented Natan with the camera. "Mr. Salat met us in Paris. His brother kept this for you when you left Switzerland for Poland."

Overwhelmed, Natan held it as if it were made of delicate crystal. "After all this time, I can't believe it. Did you take pictures?"

Jacob nudged David in the ribs. "We didn't want to damage the camera," smiled David.

Natan motioned to a tall, thin man. "Meet your Uncle Levi."

Levi grasped the boys' hands. "Welcome to Eretz Yisrael."

David opened his duffel bag and took out oranges he saved. "I brought everyone presents. They had them on the ship."

"Very kind of you," said their grandfather. He held up one and looked at it with admiration. "These oranges are special because they traveled with you on the ship."

"You're here. You're safe. It's a miracle," said Nahum.

It was no miracle, thought David. It took daring and courage for Alex and Mela to protect him and Jacob. His father, grandfather, and uncles were his family in Palestine. The Roslans would always have a special place in his heart. They were Mama Mela and Papa Alex.

Wolf Gutgeld took their hands. "Time to go home." They walked into dazzling sunshine.

The End

Epilogue
by David Gilat

> What matters in life is not what happens to
> you but what you remember and how you
> remember it.
> —Gabriel Garcia Marquez
> (1927–2014)

While reading Hans Fallada's novel *Jeder Stirbt Fur Sich Allein*
(1947), translated into English by Michael Hofmann (2009)
under the title *Every Man Dies Alone* (US edition) or *Alone
in Berlin* (British edition), it suddenly dawned on me that, as
a child, I too was once alone in Berlin. Fallada's novel, published shortly after the author's death, took place in Berlin
and explores events in the years 1941–1943 under the sniffing
noses of agents of the monstrous regime the Nazis established
in Germany. My own *alone in Berlin* affair took place several
years later, in January 1946, merely eight months after the
surrender of Nazi Germany, when the traces of what had happened remained ominously visible all over the war-torn city
of Berlin.

An eight-year-old boy, who goes astray in an unfamiliar
city, might approach a passerby and ask for help and directions to lead him back home. This is not what I chose to do
on that cold day. As a matter of fact, this obvious way to handle the situation did cross my mind, but I outright rejected it.
The people on the street were all Germans, and—be it out of
fear, pride, or embarrassment—after what I had experienced,
I wanted nothing to do with Germans. This decision, as well
as some later imprudent ones that I made, led to a three-week

adventure that almost resulted in permanent separation from my family and a good chance of my ending up in the Soviet Union.

The Russian colonel who took me under his care was generous and very kind. Nevertheless, I feared when he found the truth, his sense of duty to his country and loyalty to its government might prevail over his liking for me, and the whole unhappy episode might end up in the deportation of my entire family back to Poland. I unwisely thought that in hiding my identity I was heroically protecting my loved ones from harsh consequences. I desperately searched for someone trustworthy in whom I could confide. The colonel came close to this ideal but did not quite make it. Fortunately, my agony over facing an unknown future came to a happy ending. If there is anything I regret having neglected in the commotion and excitement of reuniting with my loved ones and saying goodbye to the gracious colonel, it is failing to note his name and address for future contact. In 1990, soon after the fall of the Soviet Union, I made an attempt to trace my colonel, but regretfully to no avail.

Out of the Storm is not a Holocaust story; it happened after the war when Ghettoes no longer existed and after the Allies liberated death camps. Nevertheless, the Berlin episode in my life, as well as the entire two-year immediate postwar period, is intimately related to my war experiences and may illustrate the effects of war on a child's psyche.

I was smuggled out of the Warsaw Ghetto in March 1943 into the protective hands and courageous good hearts of Alex and Mela Roslan and given the name Tadek (diminutive form of the quite common Polish name Tadeusz). One's name becomes a symbol of one's identity, all the more so when the name is given for the purpose of hiding one's real identity, like the name Tadek that I had to assume due to the grave circumstances of the time. It took a long while before I could confidently declare, especially to my own inner self: *"My name is not Tadek anymore; my name is David."*

I view *Out of the Storm* as a portrayal of the long, hesitant—at times painful—process of my transition from Tadek back to David. Though this never explicitly came up in our interactions, my brother Jacob must have experienced a similar elusive transition from Geniek back to Jacob. Alex and Mela continued calling us Tadek and Geniek to the very end of their lives (Mela died in 1996 and Alex in 2005). Deep down, a part of me will inevitably remain Tadek as long as I live.

Now, more than seventy-five years later and after a decades-long academic career in mathematics, I continue to wonder what would have happened had I gone to America with the Roslans and stayed Tadek rather than joining my father in Israel and turning back into David. Similarly, memories of my Berlin lost-and-found adventure of January 1946 make me wonder, perhaps even more, what would have become of me had I not been found and returned to the Roslans but ended up in the Soviet Union as an eight-year-old Russian orphan. Looking back, I have no regrets that things turned out for me as they did.

Tel Aviv, Israel

Afterword

Shortly after bidding farewell to David and Jacob in Frankfurt, Germany, Alexander and Amelia (Mela) Roslan and their daughter Marisia immigrated to the United States, settling in New York City. After a brief stint as a real estate entrepreneur, Alex joined a housing maintenance firm as a janitor in Manhattan. Impressed by his logistical skills, the company promoted him to manager of a building complex.

An influx of Polish immigrants prompted the Roslans to move to Jamaica Estates, a middle-class neighborhood in Queens, New York, where Mela gave birth to a son, Richard. The Roslans built a large home, serving as halfway house for newly arrived survivors of World War Two. They urged members of their families in Poland to visit and live with them for three to six months.

Alex hired them as maintenance workers, with wages far exceeding anything they could earn in their home country. Since living with Alex and Mela came at no cost, they returned to Poland with almost all their earnings: fifteen hundred to two thousand dollars, the equivalent in today's economy of In approximately sixteen to twenty-one thousand dollars.

Under Israel's Law of Return, Jacob and David had the right of Israeli citizenship. The nation's Israeli Defense Service Law requires all citizens who meet conscription criteria once they reach eighteen years of age to serve in the armed forces. After high school, the Israel Defense Force (IDF) gave Jacob a waiver to join the Academic Reserve permitting high school students to defer the draft and attend university before their military service. Upon graduating from Hebrew University he joined the IDF. David graduated high school in 1955, serving for a year in the army, fighting in the 1956 Sinai war. He continued his annual reserve duty until 1983. In the interim, Jacob and David corresponded with the Roslans numerous times until they lost contact.

In 1961, an Israeli acquaintance of David traveled to New York on a government mission to meet with Holocaust survivors in order to discuss immigration to Israel. A group of Polish survivors invited her to a gathering where she related the remarkable story of David and Jacob's rescue by the Roslans. Serendipitously, Alex and Mela were in the audience. Correspondence between them and the boys, now young men, resumed.

Seventy-two years after David and Jacob left Zeilsheim Displaced Persons camp in Germany, a letter from Nahum Gutgeld to Zvi Salat with the Paris office of the Jewish Agency in Jerusalem emerged. In 1960, Donia Schaumann, vice-president of the Milan Commission, Keren Kayemet LeIsrael (Jewish National Fund), a collector of Jewish artifacts and documents, discovered the letter in a trove at a Jaffa flea market.

Ms. Schaumann invited an acquaintance who was a partner of Yoram Gutgeld, a cousin of the Gilats, to view the collection. Noting the name, he informed Yoram, who recognized the letter signed by his uncle Nahum. He traveled to Israel and presented a copy to David and Jacob. David Gilat translated the letter from Hebrew to English.

Tel Aviv, 25.XI.46
Mr. Z. Salat
Paris

Respectful Sir,

I do not know if you know me personally, but you know my father and my brother . . . I have two children in Germany, lads of 13 and 8. They are there in the hands of a Polish Christian who gave them shelter and saved them during the war in Poland . . . In February 1946 they arrived to Zeilsheim . . . near Frankfurt am Main in the American zone, where they are located till present.

All the many attempts and efforts to get the children out bore no results. Originally, the Polish man wanted to come with his family to Eretz-Israel and I did my best to get a certificate [immigration permit] for him, but later he changed his mind about coming to Eretz-Israel and demanded a fair payment. I was able to get the required amount of money and as of June 1946 the funds are in the hands of the Joint [American Joint Distribution Committee]. I was later informed that in addition to money he requested an American visa for him and his family. So again I was confronted with a problem how to get a U.S. visa for him. That is how the matter evolved and I could not get my children out and bring them to Eretz-Israel, despite of the fact that already a year ago they had certificates that were initially sent to Poland and later to Paris.

In addition, on the 27th of March 1946 a cable was sent from the Aliya [immigration] department to the British Consulate in Paris to issue Eretz-Israel visas to my children Jacob and David Gutgeld. About two months ago I was informed that [he] agrees to release the children when he receives the money . . . a letter was sent and then a cable from the Joint in Jerusalem to the Joint in Paris to promptly arrange the payment

and release the children and send them to Eretz- Israel. Nevertheless, until now I have no idea if the children have already been transferred to Paris and what
has been done in the matter.

As you are in Paris, I appeal to you and ask you in
the strongest possible way to involve the Joint, talk to
them and explain the urgency of the matter . . . The
Joint in Paris has handled this affair already half a year
ago, so they are familiar with the matter. Is there anything more important and more urgent than the rescue of Jewish children? . . . Lately, the matter became
very serious and by no means can bear any further
delay. The children have to be released at the earliest.

I reiterate again: The money is in the hands of the
Joint in Paris. Eretz-Israel visas for the children are
with the British Consul in Paris, "British Passport
Control, Paris".

I repeat my request and hope that you become interested and do everything you can. I wholeheartedly
thank you in advance.

With respectful greetings,
Nahum Gutgeld. Tel Aviv."

David Gilat commented on the letter: "Alexander (Alex)
Roslan was a patriot of Poland. He supported the Polish underground Armia Krajowa (AK), the paramilitary organ of the
exiled Polish government in London, which staged the uprising against German occupiers in summer 1944 . . . his fifteen-
year-old son, Jurek, was killed in this uprising. Nevertheless,
he did not want to stay in his beloved motherland under Soviet domination. He had no definite target country in mind
but wished to deliver Jacob and me to our biological family,
so he opted initially for Palestine. I remember him repeatedly
saying: 'I saved the two Gutgeld boys, now is the time for the
Gutgeld family to help me and my family.' My father had no

interest other than reuniting with his children, so if what it took bringing the Roslans along to get them home—so be it, especially when Jacob and I related to him in no uncertain terms that we were not going anywhere without the Roslans. He was even willing to make an attempt with the British authorities in Palestine to obtain immigration permits for the Roslans.

"While already in Zeilsheim, it became clear my father's efforts were in vain and the gates of Palestine blocked for the Roslans. Return to Poland was out of the question so Alex opted for the United States . . . easier said than done! The Roslans needed Jewish help for arranging their admission to the "promised land", and again—through efforts of my father— the Joint (American Joint Distribution Committee) came to the rescue. Money was another problem. By then, earnings Alex made in Łódź had dwindled, if not completely evaporated, and there was no flow of income after we left Poland. Evidently (and rightfully) Alex refused to release us before his admission to the US and he secured a suitable funds. This is apparently what, in his letter, my father calls 'demanded payment.' My family (father and grandfather), who were barely settled in Palestine, did not have resources to reward Alex, so my father engaged Joint again. Benjamin Mintz, who at the time was active in the affairs of Holocaust survivors in Europe and later a member of the Knesset (Israeli Parliament) was instrumental in dealings with the Joint for securing the required funds. Final arrangements stipulated Alex would receive three thousand dollars upon arrival in the US. Shortly after all this (visa and money) was settled, we (Jacob and I) were sent on a train from Frankfurt to Paris.

In 1961 the Roslans greeted Jacob and his family upon their arrival at New York's Idlewild Airport, now John F.

Kennedy International. Jacob, his wife Geula and their children, remained in New York where Jacob began postdoctoral studies in physics.

Four years later David spent a week with Alex and Mela on his way to attend the University of California, Berkeley, to begin his doctoral program. On every trip from Israel to the United States, Jacob and David individually visited the Roslans, surrogate parents who had become an integral part of their lives.

After graduating from the University of California, Berkeley with his PhD, David chose to attend Columbia University in New York for postdoctoral work in order to live near the Roslans. During the academic years 1971 to 1972 he visited them weekly. He talked to the Roslans by phone every day.

Marisia (Mary) married and lived with her husband in Jamaica Estates. Eventually they moved to North Carolina. When Alex retired, he and Mela purchased a small, comfortable home surrounded by gardens in Clearwater, Florida. They led a peaceful life in a tight, insular cadre of Polish survivors.

David and Jacob filed testimonies with Yad Vashem documenting their experience under the Roslans' protection during the Holocaust, exploring compassion shown to them during the post-Holocaust era. Yad Vashem, the World Holocaust Remembrance Center, Jerusalem, Israel, verified their story recognizing the Roslans among the Righteous of the Nations.

On one of David's visits to Alex and Mela, the Clearwater edition of the *St. Petersburg Times* wrote an article relating his and Jacob's rescue by the Roslans. The story had an unexpected outcome. Several of their alleged friends in the Polish community questioned why they bothered to help Jews. Mela quoted a neighbor blithely and cruelly asking: "So what if they had killed six million and two?"

May 15, 1946, three months after David and Jacob boarded the ship sailing to the Palestine Mandate, the United States Department of State, alarmed by the eruption of antisemitism, issued a critical intelligence research paper: "The Jews in Poland since the Liberation."

> "There is little doubt that the current anti-Jewish manifestations in Poland represent a continuation of activities by right-wing groups that were at work before 1939. . . . By exploiting the surviving remnant of Polish Jewry, these elements are seeking to compromise the Government . . . even before the liberation of Poland antisemitic propaganda emerged in Polish émigré circles. . . . Polish Jews who had recently returned were again fleeing Poland because of the antisemitic excesses."

The same hatred rose out of sewers in a quiet retirement community in Florida. Facing blatant antisemitism, the Roslans left Clearwater. A Jewish real estate developer in Tampa read their story and offered them a condominium, where they lived securely the remainder of their years.

Yad Vashem memorialized Alex and Mela in the Garden of the Righteous Among Nations. The Jewish Foundation for the Righteous, founded by the late Rabbi Harold Schulweis, honored and supported the Roslans with a monthly stipend. The Museum of Tolerance, Los Angeles, inscribed their names on a memorial monument.

The Roslan's oral history is enshrined in the United States Holocaust Memorial Museum, Washington, DC, and at the University of Southern California Shoah Foundation—The

Institute for Visual History and Education. Rabbi Schulweis organized a tribute to the Roslans in 1981 at Valley Beth Shalom, Encino, California. David traveled from Israel for the celebration. In 1982 the rabbi provided financing and arrangements for the Roslans to spend Passover in Israel with Jacob, David, and their father Nahum Gutgeld. It was the first time in thirty-five years they were all reunited.

President Ronald Reagan addressed the nation at a Holocaust remembrance ceremony on April 11, 1983. He stated in his remarks:

> "During the dark days when terror reigned on the continent of Europe, there were quiet heroes, men and women whose moral fiber held firm. Some of those are called 'righteous Gentiles.' At this solemn time, we remember them. Alexander Roslan and his wife, for example, now live in Clearwater, Florida. But during the war, they lived in Poland and they hid three Jewish children in their home for more than four years. They knew the risk they were taking."

In 1990, on the forty-second anniversary of Israel's independence, Jacob, a celebrated physicist, spoke at a ceremony given by the Jewish Institute for the Righteous in New York honoring Alex and Mela Roslan:

> "When I think of days hiding in Nazi occupied Warsaw, the image that comes back is love. Yes, we had fear of death in the streets. Somehow the trauma of all those fears faded. Love persisted. Not pity, not even compassion. I do not know what gave Alex, Mela, Marisia the strength to survive overwhelming odds. I suspect it was the spirit of love permeating their household."

Mela passed away in 1996 at the age of eighty-seven. She was buried next to her son Jurek in Warsaw, Poland. Alex returned to Białystok, Poland, in 2004, where his niece Basia Roslan cared for him until his death at the age of ninety-four in 2005.

—*Michael Halperin*

ILLUSTRATIONS

Constantine I coin,
struck 313 CE.
Meisterdrucke
Kunstreproduktionen,
Austria.

Magdeburg Law, ca. tenth century. Center for Medieval
Exhibitions, Magdeburg, Germany.

Wolf Gutgeld.
Gilat Archive.

Aftermath of *Kristallnacht*,
Berlin, Germany, November 11, 1938. Yad Vashem.

Stamp collected by Jacob.
The New York Times,
April 21, 1939.

Aunt Hanka, Jacob, David, and Shalom
in the Warsaw Ghetto, 1941. Gilat Archive.

Yad Vashem certificate, February 8, 1957,
testifying to Shalom Gutgeld's death
in Warsaw, 1943. Yad Vashem.

Warsaw ruins, 1945. US Holocaust Memorial Museum.

Łódź Ghetto ruins, 1945. US Holocaust Memorial Museum.

Jacob, Alex, and David in Łódź, 1945. Gilat Archive.

Reichstag ruins, Berlin, Germany, 1945.
German News Service, Berlin.

Supreme Headquarters Allied Expeditionary Force, Frankfurt, Germany, 1946. US Army, Germany.

SHAEF shoulder patch. US Army Center of Military History

Entrance to Zeilsheim DP camp, UNRRA Team 503.
US Holocaust Memorial Museum.

Zeilsheim DP camp Holocaust Memorial, 1946.
US Holocaust Memorial Museum.

Hapoel soccer team, Zeilsheim DP camp, 1946. Yad Vashem.

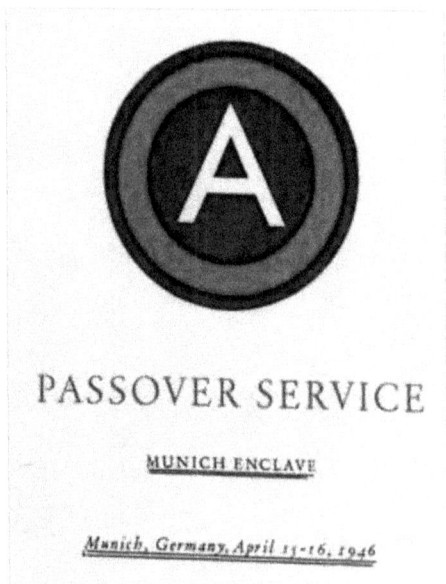

PASSOVER SERVICE

MUNICH ENCLAVE

Munich, Germany, April 15-16, 1946

Passover Service, printed by US Third Army Corps, April 15, 1946. Yad Vashem.

Zeilsheim DP camp Zionist demonstration, 1946.
US Holocaust Memorial Museum.

German refugee caravan. Bundesarchiv.

Postcard of Hotel Mirabeau, Paris.

Napoleon's tomb, Hotel des Invalides, Paris.
Halperin Archive.

Dr. Abraham (Avram) Geller Death Certificate.
(Courtesy of Yad Vashem Archives).

Jewish Refugees arriving in Marseille. Yad Vashem.

SS *Providence*-Jewish Refugees from Marseilles to Palestine.
Photo by Roman Vishniak. US Holocaust Memorial Museum.

הועד היהודי האמריקאי המאוחד לסיוע (ג'וינט)
AMERICAN JEWISH JOINT DISTRIBUTION COMMITTEE

OFFICE FOR THE MIDDLE EAST AND BALKANS   המשרד למזרח התיכון ובלקנים
CHARLES PASSMAN, DIRECTOR   ש. פסמן, מנהל הלשכה

ADVISORY COMMITTEE:
Judah L. Magnus, Chairman
Harry S. Davidowitz
Israel Kligler
Charles Passman
Julius Simon
Henrietta Szold
Harry Viteles

ref.no. 212/111

Jerusalem,   January 7th, 1946.   ירושלים.
P.O.B. 354 · PHONE 4304   354 ת.ד. · טלפון 4304

IN REPLY PLEASE REFER
TO 47/22242

American Jewish Joint Distribution Committee,
19 rue de Teheran,
PARIS

COPY TO:- A.J.J.D.C. WARSAW

Gentlemen,

Mr. Wolf GUTGELD, Tel-Aviv, Shivtei Israel Street 8,
a veteran public worker whom we know personally, approached us regarding
his two grandsons, only survivors of the entire family:-

Jakub, aged 12, and David, aged 7   -LODZ, Srodmiejska 18

Their father Mr. Nuchim GUTGELD, son of Mr. Wolf Gutgeld, is also
in Tel-Aviv at above address.

A certificate was obtained for the boys, photostatic copy of
which(ref.I/427/42)is attached.

However, meanwhile news have been received, not confirmed yet,
that the boys left Lodz accompanied by the Gentile who saved and sheltered
them, Mr. Aleksander ROSLAN, on their way to Munich.

We therefore request you to check in Lodz whether the boys and
Mr. Roslan have in fact left; on the other hand, please contact the Munich
committee and if the boys do arrive please inform us soonest, so as to
enable the family here to transfer the certificates to Paris from Warsaw.

Any help extended to the boys will be of course greatly appreciated

Sincerely yours,
A.J.J.D.C. JERUSALEM

Ro/m

American Jewish Joint Distribution Committee letter,
1946, suggesting possible survival of Jacob and David.
Gilat Archive.

Jacob's letter to Nahum, February 1946. Gilat Archive.

Jewish Distribution Committee telegram
from Łódź confirming rescue of Jacob and David,
February 14, 1946.
Gilat Archive.

הועד היהודי האמריקאי המאוחד לסיוע (ג'וינט)
AMERICAN JEWISH JOINT DISTRIBUTION COMMITTEE
OFFICE FOR THE MIDDLE EAST AND BALKANS   המשרד למזרח התיכון ובלקנים
CHARLES PASSMAN, DIRECTOR   ש. פסמן. המנהל הכללי

ref. no: 155

Jerusalem, **February 14th, 1946**   ירושלים.
P. O. B 640 PHONE 3840   ת. ד. 640 . טלפון 3840

American Jewish Joint Distribution Committee,
Warszawa
18, Chocimska

Gentlemen,

          Further to our letter No. 111 of 27.1.46, copy of which
we attach for easy reference, please note that Mr. Gutfeld
now told us that the information about his grandchildren was
not correct. He is afraid that they did not leave with Mr. Alexander
ROSLAN for Muenich; the said Gentile seems to have fled from Lodz,
taking the children with them, to some other town; he was afraid
that some friend of Mr. Gutfeld might take the children without
his getting any money for their care. It can be hoped, however,
that the children themselves will approach you. Please inform
us immediately of their present address, if you have it;
if not, please try to ascertain it, if possible, through neigh-
bours in Lodz, etc. We will be most grateful for your special
attention to this case.

                              Sincerely yours,

Re/m

                              A.J.J.D.C. JERUSALEM

COPY TO A.J.J.D.C. PARIS

JDC telegram from Łódź confirming rescue of Jacob and David,
September 3, 1946. Gilat Archive.

Nachum Gutgeld to Zvi Salat, November 25, 1946.
Gilat Archive.

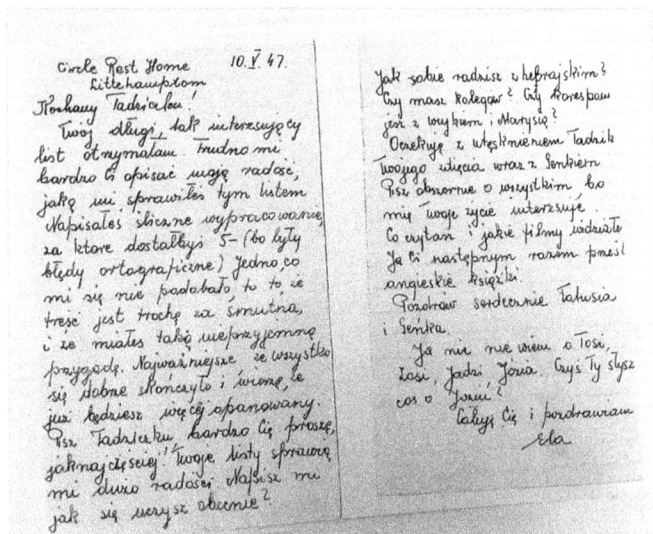

Ella Rosenberg's letter to David, May 10, 1947. Gilat Archive.

Jacob Gutgeld, Nahum Gutgeld, David Gutgeld
reunited in Palestine, 1947.
US Holocaust Memorial Museum.

METRO

Friday, October 10, 1980   Los Angeles Times

GENTILES SAVED 3 JEWISH CHILDREN

Survivor of Holocaust, Protectors Reunited

By MICHAEL SEILER
Times Staff Writer

The worst time was the night the Gestapo men came to search the house, they all agreed—Alex Roslan, his wife Mela, and David Gilat, who was 5 years old then and hiding in a kitchen cabinet with his two brothers.

The three of them—Alex, 70, Mela, 73, and Gilat, 41, were sitting in a conference room at Los Angeles International Airport Thursday, remembering.

Gilat had flown in from Israel, the Roslans from New Jersey, where they settled after World War II ended and they left Warsaw. The Roslans had not been with Gilat since the war's end, and to see him now was to see a dream and a nightmare come together before cameras, television lights and reporters.

The Roslans are gentiles and Gilat a Jew. They took in Gilat and two of his brothers after the chil-

As it was, one of the children died of smallpox and Alex and Mela's 18-year-old son was killed in 1945 fighting with the Poles who rose up and were slaughtered by the Germans before the Russians entered Warsaw.

So it was easy to understand why Mela Roslan, minutes off the plane from New Jersey, still more comfortable in her native Polish than English, was nearly at loss for words.

"I know this is my son . . . this is my son . . ." she said, bursting into tears and embracing Gilat.

Alex Roslan tried to explain why he and his wife had sheltered three Jewish boys they did not know. "When I saw how many children were dead, children dying . . . , you must do something."

For more than two years, the Roslans did what they could.

Alex Roslan, with glasses, and wife Mela are met by David Gilat.
Times photo by Ken Hively

and nothing else. Behind the other   Israel. David is a statistician at the

Michael Seiler, "Survivor of Holocaust, Protectors Reunited,"
Los Angeles Times, October 10, 1980.

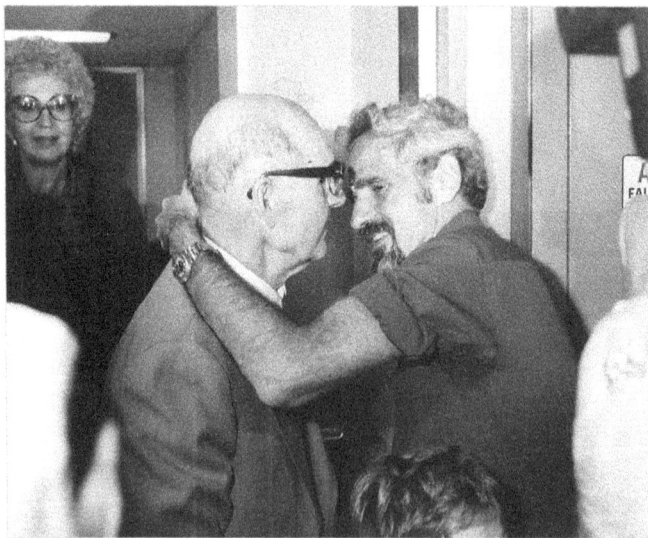

"Alex Roslan and David Gilat meet in Los Angeles, 1980,"
Los Angeles Times, October 10, 1980.

Alex Roslan, Mela Roslan, and David Gilat, 1980.
Halperin Archive.

Yad Vashem honors Alex and Mela Roslan, 1981.
Yad Vashem.

David Gilat, Tel Aviv, 2008. Halperin Archive.

Jacob Gilat, Tel Aviv, 2008. Halperin Archive.

www.ingramcontent.com/pod-product-compliance
Lightning Source LLC
Chambersburg PA
CBHW070327100426

42812CB00005B/1280